# GUIDANCE &
# COUNSELLING
# IN BRITAIN:

*a 20~year perspective*

## WINDY DRYDEN

is Professor of Counselling at Goldsmiths' College, University of London. He has authored or edited 58 books including *Rational-Emotive Counselling in Action* (Sage Publications, 1990) and *Daring to be Myself: A Case of Rational-Emotive Therapy*, written with Joseph Yankura (Open University Press, 1992). In addition, he edits eight book series in the area of counselling and psychotherapy including *Counselling in Action* (Sage Publications) and *Improve Your Counselling* (Sage Publications). His major interests are in rational-emotive therapy, eclecticism and integration in psychotherapy and, increasingly, writing short, accessible self-help books for the general public. His latest book in this genre is entitled *The Incredible Sulk* (Sheldon Press, 1992).

## TONY WATTS

is Director of the National Institute for Careers Education and Counselling, which is sponsored by the Careers Research and Advisory Centre (CRAC). A joint founder of CRAC, his books include *Diversity and Choice in Higher Education* (1972), *Counselling at Work* (1977), *Schools, Careers and Community* (with Bill Law) (1977), *Career Development in Britain* (with other colleagues) (1981), *Work Experience and Schools* (1983), *Education, Unemployment and the Future of Work* (1983), *Mirrors of Work: Work Simulations and Schools* (with Ian Jamieson and Andy Miller) (1988), *Educational and Vocational Guidance Services for the 14–25 Age-Group in the European Community* (1988), and *Rethinking Work Experience* (with Andy Miller and Ian Jamieson) (1991). He is joint chair of the Standing Conference of Associations for Guidance in Educational Settings, a Visiting Fellow at the University of London Institute of Education, and Executive Editor of the *British Journal of Guidance and Counselling*.

# GUIDANCE & COUNSELLING IN BRITAIN:

## a 20~year perspective

EDITED BY

Windy Dryden & A.G. Watts

*A selection of papers from
the first 20 years of the
British Journal of Guidance
and Counselling*

**CRAC**

HOBSONS

# CRAC

The Careers Research and Advisory Centre
(CRAC) is a registered educational charity.
Hobsons Publishing PLC produces CRAC publications
under exclusive licence and royalty agreements.

 ISBN 1 85324 720 0

© 1993 Hobsons Publishing PLC,
Bateman Street, Cambridge CB2 1LZ

Typeset by Vision Typesetting, Manchester
Printed and bound in Great Britain by
JB Offset Printers (Marks Tey) Limited


Ref: L098/v1t/A/JC

Cover design by Jane Norman graphics

HOBSONS

# CONTENTS

CONTENTS

# PREFACE

This volume commemorates the twentieth anniversary of the launching of the *British Journal of Guidance and Counselling* in 1973. The journal, familiarly known as the '*BJGC*', has seen and has charted far-reaching changes in the fields of guidance and counselling since its inception. Given its established position in these fields, the editors of this volume, with the full support of the journal's active Editorial Board, decided to mark its anniversary with a collection of some of the most important papers that have appeared in the journal's pages since 1973. The papers demonstrate not only how the *BJGC* has documented the changes that have occurred since the journal first appeared, but also how it has contributed to shaping these changes.

To this end, we sent a list of contents pages of all published issues of the journal to everyone who had served or was currently serving on its Editorial Board and Editorial Advisory Panel. We asked them to nominate twelve articles, in rank order of perceived importance, which they would like to see included in the present volume. We stressed, in our accompanying letter, that they should select papers that were not only seminal in their day, but which also had enduring value in contributing to current debates in guidance and counselling.

We received sets of nominations from, in all, thirteen people. We then met to decide on our final selection. Our task was informed by the need to include a balance of articles that demonstrated the scope of the journal. In the event, our task was a relatively easy one in that our colleagues' nominations reflected the breadth of the journal's interests, including its dual focus on guidance and on counselling.

Having made our final selection, and had this ratified at an Editorial Board meeting, we wrote to the authors of the selected articles to request permission to reprint the papers in the anniversary volume. We also asked them to submit a short postscript to be included at the end of the original article. This provided an opportunity to contextualise it and to comment on its origins, on reactions to it, and on the extent to which it still represented the author's views. Our contributors all agreed to comply with this request. Since Paul Halmos is sadly not alive to see his article reprinted, we asked Léonie Sugarman to write the commentary on his article.

The selected articles fall into three clusters. The first reflects the important point that guidance and counselling do not take place in a vacuum. They always occur in a context, and this context has an enormous impact on the content and process of the work that is undertaken. This view provides the undercurrent to the articles of Halmos, Daws (on mental health and education), and Gray.

The second cluster reflects the work published in the journal in the area of therapeutic counselling. These articles demonstrate the journal's concern with comprehensiveness (Heron, Nelson-Jones, and Norcross and Grencavage), research (Dryden) and innovation (Murgatroyd). A further strand that runs through these five papers is one that is dominating the field of counselling at present – namely, the concern with integration. This movement, which is concerned with promoting dialogue between practitioners of differing orientations and viewpoints in the hope of achieving rapprochement in an otherwise divided field, has long been a concern of the *BJGC*: these articles are excellent examples of this focus.

The contextual perspective also influences the third cluster, which covers the areas of educational and careers guidance. Three of the papers in this cluster (Roberts, Daws' reply, and Law) represent contrasting viewpoints on the limitations imposed by the social context to such guidance; a fourth (Watts and Herr) addresses its socio-political aims. The final paper in the cluster examines the place of guidance in the burgeoning field of open learning.

This volume and the journal which it commemorates would not exist without the active support of past and present members of the Editorial Board and Editorial Advisory Panel and without the loyal and continuing support of the journal's publishers, Hobsons. We take this opportunity to thank them all. The fact that the *BJGC* has reached its third decade and continues to contribute to and shape the direction of work in the fields of guidance and counselling is a testimony to their efforts. In conclusion, we hope that readers will rediscover – or, in some cases, discover for the first time – the enduring quality of some of the journal's published work as commemorated in this twentieth anniversary volume.

*Windy Dryden, London*
*Tony Watts, Cambridge*

*July 1992*

# CONTRIBUTORS

### DIANE BAILEY
is a Senior Lecturer at the Open University (Eastern Region). When she wrote her 1987 paper, she was a Research Fellow at the National Institute for Careers Education and Counselling (NICEC).

### PETER DAWS
was until recently Professor of Education in the University of Ulster at Coleraine. When he wrote his 1973 and 1977 papers, he was Senior Lecturer in Education at the University of Keele.

### WINDY DRYDEN
is Professor of Counselling at Goldsmiths' College, University of London. When he wrote his 1980 paper, he was in the Department of Educational Enquiry at the University of Aston in Birmingham.

### LISA M. GRENCAVAGE
is at the Department of Psychology in the University of Scranton, USA.

### KENNETH GRAY
was, when he wrote his 1984 paper, at the Guildford County College of Technology.

### PAUL HALMOS
was, at the time he wrote his 1970 paper, Professor of Sociology at University College, Cardiff. He has since died.

### JOHN HERON
was, when he wrote his 1976 paper, working on the Human Potential Research Project in the Department of Adult Education at the University of Surrey.

### EDWIN L. HERR
is Professor of Counselling, Educational Psychology and Career Studies at Pennsylvania State University, USA.

### BILL LAW
is a Senior Fellow at the National Institute for Careers Education and Counselling (NICEC).

### STEPHEN MURGATROYD
is Professor of Applied Psychology at Athabasca University, Canada.

**RICHARD NELSON–JONES**

is Associate Professor at the Royal Melbourne Institute of Technology, Australia. When he wrote his 1979 paper, he was in the Department of Educational Enquiry at the University of Aston in Birmingham.

**JOHN C. NORCROSS**

is in the Department of Psychology at the University of Scranton, USA.

**KENNETH ROBERTS**

is Professor of Sociology at the University of Liverpool.

**LÉONIE SUGARMAN**

is a Chartered Occupational Psychologist in Lancaster.

**TONY WATTS**

is Director of the National Institute for Careers Education and Counselling (NICEC).

# TWENTY YEARS ON: THE *BRITISH JOURNAL OF GUIDANCE AND COUNSELLING*, 1973 ~ 92

## LÉONIE SUGARMAN

### INTRODUCTION

The opening editorial of the *British Journal of Guidance and Counselling* described the journal as 'a platform for the varied interests of those who practise counselling'. This beguilingly simple description obscures many hours of discussion, correspondence and reflection as to what form such a journal should take. The present chapter looks back over the twenty years of the journal's existence, reflecting on the reasons for its establishment, on the role of the journal in mirroring and forming the developing professional identity of guidance and counselling practitioners, on the themes and changes it has instigated and recorded in its pages, and on the continuing debates that have shaped editorial policy over the years.

The chapter also strives to communicate how the journal has developed through the process of what might be termed 'controlled freedom' – being open to new ideas and perspectives whilst incorporating them into the journal in a planned and systematic manner. This has hopefully precluded the journal from, on the one hand, becoming locked into an outmoded format which is set in stone and out of step with the times, and, on the other hand, being like a feather in the wind which blows hither and thither at the slightest breeze. The aim has been to produce a journal whose format and content mirror the model of the reflective practitioner (Schon, 1987) continually spiralling round the learning cycle (Kolb, 1984) of experience, reflection, analysis and action.

### PLANNING THE BIRTH: WHY A *BRITISH JOURNAL OF GUIDANCE AND COUNSELLING?*

In the early 1970s there was a growth in the number of training courses in counselling and, of special relevance in view of the *BJGC*'s purview, counselling was being increasingly incorporated into the practice of vocational guidance. A journal explicitly concerned with both guidance and counselling was particularly timely. But what type of journal? In terms of orientation, the issue centred on the academic v. practitioner debate; in terms of focus, the decision was between a schools/education emphasis and a broader, all-encompassing scope.[1]

Since a number of practitioner-oriented journals were already in existence, the most obvious publication gap seemed to be in relation to the academic development of the disciplines on which guidance and counselling were based. The burgeoning of courses within institutions of higher education seemed likely to herald an era of theoretical advances, adding weight to the case for an academically-oriented publication. However, the aim of the Careers Research and Advisory Centre (CRAC), which was to publish the putative journal, was to service practitioners, and so the new journal needed to be compatible with this goal. In this way was born the hopefully creative tension between theory and practice which has been a hallmark of the journal's aspirations.

Prior to publication of the first issue, it was decided that the journal would have an emphasis on, but not an exclusive concern with, guidance and counselling in educational settings. This decision can be seen as the outcome of a number of inter-related factors: the overall goals and *raison d'être* of CRAC; the growth in school counselling and in training courses for school counsellors at the Universities of Exeter, Keele, Reading and Swansea; and the particular interests of the individuals who, not coincidentally, formed the initial group of editors.

The four initial editors of the *British Journal of Guidance and Counselling* were all at that stage involved in the educational field, but were also, particularly through the Standing Conference for the Advancement of Counselling (SCAC), connected to the broader field of counselling. Peter Daws, at that time Senior Lecturer in Education at the University of Keele, and Douglas Hamblin, Lecturer in Education at the University College of Swansea, sequentially assumed main editorial responsibility for the articles in the journal. Barrie Hopson, then Director of the Vocational Guidance Research Unit at the University of Leeds, took charge of Book Reviews. Tony Watts, involved with careers guidance as Head of CRAC's Research and Development Unit, pulled the disparate elements of the journal into a coherent whole. He also assumed responsibility for the Abstracts Section, which summarised papers published elsewhere concerned with different types of problems (educational, vocational, and personal), techniques and training, the roles of counsellors and the provision of services, the effects of counselling, and attitudes towards counselling. These summaries were provided by about ten readers in various locations and jobs. The Editorial Advisory Board comprised some sixteen individuals drawn from, in addition to the fields of careers guidance and education, positions in psychology, psychiatry, teaching, theology, marriage guidance, organisational behaviour, sociology and medicine. Although mainly UK-based, the Advisory Board also included Professor O'Doherty from University College, Dublin, and Professor Super from Teachers College, Columbia University, USA. In sum, those involved with the journal reflected the field of guidance and counselling as it existed at the time, and were also linked to other cognate disciplines.

## FINDING AN IDENTITY: WHAT ARE COUNSELLING AND GUIDANCE AND WHO ARE THEIR PRACTITIONERS?

By the time the *British Journal of Guidance and Counselling* was launched, the counselling profession in the UK appeared to be well-established and expanding, but there was no clearly defined and agreed definition of what the profession encompassed. The pages of the *BJGC* reflected this. Thus Mackintosh (1974) concluded, with reference to higher education, that many of those 'engaged in counselling are uncertain of their remit, and a sense of professional isolation is, at least for the present, a major occupational hazard' (p. 55). Similarly, Antonouris (1974), in a study of the careers of teachers trained as counsellors, found them to have entered a wide range of occupations and a multitude of positions: 'There is no such thing as *the* career of a counsellor-trained teacher. Similarly, there is no one definition of the counsellor's role' (p. 169).

In Volume 4, Lewis and Murgatroyd (1976) discussed counsellors' attempts to legitimate their claim to be professional, proposing collective legitimation (i.e.accreditation) as the logical next step after the attempts at individual legitimation within organisations which they saw as prevalent at the time. Mathers (1978) challenged the applicability to counselling of many of the assumptions on which claims to be a profession are based, and the implication of this for accreditation in general and the training (or learning) of counselling in particular. Professions are synonymous with assertions concerning special and exclusive suitability to carry out certain activities – they imply a monopoly on expertise. Accreditation can be seen as an attempt to assert and maintain this exclusivity. That this is not the whole story is recognised in Marteau's (1978) reply to Mathers (1978), where it is argued that accreditation 'is meant not for the benefit of the counsellor but for the protection of the public. It is concerned more with guaranteeing certain standards of ethics than with the acclamation of status' (p. 140).

During the process of forming a professional identity, professional groups may talk about protecting the lay public (i.e. those not party to their special expertise) from unscrupulous and unqualified practitioners (i.e. other 'outsiders'), and may give some (but not all) of their secrets to chosen groups of others (for example, to information assistants in guidance centres, to managers within work organisations, or to teachers within colleges). The *BJGC* has included a number of papers concerned with 'giving counselling away': i.e. with the training of professionals in other areas, para-professionals and the lay public. During the 1970s there were papers dealing with peer counselling (Ayal and Bekerman, 1978; Ward, 1978) and training in counselling for tutors in higher education (Ratigan, 1977). More recently, papers have tended to emphasise the context in which counselling takes place (for example, in the mid-decade review in 1985, and in the symposium on ethical issues in 1992), with the recognition that for many practitioners counselling may be only a part of their role. The distinction between counselling and the use of counselling skills is relevant here.

As a journal with both scholarly and practical aspirations, the *BJGC* has played its part in the definition of certain types of activity as areas of professional enterprise. This is illustrated in a number of articles dealing with careers counselling and guidance. Some papers have considered what practitioners actually do: for example, 'do careers officers give good advice?' (Cherry, 1974), 'how do careers counsellors counsel?' (Taylor, 1985), and 'which types of client are more likely to be submitted for permanent posts?' (Bradley, 1992). The continuing role of the journal in helping to forge and maintain a sense of professional identity is reflected in a recent paper (Lawrence, 1992) which considers the pressures on careers officers to modify their role. Other papers concentrate on the system in which the work occurs. For example, Watts (1980a; 1980b) produced two linked papers on educational and careers guidance services for adults, and Bradley (1990) placed the work of careers officers in its historical context. Watts (1986) discussed the changing relationship between schools and the careers service, and Bates (1990) revealed the political component in definitions of guidance – how these definitions reflect social and political values which are fought over as, for example, careers education curricula are designed, negotiated and implemented.

### FINDING A BOUNDARY: WHAT TO INCLUDE?

Despite its origins in the educational/careers sector, the *BJGC* has continuously looked beyond these areas. The retrospective review of the t journal's first dozen years (Sugarman and Watts, 1985) noted the ever-broadening scope of the articles, finding that 'virtually every issue saw the inclusion of a new topic, client group or problem area' (p. 3). This expansion of scope has continued unabated into the 1990s, with more recent papers inevitably reflecting current concerns – for example, glue sniffing (O'Connor and Britton, 1987), child abuse (Frosh, 1988) and the counselling of HIV/AIDS clients (Bor et al., 1988; 1989; 1991). Eight years ago a review paper on counselling on death and dying (Speck, 1985) made no reference to AIDS, something difficult to imagine now.

The mid-decade review published in 1985 was the outcome of an assessment of the journal's achievements during its first ten years, and an analysis of where it and guidance and counselling were heading. It considered counselling within a variety of settings – schools (Hughes, 1985), higher and further education (Thorne, 1985) and medical settings (Brown and Abel Smith, 1985); and with a variety of clients – young people (Lawton, 1985), adults (Hopson, 1985) and families (Murgatroyd et al., 1985). Pastoral counselling (Foskett, 1985) and counselling on death and dying (Speck, 1985) were also included, and a final paper dealt with training and research (Bolger, 1985). These papers, and the introduction which preceded them (Sugarman and Watts, 1985), represent a statement about the state of the art of counselling and guidance in the UK in the mid-1980s.

As well as focusing on new problem areas, the journal has also continued to give its first airing to a number of aspects of counselling and the counselling relationship – for example, the use of humour (Murgatroyd, 1987b), crying (Kingsley Mills and Wooster, 1987), and depersonalisation (Fewtrell, 1986). A wide variety of theoretical perspectives, techniques and aspects of the dynamics of counselling have been discussed – including microcounselling (Robinson and Halliday, 1987), group process (Zajicek Coleman and Clements, 1989), reversal theory (van der Molen, 1986), implosive therapy (Cowell, 1985) and cognitive counselling (Watts, 1985).

Examination of the volumes of the *BJGC* published since the mid-decade review reveals how counselling in medical settings has taken its place alongside educational institutions as a key location for the work and issues discussed. Following the paper on this topic in the mid-decade review (Brown and Abel Smith, 1985), there were several relevant papers in the 1987 symposium on counselling and health (Daniluk et al., 1987; Hanlon et al., 1987; Corney, 1987) as well as a number of other relevant papers outside this symposium (Balmer, 1987; Stewart, 1987). Also noticeable is the consideration of sources of help other than the professional counsellor (Skuy et al., 1985; Arnold et al., 1988; Cramer, 1990a; 1990b; McLennan, 1991), issues of social support (Winefield and Neuling, 1987), and the helpfulness of self-help groups (Llewelyn and

Haslett, 1986; Block and Llewelyn, 1987).

Authors in the mid-decade review were invited to predict what they believed would be the key issues for guidance and counselling during the forthcoming decade. Murgatroyd *et al.* (1985), for example, accurately predicted that boundaries between therapies would be a prominent issue. This has been discussed primarily in terms of the breaking down of these boundaries, with papers discussing how divergent approaches to counselling can enrich each other (Zajicek Coleman, 1988) and the incorporation of Gestalt concepts and methods into a psychodynamic approach (Robinson, 1991), as well as a paper (Nelson-Jones, 1985) and a symposium (Dryden and Norcross, 1989) specifically concerned with eclecticism and integration.

Similarly, Hopson (1985) predicted an increase in the resources organisations would devote to helping employees develop 'the skills of career and life management' (p. 57). There has, indeed, been a surge of interest in counselling within the workplace. Whilst providing a new career route for counsellors and undoubtably bringing comfort and assistance to many individuals, the wider social implications of this trend are more troubling, partly because of the inevitable limits that organisations place on the extent and nature of their help (including counselling), but also because assistance is usually restricted to those who actually have a job. Those without employment are normally denied access to work-based services.

In the same way as the *BJGC* has rejected a restrictive definition of content with regard to the counselling setting, so too has it eschewed a narrow definition of which aspects of counselling and guidance to address. In addition to the relationship between client and helper which is at the core of counselling practice, the *BJGC* has always included material concerning the social and political context in which this activity takes place. Thus Lawton (1985), focusing particularly on the situation of young people in the UK, offered an analysis of the first half of the 1980s as a period which saw 'an increasingly authoritarian element in British society.... There is much talk of personal responsibility, and arguably there is a developing moral climate in which this represents a reaction against what is seen as excessive personal autonomy.... Talk in education has moved from issues of autonomy and personal experience to those of standards and a return to more traditional teaching methods. If things go wrong, the emphasis is on punishment and short, sharp shock, rather than on development and change' (p. 35).

The trends which Lawton laments have intensified since then. The erosion of benefits for young people has aggravated the extent to which unemployed, disaffected young people are thrown 'into chronic dependence on the financial and emotional resources of parents who are themselves affected by that same unemployment' (p. 36). Not all families can cope, not all young people have families to turn to, and homelessness has become an evident problem in inner-city areas throughout the country. Recent troubles on several inner-city housing estates have, amongst other things, re-emphasised how 'young people with low or nil income are severely constrained in the extent to which they can participate in society' (p. 37). Again, Lawton wrote how 'a training philosophy is taking over some aspects of education, with less attention being paid to individual development and growth, and more to fitting young people to the demands of the economy and society' (p. 37). The introduction of City Technology Schools, the National Curriculum and Standardised Attainment Tests attest to the success of this takeover bid.

Thorne (1985) wrote about how, in 'optimistic moments' (p. 33) he believed careers advisers and counsellors in further and higher education could and would survive the savage cuts that were occurring in public expenditure. Thorne meant 'survive' in spirit as well as in body. By 1990 (Thorne, 1990a) he described the attack on counselling services as more subtle, coming also from those purporting to support them through admonitions to ensure their survival by proving themselves to be efficient and cost-effective and able to face the implications of accountability. Thorne derived comfort from the knowledge that counselling enabled some clients to find the language to challenge the bases of a consumerist society. But whereas in 1985 he had optimistic moments, five years later he referred only to the consolation of a dream of what counsellors and their clients might achieve. The brave new world of demonstrating cost-effectiveness and efficiency is reflected in several papers published during the subsequent years – for example, Aldridge and Legge (1990) on performance indicators for student services, and Watts and Sampson (1989) on strategic planning and performance measures.

Whilst it has been change and expansion that has been particularly noted in this chapter, this is not to imply that the *BJGC* has lost touch with its roots. As well as all the new blooms, many hardy perennials continue to be found in its pages. These include:

❖ **Career-related topics**, such as computer-assisted careers counselling (Hesketh *et al.*, 1987; 1989; Sampson and Reardon, 1991; Watts *et al.*, 1991); career decision-making (Pryor, 1985; 1987; Cox and Morgan,

1985; Siann *et al.*, 1990; Hesketh and McLachlan, 1991; Kelly, 1989; Arnold and Bye, 1989); career indecision (Downing and Dowd, 1988); and careers education (Ross, 1988; Guichard, 1989; Prout, 1990).

❖ **Marriage guidance counselling** (Baird and Walker, 1986; Walker and Baird, 1988; Corney, 1987; Patten and Walker, 1990; Walker and Patten, 1990).

❖ **Training and its assessment** (Wooster *et al.*, 1986; Small and Manthei, 1988; Jacobs, 1990; Sharpley and Ridgway, 1991; Baird and Walker, 1986; Walker and Baird, 1988; Pates and Knasel, 1989; Gallagher and Hargie, 1989).

❖ **Testing** (Cramer, 1986; Pryor, 1986; Taylor and Pryor, 1986; Hesketh *et al.*, 1987; Porteous and Aherne, 1990).

## FINDING A VOICE: HOW TO COMMUNICATE WITH THE READER?

Recognising that in communication the music can be as important as the words, the format of the *BJGC* has been regularly reviewed by the Editorial Board. The goal has been to retain contact with detached analysis and critical evaluation (Sugarman and Watts, 1985), whilst not restricting the journal to statistical studies of a traditional positivist kind, nor excluding material which, in appropriately rigorous ways, provides access to the less tangible aspects of the experience of guidance and counselling. The result has been that over the years there have been several innovations with regard to the style and format of papers.

Prior to the mid-decade review, symposia or special issues appeared on a rather *ad hoc* basis. Four were published during the journal's first twelve years, dealing with the counselling of disturbed children (1975), study skills in higher education (Thorne, 1979), unemployment (1981), and intervention in marriage (Hooper, 1984). The positive reception accorded to these issues, and the opportunity symposia provide for wider and deeper discussion of topics, led to the policy decision to include and commission symposia on a regular basis. Since 1985 at least one symposium has been included every year: on counselling and computers (Sugarman, 1986), counselling and health (Murgatroyd, 1987a), career issues in organisations (Brown, 1988), eclecticism and integration in counselling (Dryden and Norcross, 1989), spiritual dimensions in counselling (Thorne, 1990b), counselling in disaster situations (Taylor, 1991; Lane, 1991), policy challenges confronting careers guidance (Pryor, 1991) and ethics in counselling practice (Cooper, 1992). Symposia provide the opportunity to present different perspectives and opinions on the same topic; as such, they enhance the role of the journal as a platform of debate. Further symposia are planned.

Another innovative section to the journal, the 'personal view', also encourages publication of a wider range of material and perspectives. The 'personal view' is described in the editorial statement introducing it in 1989 as a commissioned 'personal statement about a topical issue which the author feels needs airing in relation to the development of guidance and counselling. It should be opinionated but informed . . .; it may also be controversial and speculative.' It is, therefore, a publication outlet for those with something important to say who do not wish to develop an academic treatise. Three of the eight statements published during the following three years have dealt with aspects of the professional role of the counsellor: the magic and constraints of counselling (Charles-Edwards, 1989), the challenges and dangers brought by the emergence of counselling psychologists as a professionally recognised group (Allen, 1990), and a plea for co-operation rather than in-fighting between counsellors with different theoretical perspectives (Houston, 1991). Three further statements have dealt with the inauspicious context in which counselling operates today: the pernicious effect of the consumerist ideology pervading much of our society (Thorne, 1990a), the nonsense of anti-collectivist 'enterprise' as the basis of a healthy society (Law, 1990), and the relevance of the concept of 'career' during times of recession (Herriot, 1992). What, above all, shines through these contributions is the energy and commitment with which the authors state their case. Released from the constraints of formal academic writing, the authors have been free to expound on a topic about which they have both much knowledge and strong feelings.

The most recent major review of editorial policy, reported in the opening issue of 1990, considered both the scope and level of the journal's coverage. It was decided to retain the *BJGC*'s distinctively broad scope and to attempt to increase its attractiveness to practitioners other than the journal's stable readership of 'researchers, theoreticians, trainers and practitioners actively involved in fostering professional development of the field'. Encouraging full-time practitioners to record their experiences for journals is notoriously difficult – it tends not to be a high priority in their busy schedules, and in any case it is frequently not where such people see their strengths as lying. And yet it is just such material that would encourage a wider practitioner readership. The recently initiated interview section of the journal is one possible way of bringing the experience of these people to a wider audience. To date three interviews have appeared – dealing with the issue of therapist sexual abuse (Dryden, 1991), and with counselling in South Africa (Dryden, 1990) and Japan (Sugarman, 1992). It is unlikely that the material covered in these interviews would have reached the pages of the *BJGC* in any other form.

Despite the introduction of the personal view and interview sections, the balance between the different types of paper published in the *BJGC* has remained fairly constant. Bolger (1985), in an analysis of papers published during the journal's first ten years, counted 93 articles, of which 45% were research papers. During the following ten years (1983–92), a further 247 papers were published, with 100 (40%) being primarily accounts of research. The increase in 1985 from two to three issues a year explains the higher overall number of publications, assisted by the fact that the personal views tend to be shorter than the average article. Of the 147 papers in the later period that were not primarily research studies, just over 15% (23) described fieldwork or case-studies. Classification of articles as 'research', 'fieldwork or case-studies' or 'discursive' is not always clear-cut, reflecting the journal's policy of flexibility with regard to the type of material considered. Thus, for example, a predominantly discursive paper (Murgatroyd, 1983) included a fairly detailed consideration of a case-study, while a piece classified as fieldwork (Pearson, 1988) included some evaluative research. Again, research studies (e.g. Robinson, 1991) have sometimes included a substantial amount of more general discussion of a topic.

## FINDING A POLICY: THE EDITORIAL BOARD AS EXPERIENTIAL LEARNERS

The introduction to the mid-decade review (Sugarman and Watts, 1985) likened the policy reviews of the *BJGC* to re-evaluation points in people's lives – opportunities to take stock of who they are and what they wish to become. The Editorial Board of the journal, in consultation with the Editorial Advisory Panel and the readers, has chosen regularly to review its aims and how to achieve them. Major policy reviews took place in 1975–76, 1983 and 1989. Policy is also continuously monitored and modified via the now six-monthly Editorial Board meetings – as, for example, when it was decided in the mid-1980s to introduce a policy of non-sexist language use. Changes in the composition of the Editorial Board, and the practice of regularly inviting a member of the Editorial Advisory Panel to attend each meeting, also help to ensure that editorial policy review is kept simmering like a bubbling pot.

Having launched the journal in 1973 with a policy of straddling the boundary between theory and practice, and focusing on the educational and careers setting whilst not ignoring other areas, this editorial policy was reviewed on the journal's third birthday. A readers' feedback questionnaire accompanied the July 1975 issue, with the results helping to shape the content and format of the journal over subsequent years. Readers supported the overall aims of and choice of material for the journal, whilst expressing a demand for more fieldwork studies. The results of the survey also suggested that the increase in subscription costs consequent upon raising the number of issues from two to three a year would probably result in the loss of a significant number of individual subscribers; the number of issues a year was accordingly kept at two. Whilst the Editorial Board had considered dropping the abstracts section in favour of a greater number of articles, readers' support for this section resulted in its being retained.

The issues addressed in this first formal review of *BJGC* policy have continued to exercise the minds of the Editorial Board over subsequent years. In 1985 the number of issues was increased from two to three a year. By that time the subscription rate for two issues a year had increased from £2.20 (post free) in 1973 to £10.95 (plus £1.50 postage and packing) in 1984, and the proportion of individual in relation to institutional subscribers had already decreased. There was more than enough good-quality material available to justify three issues a year, and it was felt that the increase in subscription cost would not have the same negative effect on sales that had been feared in the mid-1970s.

We eventually bade farewell to the abstracts section in 1989. With the expansion in the number of relevant journals that had occurred, it had become extremely difficult to offer anything approaching a comprehensive coverage. Furthermore, the economic situation was such that publishers were increasingly reluctant to offer complimentary copies of their journals to would-be abstracters. Without that inducement it was difficult to recruit sufficient readers to submit summaries of relevant articles. In short, the abstracts section was no longer tenable. Its demise released more space for other material, notably book reviews.

The journal has constantly aspired, with limited success, to encourage the submission of more fieldwork and case-study articles. In 1991 the decision was made to allocate a member of the Editorial Board special responsibility for this area, and hopefully this attempt to stimulate and support appropriate material will produce results in the future.

As the counselling profession developed, the *BJGC* established formal links in 1985 both with the British Association for Counselling and with the Counselling Psychology Section (now the Special Group in Counselling Psychology) within the British Psychological Society. These links continue today, with both organisations nominating members to the *BJGC* Editorial Board. Also in 1985, as a result of the editorial policy review triggered by the journal's tenth anniversary in 1983, co-operative links were established between the *BJGC* and the BAC journal *Counselling*, clarifying the distinct but related roles of these two publications. Thus whilst (to quote from the 1985 announcement of these links) the role of the *BJGC* is primarily 'in publishing research and acting as an academic/professional journal to further the standing and quality of counselling', *Counselling* is 'focused more immediately towards counselling practice'.

Like the *BJGC*, other publications in the field also reflect the developing profession. For example, with the establishment in 1986 of a Counselling Psychology Section within the British Psychological Society came the publication of a Section 'Newsletter'. This rapidly metamorphosed into a Section 'Review', and during 1989 the title was changed again, becoming the *Counselling Psychology Review*. This reflected the move to having a Special Group rather than a Section concerned with Counselling Psychology, and denoted the continued upgrading of the publication. In the light of this and other initiatives, such as the launch of the *Counselling Psychology Quarterly* in 1987, the *BJGC*'s editorial policy was further reassessed.

The revised mission statement published in 1990 represents the most recent statement of the aims and objectives of the *British Journal of Guidance and Counselling* and is therefore worth quoting in full. This statement, reprinted in the 'Notes for Contributors' on the inside back cover of all issues of the journal, defines the journal as 'existing to communicate theoretical and practical writing of high quality in the guidance and counselling field. In particular, the journal is concerned to promote development in this field by providing a forum for:

❖ Debate between academics, trainers and practitioners on topical and/or controversial issues related to:
~ the theory and practice of guidance and counselling;
~ the provision of guidance and counselling services;
~ training and professional issues.
❖ Reporting of empirical studies relating to the practice of guidance and counselling – drawing on a variety of disciplines, encompassing both qualitative and quantitative methodologies and ranging in scope from

large-scale surveys to single case-studies.

❖ Exploration of the interface between the various areas of guidance and counselling and their relationship to such cognate fields as education, psychotherapy and social work.'

These aims are directed at fulfilling the *BJGC*'s goal as summarised in the opening paragraph of this chapter.

## CONCLUSION

During the 1960s and 1970s the profession of counselling was expanding and gaining in respectability. Despite the limited number of counselling posts available, counsellors were able to find positions which enabled them to utilise their skills and incorporate the value basis of counselling into their work. In particular, the education sector was marrying the values and practices of counselling with the already established principles and practices of guidance. The launch of the *British Journal of Guidance and Counselling* in 1973 was emblematic of the more general pluralisation of institutions, questioning of traditional disciplinary boundaries and blurring of genres (Geertz, 1983) that characterised this era. In debating the preoccupations of the time, the journal both reflected and contributed to the developing sense of professional identity amongst guidance and counselling practitioners.

The scope of coverage of the journal has continuously expanded. This was consistent with the centrifugal forces of the times in which it was initiated, and has been maintained in the face of the more centripetal forces of later years, which have led to debate as to whether the journal should reduce its breadth of coverage and become, for example, a journal of careers guidance, of guidance in education, of counselling in the workplace, and so on. These forces emanated from the need to maintain an adequate level of subscriptions, and also from a concern as to whether in retaining a broad coverage the journal was slipping between too many cracks – pleasing no-one by trying to please everyone. In the end these forces have always been resisted on the grounds of keeping the profession as a whole together and encouraging dialogues between different elements within it. The question of whether such eclecticism creates a Tower of Babel rather than a useful dialogue between different cognate areas is kept continuously under review. The attempts of Industry Lead Bodies (MSC, 1981) to define standards of competence in the areas of guidance and counselling (McNair, 1992) is likely to ensure that this issue remains on the agenda.

There are analogies between the evolution of the *BJGC* and the process of life career planning. The overall goal, or mission, has been regularly scrutinised; current strategies designed to work towards this goal have been regularly evaluated; and new or potentially more effective strategies have been regularly brainstormed and implemented. Wide-ranging articles (both discursive and research-based), and book reviews, constitute the traditional and enduring strategies. Other strategies may be deemed to be effective but difficult to implement (fieldwork reports and case-studies), to have outlived their usefulness or feasibility (abstracts) or to be useful ways of contributing to the achievement of the overall goal (symposia, personal views and inter-views). These strategies are implemented through a combination of serendipity (the unsolicited papers submitted to the journal) and planning (commissioned symposia, invited personal views, etc.). Hope-fully the combination of a lack of complacency and a willingness to re-evaluate goals and the mechanisms for achieving them will lead the *British Journal of Guidance and Counselling* into the twenty-first century and towards its thirtieth anniversary.

### NOTES

1 I am grateful to Tony Watts for information and discussions concerning the establishment and history of the journal.

### REFERENCES

(For the purposes of this chapter only, the title of the *British Journal of Guidance and Counselling* has been abbreviated.)

Aldridge, S., and Legge, D.: 'Performance Indicators for Student Services'. *BJGC*, Volume 18 No.1, 1990, pp. 3–12.

Allen, J.: 'Counselling Psychologists and Counsellors: New Challenges and Opportunities'. *BJGC*, Volume 18 No.3, 1990, pp. 321–325.

Antonouris. G.: 'Subsequent Careers of Teachers Trained as Counsellors'. *BJGC*, Volume 2 No.2, 1974, pp. 160–170.

Arnold, J., Budd, R.J., and Miller, K.: 'Young People's Perceptions of the Uses and Usefulness of Different Sources of Careers Help'. *BJGC*, Volume 16 No.2, 1988, pp. 83–90.

Arnold, J., and Bye, H.: 'Sex and Sex Role Self-Concept as Correlates of Career Decision-Making Self-Efficacy'. *BJGC*, Volume 17 No.2, 1989, pp. 201–206.

Ayal, H., and Beckerman, R.: 'Peer Counselling – a Means of Actualising Adolescents' Helping Potential'. *BJGC*, Volume 6 No.2, 1978, pp. 204–211.

Baird, P., and Walker, G.: 'Perceived Marital Changes Following Marriage Guidance Training'. *BJGC*, Volume 14 No.2, 1986, pp. 205–11.

Balmer, D.H.: 'Counselling in a Hospital Setting: an Introduction to the CARE Project'. *BJGC*, Volume 15 No.2, 1987, pp. 150–158.

Bates, I.: 'The Politics of Careers Education and Guidance: a Case for Scrutiny'. *BJGC*, Volume 18 No.1, 1990, pp. 66–83.

Block, E., and Llewelyn, S.: 'Leadership Skills and Helpful Factors in Self-Help Groups'. *BJGC*, Volume 15 No.3, 1987, pp. 257–270.

Bolger, A.W.: 'Training and Research in Counselling'. *BJGC*, Volume 13 No.1, 1985, pp.112–124.

Bor, R., Miller, R., and Perry, L.: 'AIDS Counselling: Clinical Application and Development of Services'. *BJGC*, Volume 16 No.1, 1988, pp. 11–20.

Bor, R., Miller, R., Scher, I., and Salt, H.: 'The Practice of Counselling HIV/AIDS Clients'. *BJGC*, Volume 19 No.2, 1991, pp. 129–138.

Bor, R., Perry, L., and Miller, R.: 'When the Solution Becomes a Part of the Problem in the Psychological Management of an AIDS Patient'. *BJGC*, Volume 17 No.2, 1989, pp. 133–137.

Bradley, S.: 'The Careers Service: Past, Present and Future'. *BJGC*, Volume 18 No.2, 1990, pp. 137–155.

Bradley, S.: 'A Case-Study of the Careers Service Placement Function'. *BJGC*, Volume 19 No.1, 1992, pp. 90–107.

Brown, P.T.: 'Career Issues in Organisations: Introduction'. *BJGC*, Volume 16 No.3, 1988, pp. 225–227.

Brown, P.T., and Abel Smith, A.E.: 'Counselling in Medical Settings'. *BJGC*, Volume 13 No.1, 1985, pp. 75–88.

Charles-Edwards, D.: 'A Personal View: Counselling Pearls and Priorities'. *BJGC*, Volume 17 No.1, 1989, pp. 2–7.

Cherry, N.: 'Do Careers Officers Give Good Advice?'. *BJGC*, Volume 2 No.1, 1974, pp. 27–40.

Cooper, G.F.: 'Ethical Issues in Counselling and Psychotherapy: the Background'. *BJGC*, Volume 20 No.1, 1992, pp. 1–9.

Corney, R.H.: 'Marriage Guidance Counselling in General Practice in London'. *BJGC*, Volume 15 No.1, 1987, pp. 50–58.

Cowell, D.: 'Implosive Therapy in the Counselling of a Pupil Who Sets Fires'. *BJGC*, Volume 13 No.2, 1985, pp. 157–165.

Cox, T., and Morgan, K.: 'The Career Aspirations and Occupational Interests of Culturally Disadvantaged Children'. *BJGC*, Volume 13 No.2, 1985, pp. 191–203.

Cramer, D.: 'An Item Factor Analysis of the Revised Barrett-Lennard Relationship Inventory'. *BJGC*, Volume 14 No.3, 1986, pp. 314–325.

Cramer, D.: 'Disclosure of Personal Problems, Self-Esteem, and the Facilitativeness of Friends and Lovers'. *BJGC*, Volume 18 No.2, 1990(a), pp. 186–196.

Cramer, D.: 'Helpful Actions of Close Friends to Personal Problems and Distress'. *BJGC*, Volume 18 No.3, 1990(b), pp. 281–293.

Daniluk, J.C., Leader, A., and Taylor, P.J.: 'Psychological and Relationship Changes of Couples Undergoing an Infertility Investigation: Some Implications for Counsellors'. *BJGC*, Volume 15 No.1, 1987, pp. 29–36.

Downing, K.R., and Dowd, E.T.: 'Career Indecision: a Summary of the Research and Implications for Counselling'. *BJGC*, Volume 16 No.2, 1988, pp.145–157.

Dryden, W.: 'Counselling Under Apartheid: an Interview with Andrew Swart'. *BJGC*, Volume 18 No.3, 1990, pp. 308–320.

Dryden, W.: 'Therapist Sexual Abuse: an Interview with Jill Sinclair'. *BJGC*, Volume 19 No.3, 1991, pp. 320–332.

Dryden, W., and Norcross, J.C.: 'Eclecticism and Integration in Counselling and Psychotherapy: Introduction'. *BJGC*, Volume 17 No.3, 1989, pp. 225–226.

Fewtrell, W.D.: 'Depersonalisation: a Description and Suggested Strategies'. *BJGC*, Volume 14 No.3, 1986, pp. 263–269.

Foskett, J.: 'Pastoral Counselling'. *BJGC*, Volume 13 No.1, 1985, pp. 98–111.

Frosh, S.: 'No Man's Land?: the Role of Men Working with Sexually Abused Children'. *BJGC*, Volume 16 No.1, 1988, pp. 1–10.

Gallagher, M.S., and Hargie, O.D.W.: 'An Investigation into the Validity of Role Play as a Procedure for Counsellor Skill Training'. *BJGC*, Volume 17 No.2, 1989, pp.155–164.

Geertz, C.: *Local Knowledge: Further Essays in Interpretative Anthropology*. New York: Basic Books, 1983.

Guichard, J.: 'Career Education in France: New Objectives and New Methods'. *BJGC*, Volume 17 No.2, 1989, pp. 166–178.

Hanlon, R.B., Turk, D.C., and Rudy, T.E.: 'A Collaborative Approach in the Treatment of Chronic Pain'. *BJGC*, Volume 15 No.1, 1987, pp. 37–49.

Herriot, P.: 'Careers in Recession?'. *BJGC*, Volume 20 No.2, 1992, pp. 231–238.

Hesketh, B., Gleitzman, M., and Pryor, R.: 'Tailoring Computerised Interventions to Client Needs'. *BJGC*, Volume 17 No.1, 1989, pp. 19–33.

Hesketh, B., and McLachlan, K.: 'Career Compromise and Adjustment Among Graduates in the Banking Industry'. *BJGC*, Volume 19 No.2, 1991, pp. 191–208.

Hesketh, B., Wilson, L., Faulkner, A., and Jackson, C.: 'GRADSCOPE: an Analysis of the Item Structure and a Survey of Usage'. *BJGC*, Volume 15 No.2, 1987, pp. 198–213.

Hooper, D.: 'Intervention in Marriage – an Introduction'. *BJGC*, Volume 12 No.1, 1984, pp. 46–51.

Hopson, B.: 'Adult Life and Career Counselling'. *BJGC*, Volume 13 No.1, 1985, pp. 49–59.

Houston, G.: 'Ouch Ouch Stop it'. *BJGC*, Volume 19 No.2, 1991, pp. 209–212.

Hughes, P.: 'Guidance and Counselling in Schools'. *BJGC*, Volume 13 No.1, 1985, pp. 11–21.

Jacobs, M.: 'A Controlled Explosion? – a Decade of Counselling Training'. *BJGC*, Volume 18 No.2, 1990, pp. 113–123.

Kelly, A.: '"When I Grow Up I Want to Be ..."': a Longitudinal Study of the Development of Career Preference'. *BJGC*, Volume 17 No.2, 1989, pp. 179–200.

Kingsley Mills, C., and Wooster, A.D.: 'Crying in the Counselling Situation'. *BJGC*, Volume 15 No.2, 1987, pp. 125–130.

Kolb, D.A.: *Experiential Learning: Experience as the Source of Learning and Development*. Englewood Cliffs, NJ: Prentice-Hall, 1984.

Lane, D.A.: 'Psychological Aspects of Disasters. Issues for the 1990s'. *BJGC*, Volume 19 No.1, 1991, pp. 31–43.

Law, B.: 'Deconstructing the Enterprise Culture'. *BJGC*, Volume 18 No.2, 1990, pp. 201–208.

Lawrence, D.: 'Under Pressure to Change: the Professional Identity of Careers Officers'. *BJGC*, Volume 20 No.3, 1992, pp. 257–273.

Lawton, A.: 'Youth Counselling'. *BJGC*, Volume 13 No.1, 1985, pp. 35–48.

Lewis, D.G., and Murgatroyd, S.: 'The Professionalisation of Counselling in Education and its Legal Implications'. *BJGC*, Volume 4 No.1, 1976, pp. 2–15.

Llewelyn, S.P., and Haslett, A.V.J.: 'Factors Perceived as Helpful by Members of Self-Help Groups: an Exploratory Study'. *BJGC*, Volume 14 No.3, 1986, pp. 252–262.

Mackintosh, J.: 'Counselling in Higher Education: Some Basic Issues'. *BJGC*, Volume 2 No.1, 1974, pp. 55–63.

McLennan, J.: 'Formal and Informal Counselling Help: Students' Experience'. *BJGC*, Volume 19 No.2, 1991, pp. 149–159.

McNair, S.: 'New Maps for Old: Guidance and the Reform of Vocational Qualifications'. *BJGC*, Volume 20 No.2, 1992, pp. 129–149.

Manpower Services Commission: *A New Training Initiative: Consultative Document*. Sheffield: MSC, 1981.

Marteau, L.: 'Accreditation: a Reply to Mathers'. *BJGC*, Volume 6 No.2, 1978, pp. 140–146.

Mathers, J.: 'The Accreditation of Counsellors'. *BJGC*, Volume 6 No.2, 1978, pp. 129–139.

Murgatroyd, S.: 'Training for Crisis Counselling'. *BJGC*, Volume 11 No.2, 1983, pp. 131–144.

Murgatroyd, S.: 'Counselling and Health: an Introduction'. *BJGC*, Volume 15 No.1, 1987(a), pp. 1–5.

Murgatroyd, S.: 'Humour as a Tool in Counselling and Psychotherapy: a Reversal-Theory Perspective'. *BJGC*, Volume 15 No.3, 1987(b), pp. 225–236.

Murgatroyd, S., Cade, B., and Shooter, M.: 'Family Relationships and Counselling'. *BJGC*, Volume 13 No.1, 1985, pp. 60–74.

Nelson-Jones, R.: 'Eclecticism, Integration and Comprehensiveness in Counselling Theory and Practice'. *BJGC*, Volume 13 Nc.2, 1985, pp. 129–138.

O'Connor, D.J., and Britton, P.G.: 'Counselling Glue Sniffers and Solvent Abusers'. *BJGC*, Volume 15 No.3, 1987, pp. 271–284.

Pates, A., and Knasel, E.: 'Assessment of Counselling Skills Development: the Learning Record'. *BJGC*, Volume 17 No.2, 1989, pp. 121–132.

Patten, M.I., and Walker, L.G.: 'Marriage Guidance Counselling: I. What Clients Think Will Help'. *BJGC*, Volume 18 No.1, 1990, pp. 28–39.

Pearson, R.W.: 'Creating Flexible Careers: Some Observations on a "Bridge" Programme for Unemployed Professionals'. *BJGC*, Volume 16 No.3, 1988, pp. 250–267.

Porteous, M.A., and Aherne, H.A. 'An Evaluation of the Concurrent Validity of the Porteous Checklist Using a Structured Interview Schedule'. *BJGC*, Volume 18 No.2, 1990, pp. 197–200.

Prout, G.A.: 'Developing Careers Education and Guidance in a Tertiary College'. *BJGC*, Volume 18 No.1, 1990, pp. 84–95.

Pryor, R.G.L.: 'Towards a Composite Theory of Career Development and Choice'. *BJGC*, Volume 13 No.3, 1985, pp. 225–237.

Pryor, R.G.L. 'Psychological Test Interpretation: Integrative or Disintegrative?'. *BJGC*, Volume 14 No.3, 1986, pp. 270–279.

Pryor, R.G.L.: 'Compromise: the Forgotten Dimension of Career Decision-Making'. *BJGC*, Volume 15 No.2, 1987, pp. 158–168.

Pryor, R.G.L.: 'Policy Challenges Confronting Careers Guidance: Introduction'. *BJGC*, Volume 19 No.3, 1991, pp. 225–229.

Ratigan, B.: 'Counselling Training for Tutors in Higher Education'. *BJGC*, Volume 5 No.1, 1977, pp. 98–101.

Robinson, J.: 'Towards a State of Being Able to Play: Integrating Gestalt Concepts and Methods into a Psychodynamic Approach to Counselling'. *BJGC*, Volume 19 No.1, 1991, pp. 44–65.

Robinson, V., and Halliday, J.: 'A Critique of the Microcounselling Approach to Problem Understanding'. *BJGC*, Volume 15 No.2, 1987, pp. 113–124.

Ross, R.P.: 'Establishing Careers Education within a Modular Degree System'. *BJGC*, Volume 16 No.2, 1988, pp. 203–209.

Sampson, J.P., and Reardon, R.C.: 'Current Developments in Computer-Assisted Careers Guidance in the USA'. *BJGC*, Volume 19 No.2, 1991, pp. 113–128.

Schon, D.A.: *Educating the Reflective Practitioner*. San Francisco, Calif.: Jossey-Bass, 1987.

Sharpley, C.F., and Ridgway, I.R.: 'The Relevance of Previous Knowledge of Psychology to Training in Basic Counselling Skills'. *BJGC*, Volume 19 No.3, 1991, pp. 298–306.

Siann, G., Knox, A., Thornley, E., and Evans, R.: 'Parents, Careers and Culture: the Views of Ethnic-Minority and Ethnic-Majority Girls'. *BJGC*, Volume 18 No.2, 1990, pp. 156–169.

Skuy, M., Hoar, R., Oakley-Smith, T., and Westaway, M: 'Perceptions of the Guidance Teacher as Preferred Helping Agent in some South African Schools'. *BJGC*, Volume 13 No.3, 1985, pp. 266–274.

Small, J.J., and Manthei, R.J.: 'Group Work in Counsellor Training: Research and Development in One Programme'. *BJGC*, Volume 16 No.1, 1988, pp. 33–49.

Speck, P.: 'Counselling on Death and Dying'. *BJGC*, Volume 13 No.1, 1985, pp. 89–97.

Stewart, W.: 'Counselling and Pain Relief'. *BJGC*, Volume 15 No.2, 1987, pp. 140–149.

Sugarman, L.: 'Counselling and Computers: Introduction and Overview'. *BJGC*, Volume 14 No.1, 1986, pp. 1–11.

Sugarman, L.: 'Counselling Behind the Inscrutable Mask: an Interview with Agnes Mieko Watanabe'. *BJGC*, Volume 20 No.3, 1992, pp. 352–364.

Sugarman, L., and Watts, A.G.: 'The BJGC and Guidance and Counselling in Britain 1973–1985'. *BJGC*, Volume 13 No.1, 1985, pp. 1–10.

Taylor, A.J.W.: 'The Field of Disasters and Disaster Stress'. *BJGC*, Volume 19 No.1, 1991, pp. 1–7.

Taylor, N.: 'How Do Careers Counsellors Counsel?' *BJGC*, Volume 13 No.2, 1985, pp. 166–177.

Taylor, N.B., and Pryor, R.G.L.: 'The Conceptualisation and Measurement of Vocational and Work Aspect Preferences'. *BJGC*, Volume 14 No.1, 1986, pp. 66–77.

Thorne, B.: 'Study Skills – a Symposium of Practical Applications in Higher Education: Introduction'. *BJGC*, Volume 7 No.1, 1979, pp. 64–65.

Thorne, B.: 'Guidance and Counselling in Further and Higher Education'. *BJGC*, Volume 13 No.1, 1985, pp. 22–34.

Thorne, B.: 'Counselling and the Grocer's Shop on Campus'. *BJGC*, Volume 18 No.1, 1990(a), pp. 96–100.

Thorne, B.: 'Spiritual Dimensions in Counselling: Editor's Introduction'. *BJGC*, Volume 18 No.3, 1990(b), pp. 225–232.

van der Molen, P.P.: 'Reversal Theory, Learning and Psychotherapy'. *BJGC*, Volume 14 No.2, 1986, pp. 125–139.

Walker, L.G., and Baird, P.: 'Marriage Guidance Training and the Trainer's Own Marriage: a Prospective Study'. *BJGC*, Volume 16 No.2, 1988, pp. 176–189.

Walker, L.G., and Patten, M.I.: 'Marriage Guidance Counselling: II. What Counsellors Want to Give'. *BJGC*, Volume 18 No.3, 1990, pp. 294–307.

Ward, R.: 'Towards Community Self-Help in Higher Education'. *BJGC*, Volume 6 No.1, 1978, pp. 95–101.

Watts, A.G.: 'Educational and Careers Guidance Services for Adults: I. A Rationale and Conceptual Framework'. *BJGC*, Volume 8 No.1, 1980(a), pp. 11–22.

Watts, A.G.: 'Educational and Careers Guidance Services for Adults: II. A Review of Current Provision'. *BJGC*, Volume 8 No.2, 1980(b), pp. 188–211.

Watts, A.G.: 'The Careers Service and Schools: a Changing Relationship'. *BJGC*, Volume 14 No.2, 1986, pp. 168–186.

Watts, A.G., Kidd, J.M., and Knasel, E.: 'PROSPECT (HE): an Evaluation of User Responses'. *BJGC*, Volume 19 No.1, 1991, pp. 66–80.

Watts, A.G., and Sampson, J.P.: 'Strategic Planning and Performance Measurement: Implications for Careers Services in Higher Education'. *BJGC*, Volume 17 No.1, 1989, pp. 34–48.

Watts, F.N.: 'Individual-Centred Cognitive Counselling for Study Problems'. *BJGC*, Volume 13 No.3, 1985, pp. 238–247.

Winefield, H.R., and Neuling, S.L.: 'Social Support, Counselling and Cancer'. *BJGC*, Volume 15 No.1, 1987, pp. 6–16.

Wooster, A.D., Hall, E., and Woodhouse, D.A.: 'In-Service Courses in Human Relations: One Teacher's Learning'. *BJGC*, Volume 14 No.1, 1986, pp. 78–87.

Zajicek Coleman, E.: 'Room to Grow: How Divergent Approaches to Counselling Can Enrich One Another'. *BJGC*, Volume 16 No.1, 1988, pp. 21–32.

Zajicek Coleman, E., and Clements, J.: 'Group Process: a Developmental View'. *BJGC*, Volume 17 No.2, 1989, pp. 138–154.

# 1: THERAPEUTIC COUNSELLING

# A SIX-CATEGORY INTERVENTION ANALYSIS

## JOHN HERON

*Six categories of intervention are briefly defined, together with a definition of the term 'intervention', and some general comments on their application to practitioner–client situations. Each of the six categories is then defined more thoroughly, and a characterisation of different sorts of intervention under each category is given. The analysis concludes with a review of some principles for using the categories in practice.*

### INTRODUCTION

The analysis described in this article was originally inspired by Blake and Mouton (1972). Their Diagnosis and Development Matrix offered five kinds of interventions that 'characterise what applied behavioural scientists do as they work with people in organisations': cathartic, catalytic, confrontation, prescriptive, principles/theories/models. I have altered this scheme to make it both more comprehensive, by adding two further types of intervention (informative and supportive), and to make it more internally coherent, by regarding their principles/theories/models as a sub-species of the catalytic type of intervention.

What is now offered therefore are six basic intervention categories. They have been developed by me in ways that are quite independent of Blake and Mouton, whose focus is primarily on interventions in organisational life; mine is primarily on one-to-one interventions. The following claims are made for the categories:

**1.** That they apply equally to one-to-one, one-to-group and inter-group interventions.

**2.** That they apply across the board to consultancy, tutoring, counselling, interviewing, therapeutic, training, individual or group facilitation, clinical and all professional interventions.

**3.** That they are exhaustive of all desirable and worthwhile types of intervention: that is, they exclude only negative and destructive types of intervention – although they themselves do have their perverted forms (see Heron, 1975).

**4.** That they constitute a powerful analytic training tool for anyone who wishes to build up intervention skills in any and every professional field where they are called for. In particular, they aid the development of

---

First published in the *British Journal of Guidance and Counselling*, Volume 4 No.2, July 1976.

self-assessment and self-monitoring in the helping professions.

The term 'intervention' is not entirely fortunate since normally it connotes some element of interference. It may be as well therefore to define the sense in which it is here used:

**1.** It implies there is some formal differentiation of roles between the one who is practising the intervention, and his client – for example, between trainer and trainee. The differentiation is such that the practitioner is offering some kind of enabling service and skill to the client.

**2.** It implies there is a clear and explicit voluntary contract between practitioner and client, to the effect that the client freely elects to avail himself of the services of the practitioner, and that the practitioner likewise freely elects to provide them.

The second point is particularly important since if the client has not freely chosen to receive the attention of the practitioner, then the latter's interventions will indeed constitute a subtle kind of interference. The term 'intervention' is accordingly used here in a technical sense which excludes the notion of unsolicited interference. From the point of view of this paper, both the term and the practice to which it refers *degenerate* when any element of unsolicited interference enters in.

### THE SIX CATEGORIES

The six categories fall into two groups:

#### Authoritative

**1.** *Prescriptive:* Give advice, be judgmental/critical/evaluative. A prescriptive intervention is one that explicitly seeks to direct the behaviour of the client, especially (though not exclusively) behaviour that is outside or beyond the practitioner–client interaction.

**2.** *Informative:* Be didactic, instruct/inform, interpret. An informative intervention seeks to impart new knowledge and information to the client.

**3.** *Confronting:* Be challenging, give direct feedback. A confronting intervention directly challenges the restrictive attitude/belief/behaviour of the client.

#### Facilitative

**4.** *Cathartic:* Release tensions in, encourage laughter/crying/trembling/storming. A cathartic intervention seeks to enable the client to abreact painful emotion.

**5.** *Catalytic:* Be reflective, encourage self-directed problem-solving, elicit information from. A catalytic intervention seeks to enable the client to learn and develop by self-direction and self-discovery not only within the context of the practitioner–client situation, but also beyond it.

**6.** *Supportive:* Be approving/confirming/validating. A supportive intervention affirms the worth and value of the client.

The first three I call 'authoritative' since in each case the practitioner is taking a more overtly dominant or assertive role; also, the emphasis in the definition is more on what the practitioner is doing. The second set of three I call 'facilitative' since the role of the practitioner is less obtrusive and more discreet, seeking to elicit some state of being in the client; the emphasis in the definition is on the effect of the intervention on the client.

At this point the following general comments should also be made:

**1.** As presented above, the six categories and their designations as either authoritative or facilitative are value-neutral: there is no implication that any one category is either more or less significant and important than any other; nor is there any implication that authoritative and facilitative interventions can be distinguished by any differences of value. The value of an intervention is a function of the total situation at the time, and of the point and purpose of the practitioner's role in relation to his client. Each of the six in an appropriate context can have a high value.

**2.** In general my experience of using the six categories as a training tool with general practitioners, dentists, college tutors, social workers, group facilitators, psychiatric professionals of various kinds, and community health workers of various kinds, has been that they tend to show a much greater deficit in the skilful use of facilitative interventions than they do in the skilful use of authoritative ones (Heron, 1974a). The lowest level of competence, I have found, is in the handling of cathartic interventions.

**3.** I consider that the cultivation of competence in all six types of intervention including the cathartic falls within the province of continuing education in its widest sense. More specifically it is an aspect of human relations training, or interactive skills training, or professional development training. There is a great need for the cultivation of such competence among many professional groups.

**4.** The categories are not totally exclusive of each other. While each has one or more relatively pure forms that entitle it to be clearly distinguished from the others, nevertheless the six types of intervention are significantly and necessarily interdependent. This will be evident in the more detailed analysis that follows later in this paper. Thus an effective confrontation is one that is rooted in a fundamentally supportive attitude; certain predominantly catalytic interventions may have a subordinate but important informative and/or prescriptive element; and so on. Nonetheless, in practice it is invariably clear what the main thrust of an intervention is, however much other categories may be introduced in a subordinate role.

**5.** The most general statement I can make about the truly skilful practitioner in whatever profession is that (**a**) he is equally proficient in each of the six types of intervention, (**b**) he can move elegantly and cleanly from one type of intervention to any other as the developing situation and the purposes of the interaction require, and (**c**) he is aware at any given time of what type of intervention he is using and why. These three together comprise an important aspect of the practitioner's conscious and effective use of his own human resources.

**6.** The six categories transcend any distinctions between schools of counselling, tutoring, interviewing, therapy, personal growth, and so on. Thus they constitute an analytic tool for comparing, contrasting and evaluating the varying approaches of different schools. My own detailed analysis of the categories, however, will disclose directly or by implication a good deal of my own theory and practice of reciprocal counselling (Heron, 1974b).

**7.** The six types of intervention are only of any real value if they are rooted in care and concern for the client. They are of disvalue when used manipulatively. A manipulative use is one in which the practitioner intervenes exclusively to meet his own needs and interests regardless of, or to the actual detriment of, the needs and interests of the client.

### SOME VALID FORMS OF THE SIX CATEGORIES

I will now consider each category in more depth and detail. The following analysis does not claim to be exhaustive of all that can be said under each category (although I regard the basic categories as exhaustive), but it does intend to be reasonably comprehensive. Thus it constitutes some kind of check list for analysis of skills and for awareness of possible sorts of interventions. It is only a look at *sorts* of intervention under each category: it necessarily omits *content* (what is said and done within the given sort) and *manner* (how it is said and done – timing, verbal mood, non-verbal behaviour), since these are situation-specific, and their grasp requires the use of experiential training techniques. All the interventions listed are only validly used when they are appropriate to the type of practitioner–client situation and to its particular phase of development, and also when the content and manner are similarly appropriate. The determination of such validity is a matter of experiential enquiry (Heron, 1972).

**Prescriptive interventions** do not encroach on the self-determining competence of the client and are presented in such a way that the client feels free to acknowledge that they do (or do not) accord with his own true needs and interests. Sorts of prescriptive intervention include:

**1.** With respect to the client's *future* behaviour, the practitioner may (**a**) give advice, (**b**) suggest or commend, (**c**) request, (**d**) demand or command (the situation may legitimate this), (**e**) demonstrate how to do it before the client does it, (**f**) lead the way so that the client subsequently follows.

**2.** With respect to the client's *current* (actually occurring) behaviour, the practitioner may (**a**) verbally direct/monitor/correct/evaluate the client's performance, (**b**) non-verbally do the same by touch, gesture or eye-contact, (**c**) demonstrate the appropriate behaviour concurrently.

**3.** With respect to the *level* of intervention in client behaviour, the practitioner may prescribe (**a**) general values and/or general norms, (**b**) particular means, (**c**) particular ends. Or to put it another way, he may prescribe (**a**) beliefs and attitudes about behaviour, (**b**) particular behaviours, (**c**) particular goals to be achieved.

**Informative interventions** are seen by the client to be relevant to his needs and interests. They do not suppress but positively enhance the client's needs to participate actively in the learning process in a self-directing manner. Sorts of informative intervention include:

**1.** Giving general knowledge to the client – factual, practical, theoretical. This is any kind of knowledge that is not specifically or exclusively about or relevant to the client.

**2.** Giving information to the client that he specifically needs to fulfil his needs and interests.

**3.** Giving information to the client that is specifically about the client or about the situation in which he is very closely involved. This may extend to giving the client a prediction about himself.

**4.** Giving an interpretation to the client of the client's past and/or present experience and behaviour. This shades over into a more confronting version (see below).

**Confronting interventions** reach out to and are supportive of the person, while throwing into relief his rigidities and defences so that he can experience his own insight into their role as defences. Sorts of confronting intervention include:

**1.** 'Direct feedback'. The practitioner shares with the client his impressions of restrictive client behaviour and shares also his feeling reactions to those impressions. This is done in a non-punitive, non-judgmental way, stripped clean of any pseudo-objective critical appraisal of the client's 'character'. However chastening the content of what he says, the practitioner says it supportively: 'Right or wrong, this is the impression you make on me, and this is what that impression does to me. Maybe this is feedback which you can use.'

**2.** 'Interrupt the pattern'. The client is playing an old negative recording, lost in the dramatisation of his distresses. Without attack, remaining supportive in attitude, the practitioner interrupts the pattern by quickly and deftly (**a**) drawing attention to something in the environment, or (**b**) introducing and sustaining a totally different topic, or (**c**) contradicting by the use of unqualified positive statements the negative assertions the client is making about himself, his life, or the world at large, or (**d**) proposing a total change of activity, a new address to the environment, or (**e**) drawing attention by the use of the eyes to the client's non-verbal agitations and tensions.

**3.** 'Holding up a mirror'. The practitioner holds up a mirror to the client's negative verbal and non-verbal behaviour by mimicking it back to him, piece by piece as it occurs. But he does this with supportive attention, not in any kind of mocking spirit. It can be very powerful if the practitioner is really attuned to the person of the client while doing it, and can be used cathartically (see below).

**4.** 'Direct question'. The practitioner aims a direct question at the client's concealed data, data that the client is defending against acknowledging either to himself or to others or to both: 'When did you last have an orgasm?' 'When did you last tell your daughter you loved her?'

**5.** 'Rattle and shake'. The practitioner asks questions that challenge the restrictive attitudes, beliefs, intentions, actions of the client, but is attuned to the person of the client while posing them: 'Do you really believe/think/feel/intend X, Y or Z?' 'Are you aware of the inconsistency/incoherence of . . .?' 'What evidence do you have for . . .?' This shades over into catalytic questioning.

**6.** 'Unmask'. The practitioner directly confronts the client with information about the client which the latter has tried to conceal and to which the practitioner has independently gained access.

**7.** 'Interpretation'. The practitioner gives the client an interpretation of the latter's defences and restrictions of being.

**8.** 'Discharge feedback'. The practitioner, without in any way verbally attacking or invalidating the client, displays before him a full and complete discharge in sound and movement of pent-up anger and frustration. This is a radical step but can be effective if the situation merits it and if the practitioner moves straight back into the relationship with open and free attention, ready to continue to work for constructive, caring interaction.

When confronting interventions become punitive and attacking, they generally fail since the client recoils, the defences harden, and a counter-attack is soon under way. They are effective usually only when the practitioner is felt by the client to be on his side against his defences and rigidities.

**Cathartic interventions** facilitate the client to abreact painful emotions such as anger (in 'storming' sounds and movements), grief (in tears and sobbing), fear (in trembling and shaking), and embarrassment (in laughter). They are pitched at a level of distress which the client is ready to handle in a relatively undisruptive way. They are followed through systematically so that there is a sufficient release of accessible painful emotion for the client to be free of its disabling effects. Space is given for the verbalisation of spontaneously-generated client insight. Sorts of cathartic intervention include:

**1.** 'Literal description'. The client is invited to describe in literal detail a traumatic event. He does not talk about it analytically from the top of his head, but evokes it by recall of sights, sounds, what people said and did. He stays close to the immediate texture of the event. The distressful emotion is invariably impacted in the interstices of the literal details. Evocation of the scene is helped if the client describes it in the present tense as if he is witnessing it now. He may need to repeat the description many times. He can be helped by discreet questions to get closer to the immediate and traumatically crucial goings-on in the scene. This intervention alone may induce catharsis, but it combines well with the next one.

**2.** 'Repetition'. The client is invited, especially during literal description of some traumatic event, to repeat words or phrases that carry – especially as indicated by paralinguistic and non-verbal cues – a charge of emotional tension. The cues may be a faltering tone of voice, a puckering of the mouth or eyes, a twitching of the fingers or the limbs, a sudden change of posture, and so on. If the client repeats the phrases several times – especially with an increase in volume beyond a level which he finds comfortable – he may discharge the underlying painful emotion with sobbing, or storming movements and sounds, or trembling, or laughter, or some combination of these, depending on the trauma.

**3.** 'Association'. The client is invited by a quick, deft intervention to verbalise a sudden and unbidden thought or to repeat a slip of the tongue. This will often produce light catharsis in laughter and may lead into frutiful areas for further cathartic release. The signs in the client of unbidden associations are unmistakable: he suddenly looks across the room, or to the floor, or to the ceiling, or out of the window; there is a quick fleeting pensiveness, a rearrangement of face, posture, hands. Also, the thoughts, images, memories which are released spontaneously after a cathartic episode, if given space for verbal expression, may themselves lead on directly or ultimately to further cathartic release.

**4.** 'Acting into'. If the distressful emotion is near the surface and the client is starting to feel it, he may be enabled to discharge it by acting into the discharge. That is, he initially acts the sounds and movements of catharsis, which has the effect of precipitating a genuine cathartic episode. So he may be invited to act a shudder and trembling movement when he feels fear rising, and then a real trembling takes over as the fear runs off; or to act storming sounds and movements when he feels buried anger rising, and then the real danger discharge takes over.

**5.** 'Mobilising body energy'. Unresolved painful emotion from old trauma may be impacted in chronic muscular spasm and tension and in restricted breathing habits. The client may be invited to breathe deeply, to hyperventilate, to arch and stretch the spine over pillows and covered stools, to thrash the arms and legs and head, with loud sounds. This total loosening of physical structures and mobilisation of body energy may itself precipitate cathartic release, often of painful emotion which has been suppressed long before.

**6.** 'Self-role-play'. This is one of the most basic forms of cathartic intervention. As the trauma is brought into focus by literal description and other strategies, the client is invited to become himself in the traumatic scene and to say and express now what was left unsaid, suppressed and denied at the time. The practitioner can stand in for the person from the past who was in the crucial trauma-inducing role; or, as in psychodrama, group members may help reconstruct the family scene from the past. In such a context, the client finds a way to express and abreact the painful emotion which he suppressed at the time, in a manner that is *directed at* (though in no way physically harming) the role-played oppressor from the past. Classically, the 'oppressor' is the client's mother or father; as the early distress is surfacing it may be sufficient for the client simply to cry out 'Mummy' or 'Daddy' loudly several times to precipitate a powerful cathartic release, especially if this is combined with physical holding (see below) by the practitioner. This intervention has been variously developed in psychodrama, psychomotor therapy, primal therapy, co-counselling, neo-Reichian therapy and so on. In a sense, every cathartic release is a return to oneself in the past to complete unfinished business.

**7.** 'Monodrama'. The client is invited to play the two sides of an internal conflict. This may be a role conflict – for example, a person who is in conflict about his role as doctor and his role as husband. Or it may be a more radical conflict such as that between internal oppressor and internal victim. The client has a chair for each protagonist in the conflict, and switches from chair to chair as he creates a dialogue between the two. The method can rapidly become cathartic if the client is skilfully facilitated to use repetition, increased volume and acting-into on key phrases used by either side of his conflict.

**8.** 'Contradiction'. The client is invited to use phrases and/or to use a manner that contradicts, without qualification, his deeply-ingrained negative self-image. This negative self-image or internally invalidating piece of programming, is the ultimate suppressor of painful emotion – it is the introjected or internalised parental rejection of the child's need for cathartic release, together with all the internalised invalidations the child has received down the years. Contradiction can work in at least three ways:

(**a**) 'Full contradiction'. The client is invited to make an unqualified self-appreciative statement which contradicts the negative feeling he has about himself, in a self-appreciative tone of voice, and with self-appreciative facial expression, gestures and posture.

(**b**) 'Partial contradiction'. The client expresses the negative view he has about himself but does so in a very pleased tone of voice with pleased and delighted facial expression, gesture and posture.

(**c**) 'Double negative'. The client exaggerates the negative statement about himself with exaggeratedly negative tone of voice, and exaggeratedly negative facial expression, gesture and posture.

More generally, any way the client can be enabled to say and do things (i.e. behave verbally and non-verbally) in ways that contradict the ingrained negative and rigid suppressive way he has of *not* being his dynamic, creative and joyful self, will tend to facilitate cathartic release. Well-conceived contradiction always has a cathartic effect – initially light, then deeper – if the client will put enough energy into it. But precisely because it is so effective, his defences and controls will at first baulk heavily at it.

**9.** 'Phantasy'. The client can be invited to use phantasy in a variety of ways to reach down to and loosen up material for cathartic work. Phantasy can quickly sidestep a lot of analytic, rational controls.

**10.** 'Relaxation and reverie'. The client is invited to relax into a reverie, then to pick up associations, and to work with phantasy or spontaneous body movements. With suitable encouragement, autogenic catharsis can occur.

**11.** 'Transpersonal work'. The client may be invited to pursue meditation or enlightenment methods which can have incidentally cathartic effects.

**12.** 'Physical holding'. For the client to start working in the practitioner's arms on certain kinds of material will facilitate eventual abreaction. When the client is on the verge of tears and sobbing, if the practitioner reaches out to embrace him supportively, the floodgates will open. Similarly with emerging fear, if the client is held this may facilitate the fear running off, especially if he is invited to dig his fingertips into the practitioner's back. For working on double-bind material related to either parent, the client can be invited to hold and be held by the practitioner, discharging anger by pounding the practitioner's back with the flat of the closed fists, together with appropriate words and sound.

**13.** 'Physical pressure'. When the client is discharging grief in the practitioner's arms, a discreetly-timed but very firm pressure applied in certain parts of the dorsal spine will often intensify the release. Deep friction or pressure applied by the practitioner to certain areas of tension, especially those adjacent to the spinal column, can reach and release suppressed painful emotion if the client is encouraged to react to the initial physical pain of the pressure with uninhibited sound and movement of the limbs. Various forms of light and heavier relaxing massage, if combined with attention to breathing and the verbalising of associations, can also have a cathartic effect.

**14.** 'Mimicry'. As in 'holding up a mirror' (see under 'confronting interventions' above). This rapidly produces cathartic laughter in the client if executed and timed well, and is on the side of the client against his redundant controls.

**15.** 'Primary contact'. Gazing into the client's eyes and simultaneously holding his hands with abundant free attention is an incipiently cathartic intervention.

**16.** 'Immersion'. The client may be invited to immerse himself in water and use energy-mobilising exercises through sound, breathing and movement.

**17.** 'Hallucinogens'. LSD, for example, can be a powerful abreactive drug if the client is appropriately facilitated when under its influence. Its general use is however currently illegal.

**18.** 'Balance of attention'. The client cannot discharge old painful emotion unless he has sufficient attention outside that material. The client who is in a very heavy, negative, woe-begotten state of mind has no attention available for effective cathartic work: his attention has sunk into, has been swamped by, the old miasmic distresses. The practitioner will then need to switch to a light level of working, using contradiction in one of its forms or generating attention techniques (see below), to build up a reservoir of attention outside and away from the buried distress. If the client remains open to that distress and gets the balance right between awareness of it and what his attention is engaged with outside it, then the distress will tip into discharge. Some disidentification from the pain is necessary before it can be discharged.

**19.** 'Generating attention techniques'. Where the client is over-identified with old impacted painful emotion, the practitioner can help him generate some attention, in order to get the balance of attention right for discharge. He can do this by inviting him to describe the practitioner, or to describe the immediate environment, or to move around in the environment, or to change the immediate environment, or to describe recent pleasant events, or to relax and do deep breathing, or to release his imagination and phantasy, and so on. Also any light cathartic release in laughter – for example, following the use of contradiction – will generate distress-free attention. Sustained catharsis liberates abundant distress-free attention so that the client is very much alive to the fullness of present-time reality.

**Catalytic interventions** facilitate the emergence of impending client-generated change, never overstay their welcome, and are alive with active empathy. Sorts of catalytic intervention include:

**1.** 'Free attention'. The practitioner gives to the client all his available attention – that is, all his attention that is not distracted by other events in the environment and that is not distracted inwards by his own internal psychological noise (negative thoughts, feelings and preoccupations). Giving free attention is a subtle and intense activity of being present for the client; it involves gaze, posture, facial expression, maybe touch. It has the qualities of being supportive – out there with the client; of being expectant – waiting for the human being to emerge in ways that are meaningful to him and his fulfilment; and of being non-anxious – the practitioner is free of claims and demands, of any harrying attitude towards the client. It is always wider and deeper than the content of the client's speech, being attuned to his emerging potential as well as his actual behaviour.

**2.** 'Reflection'. The practitioner simply echoes back to the client the last few words the client said before pausing. Or he may rephrase the last few words, expressing the same meaning as the client but in different words. The reflection is a way of conveying to the client – when the client pauses in the development of his theme – that the practitioner is paying attention, is interested, and above all wishes the client to continue to any way that is meaningful to himself (the client). It is an intervention that gives space and support to the client to unfold his story or his thinking in his own way. A direct question takes the client in a certain direction, so that his options for developing his theme are immediately restricted. The combination of reflection and free attention represents a pure catalytic intervention.

**3.** 'Selective reflection'. Reflection as above echoes the last few words the client says before a pause in his delivery. Selective reflection picks out from the whole body of statements he has just made a few words or phrases that seem to carry a suppressed emotional charge, that were accompanied by noticeable non-verbal agitation, or that were sudden impromptu asides or seeming slips of the tongue. These words are simply echoed back literally to the client, with free attention. He then has space to explore their deeper implications if he so wishes, in any way he chooses.

**4.** 'Checking for understanding'. This is slightly more elaborate than reflection and for similar though slightly different motives. The practitioner gives in his own words a resumé of the point of view, the orientation within the problem, which the client has just expressed. In doing this, the practitioner is (**a**) checking to make sure he has understood the client, (**b**) giving evidence of his empathy in getting under the skin of the client's way of construing his world, and (**c**) inviting the client to elaborate and develop the theme in any way that seems appropriate after that theme has been seen to pass through the prism of another's understanding mind.

**5.** 'Client-centred questioning'. The practitioner, sensitive to the areas of potential development in the client's thinking, feeling and decision-making, times and conceives questions that enable the client to open up these areas in a spirit of genuine self-discovery and self-directed problem-solving. The question points in a discreet and timely way to an emerging area of growth, but it does not pre-empt any issues about how the client will develop such an area. This intervention will normally combine with the four previous sorts of catalytic intervention.

**6.** 'Discreet self-disclosure'. Disclosure begets disclosure. If the practitioner discloses some of his experiences and concerns in the area that the client is addressing, this may facilitate client disclosure through raising the level of trust, openness and risk-taking. It constitutes authentic, intimate sharing.

**7.** 'Problem-solving structures'. The practitioner offers a structured exercise, a formal procedure, by the use of which the client is invited to seek to solve his problem or resolve his task. It may be a scheme for analysing relevant phenomena and experience, for generating or evaluating ideas, for goal-setting and role-definition, for decision-making and action-planning, and so on. The practitioner simply offers a procedural form which the client fills with his own content. Organisation development consultants have many exercises of this kind available for their clients, and there are also parallels with staff-student contracts for self-directed learning schedules.

**8.** 'Self-discovery structure'. The practitioner offers a structured exercise by means of which the client may increase his personal and interpersonal awareness and development. Reality games, growth games, human relations training exercises – all fall within this sort of intervention. The client is self-directing in his exploration of the exercise within the limits set by the exercise, and is free to make his own discoveries in his own way. After the exercise, the client needs space to verbalise and discuss his experiences. This intervention shades over into structured exercises that have a cathartic effect, e.g. co-counselling training. It includes all self-directed transpersonal exercises.

**9.** 'Theoretical structure'. The practitioner offers theories, conceptual models, that facilitate the client's orientation within some domain of experience and practice. The theories and models give the client ground-plans that enable him to become more intelligently self-directing in some area of concern to him. The theories are general: they include, but are not exclusively relevant to, the client's situation.

**10.** 'Analysis of variables'. The practitioner offers the client an analysis of what he sees to be some of or all the situation-specific variables that have a bearing on some process or task with which the client is involved. The analysis is offered to aid client resolution of the situation, but does not itself constitute any kind of solution. This sort of intervention includes process comments in groups.

**11.** 'Analysis of options'. The practitioner outlines what he conceives to be some of or all the relevant options or possibilities open to the client with respect to some specific decision the client has to take. The analysis is offered as a means of facilitating a client-generated decision; it does not itself constitute any kind of decision. Or the intervention may alert the client to unacknowledged but urgent decisions he needs to take or to life-enhancing possibilities that had never occurred to him.

On the last three sorts of intervention, the informative and the catalytic coalesce. This is also the case, on another level, with the traditional 'teacher of wisdom' whose informative utterances may have a powerful catalytic effect: the listener is moved to inaugurate significant changes in the way he directs his life, for his own inner initiative is stirred by the impact of what he has heard.

**Supportive interventions** do not collude with the person's rigidities, defences and negative misidentifications. They are intimate, authentic and caring. Sorts of supportive intervention include:

**1.** 'Free attention' (see under 'catalytic interventions' above). This is the fundamentally supportive act of being present for the client with the expectation only that he shall become ever more fully his authentic self. It is, I believe, the *sine qua non* of all other sorts of interventions if they are to be truly and effectively human.

**2.** 'Touch'. From a fleeting touch with the fingers to a full embrace, the use of touch is one of the most immediate ways of expressing support, solidarity and fellow-feeling. Often grossly under-used because the practitioner mistakenly supposes that touch necessarily has primary erotic implications. Wise practice however distinguishes between nurturance needs – for closeness, warmth, human nourishment – and sexual needs. The former is assuaged by sensitive, aware, caring person-to-person physical holding and contact in which the sexual component is invariably absent, marginal or entirely secondary.

**3.** 'Expressions of positive feeling'. This involves the direct verbal expression to the client of feelings of love, affection, liking, fondness.

**4.** 'Expressions of care and concern'. The practitioner makes unequivocally clear in words to the client his care about the client, his wish to reach out, relate to, work with, and give support and facilitation to him.

**5.** 'Validation'. The practitioner verbally affirms to the client, without qualification, the intrinsic value of the client either in general terms or in terms of specific worthwhile qualities, attitudes, achievements, and ways of being which the client is blind to or denigrates in himself.

**6.** 'Sharing'. The practitioner shares the good things in his experience with the client.

**7.** 'Self-disclosure'. The practitioner discloses some of his own Sturm and Drang, past and present, to the client as an expression of human solidarity. This is closely related, of course, to the catalytic use of self-disclosure as given above.

It may often be difficult for the client really to hear and accept supportive interventions. They tend to bounce off the hardened shell of his negative self-image. He will often rapidly disown them or drive them away with a fast compliment in return. It is a cathartic intervention to invite him to find some way of accepting, say, the validation: if he really opens to it and allows himself to hear it, he will invariably discharge some embarrassment in laughter.

### SOME FINAL GENERAL POINTS

**1.** As I pointed out earlier, none of the six categories are entirely independent of each other. The supportive category, especially, is a vital substratum of all the others, for unless the manner of intervention breathes support for the worth of the client, the intervention itself is either valueless or disvaluable.

**2.** Sorts (7) to (11) inclusive under 'catalytic interventions' provide a basic core of interventions for introducing experiential and self-directed learning into education at all levels.

**3.** The different categories and sorts can be woven together in an endless variety of ways depending upon the type of practitioner–client relation, the way the given relation is developing, the emerging potential of the client, the creativity and insight of the practitioner. One category or sort may merge imperceptibly into another. Or there may be a sudden and distinctive change of intervention.

**4.** Conscious use of the self enhances and does not inhibit spontaneity and creativity. The greatest improvisors are those who have a clear conscious grasp of the full range of the medium's resources.

**5.** The whole purpose of the analysis, its preparatory application through training, and its practical application in life, is to release more and more of the potential of a person-to-person relation within the practitioner–client relation.

**6.** The creation of any kind of long-term dependency of a psychologically debilitating kind – which upsets a healthy balance between autonomy and inter-dependence – is against the whole spirt of the analysis. Hence all the sorts and categories of intervention, as well as being fundamentally supportive of the value of the person, need also to have an implicit catalytic thrust – they need directly or indirectly to work toward increasing the capacity of the client for creative self-direction in a context of mutual aid.

**7.** A fundamental issue arises with respect to the appropriate application of prescriptive interventions of the advice-giving variety as against catalytic interventions that facilitate self-directed problem-solving. Giving advice seems more appropriate where the practitioner is an expert in some area of technicality – the law, finance, medicine, technology, architecture, etc. – beyond the range of the client's experience and knowledge. It seems less and less appropriate where the practitioner is concerned to aid the client to achieve full human stature – as in psychotherapy, counselling, and their variants.

**8.** The validation of the various sorts of intervention is ultimately a matter of experiential research (Heron, 1972). I have listed only those which I have field-tested and which other persons whom I judge to be reliable in experiential work have field-tested.

### REFERENCES

Blake, R., and Mouton, J.: *The D/D Matrix*. Austin, Texas: Scientific Methods, 1972.

Heron, J.: *Experience and Method*. Human Potential Research Project, University of Surrey, 1972 (mimeo).

Heron, J.: *Course for New Teachers in General Practice II*. Human Potential Research Project, University of Surrey, 1974(a) (mimeo).

Heron, J.: *Reciprocal Counselling*. Human Potential Research Project, University of Surrey, 1974(b) (mimeo).

Heron, J.: *Six Category Intervention Analysis*. Human Potential Research Project, University of Surrey, 1975 (mimeo).

## POSTSCRIPT

The article above was a digest of a somewhat longer monograph published by the Human Potential Research Project, University of Surrey, in 1975. I had founded this Project in November 1970, in the then Centre for Adult Education (now the Department of Educational Studies) as a focus for extramural personal and professional development courses. In 1973 I was approached by the course organisers of the GP Vocational Training Scheme for the South West Thames Region to put on a 6-month, half-day release course to train senior General Practitioners to become trainers of young hospital doctors entering general practice for the first time.

The course was designed by consultative planning with the participants, and it included experiential, interpersonal skills training, for which I agreed to be responsible. I looked around for an adequate behaviour category system to use as a basis for this training, but could not find one. Perhaps Bales' system was nearest, but for various reasons it did not suit. So I started from scratch with an obvious distinction between authoritative behaviour ('I'm telling you') and facilitative behaviour ('I invite you to tell me'). Simple exercises built round this proved very fruitful, since the GPs could quickly see that their attempts at being facilitative were in a thinly veiled authoritative manner ('Don't you think it would be best here to . . . ?').

We all realised early on that many of the trainer–trainee relationship issues between senior GP and fledgling GP mirrored very exactly important aspects of the GP–patient relationship. By keeping an eye on this parallelism during the first course, I turned the authoritative category into a set of three (prescriptive, informative and confronting) and the facilitative category into another set of three (cathartic, catalytic and supportive). The flash point for this conversion was reading Blake and Mouton's *Diagnosis and Development Matrix*, as the article explains.

Through the 1973 GP Trainers' Course, and more so during the 1974 Course, *each* of the six categories spawned a set of quite specific interventions, so that there was eventually a large number of particular interventions of six basic different sorts. By the end of 1974, the whole thing had been quite thoroughly field-tested, and this in three ways: by the training exercises on the courses; by trainer–trainee relationships within the GPs' practices; and perhaps most fundamentally by the doctor–patient relationship itself. For with a weekly half-day release course we could get feedback on both these last two applications. During this year, too, I had started to run Six Category Workshops for mixed professional groups, and so was developing its general, all-purpose use. By 1975 it was time to write up the whole model and publish it through the University of Surrey. The article for *BJGC* followed shortly afterwards.

As a conceptual framework for basic interpersonal skills training, the Six Category model has been very durable and popular. I think this is because the categories are in the mid-range of human *intention* between general qualities (empathy) and specific behaviours (ask an open question). This makes them both readily accessible and widely applicable. People can quickly learn the basic repertoire, and use it to assess their strengths and weaknesses, and to build up at least some minimal and modest skill in areas of weakness. Just as a matter of interest, in passing, the vast majority of professional helpers who have attended workshops in the UK and Europe assess themselves as weakest in cathartic and confronting interventions.

I ran a steady series of same profession and mixed profession Six Category Workshops through the University of Surrey, the British Postgraduate Medical Federation in the University of London, and at other centres in the UK and in Europe from 1974 to 1986. I and especially my successors at the Human Potential Research Project (now the Human Potential Resource Group) evolved a combination of basic training, advanced training and trainer training, which is still going strong at the University of Surrey eighteen years after the model was first mooted.

As a result, for many years there have been large numbers of trainers using the method for basic and trainer training in a wide diversity of professional settings: medicine (especially general practice), nursing (especially psychiatric nursing), social work, psychotherapy and counselling training, professional supervision, teaching (especially in higher and continuing education), police, youth and community work, management training in industry. It is by now impossible to keep track of all the ramifications of usage. And while it has been widely adopted in practice, with books and training manuals based on it, it has been virtually ignored, so far as I am aware, in the general literature of its field.

The original monograph was very extensively enlarged in 1986, revised again in 1989, and most recently in 1990, when it was published as *Helping the Client: a Creative, Practical Guide* (London: Sage). For me, the basic conceptual model is still valid and remains entirely unchanged (unlike, for example, the companion *Dimensions of Facilitator Style*, whose deep structure I radically overhauled in 1989). But the number of interventions under each category has been greatly expanded. And there are numerous additions including: issues and agendas to do with the use of each category; the sequencing of interventions; their degenerate forms; client categories; states of personhood; practitioner process; the nature of helping; the relationship between catharsis and transmutation; illustrative diagrams; and training methods.

The article claims that the model applies to one-to-group and inter-group interventions as well as one-to-one. This is quite wrong. It is exclusively a one-to-one model. Re-reading the 1976 article now in the light of the 1990 edition of the book, it all appears rather minimalist and thin on the ground. The definitions of each of the categories are all right as far as they go, but don't go very far. The accounts of the prescriptive and informative categories are underdeveloped; the confronting, cathartic and catalytic categories have all been substantially enriched and enlarged in the 1990 version.

My final point is this. The Six Category approach to interpersonal skills training affirms then and now an important truth: people in our society can significantly extend the range of their effective helping simply by learning a comprehensive repertoire of helping behaviours, using it to identify behaviours they omit or do badly, and to acquire new and improved skills through practice and feedback, in the light of good modelling. Sooner or later, of course, some in-depth personal development work is called for to underpin and advance the whole enterprise. But nothing whets the appetite for this more than taking behaviour to the outer limits of what can be accomplished without it.

# GOALS FOR COUNSELLING, PSYCHOTHERAPY AND PSYCHOLOGICAL EDUCATION: RESPONSIBILITY AS AN INTEGRATING CONCEPT

## RICHARD NELSON-JONES

*Responsibility may be viewed as a central integrating concept in counselling, psychotherapy, and psychological education. A distinction is made between responsibility to and responsibility for. The ultimate goal of counselling is to help clients towards taking effective responsibility for their own self-realising. Four mediating goals toward higher levels of self-realising are described: realism, relatedness, rewarding activity, and right-and-wrong (an ongoing process of ethical living). Some central sub-goals are suggested for these four areas, in each of which responsibility may be avoided or assumed.*

As counsellors we frequently use terms like 'personal growth' and 'personal development'. It is important that we clearly understand what we mean by such terms as a basis for effective intervention with clients, and also for our own lives. In this paper on goals I will present a view of counselling, psychotherapy and psychological education in which responsibility is regarded as a central integrating concept. In a functional way I will attempt to identify and associate relevant themes among the goals of existing therapies, as well as to offer a more focused emphasis on responsible attitudes and behaviour.

At first glance there appears to be a plethora of goals in counselling and psychotherapy. Mahrer (1967) defined psychotherapeutic goals as the long-range, ultimate aims and purposes, directionalities and outcomes of therapy. Jahoda (1958), in her review of the literature on positive mental health, identified six major categories of concepts, to which all ideas on the topic could be assigned with relative ease, even though there might be some overlap. These categories were: (**1**) the individual's attitudes towards his own self; (**2**) his style and degree of growth, development, or self-actualising; (**3**) his degree of integration, this being a central synthesising psychological function; (**4**) his autonomy or degree of independence from social influences; (**5**) the adequacy of his perception of reality; and (**6**) his degree of environmental mastery. Jahoda further sub-divided each of these categories into differing dimensions.

For a number of reasons, the concept of positive mental health does not seem an appropriate integrating focus. First, it is a vague concept

First published in the *British Journal of Guidance and Counselling*, Volume 7 No.2, July 1979.

which is open to numerous interpretations. Second, despite the use of the word 'positive', it has connotations of a sickness model in which someone from outside provides a cure. Third, it is difficult for individuals in our culture to acknowledge deficiencies in their mental health, since the term 'mental health' is so value-laden. And fourth, use of the word 'health' may overemphasise the contribution which the medical profession can make in helping people with psychological concerns as contrasted with that of other helping professions and with self-help.

The concept of responsibility may provide a better focus. It is a theme running through all six of Jahoda's concept of positive mental health categories, but does not imply psychiatric sickness and the need for medical attention. Also, it has connotations of self-help rather than reliance on others for a cure. Furthermore, unlike the term 'mental health', responsibility is central to the means as well as to the ends of effective living.

The idea of responsibility is implicit if not explicit in the goals of a number of humanistic psychologists, such as Maslow's (1970) 'self-actualising', Rogers' (1961) 'fully-functioning', Combs and Snygg's (1959) 'adequate' persons, and Fromm's (1976) 'new man'. It is central in existential psychology, where man, within the confines of death and destiny, is responsible for fashioning his life (Frankl, 1946); and is also emphasised by Christian writers such as Paton (1968), Bonhoeffer (1953) and Tillich (1952), the last of whom writes of 'courage' to describe man's self-affirmation of being in spite of the fact of non-being. Furthermore, concepts like responsibility and self-efficacy are increasingly being used by behavioural psychologists (Bandura, 1977; Thoresen and Coates, 1978).

A useful distinction can be drawn between responsibility *to* and responsibility *for*, though it is a difference of emphasis rather than a distinction between discrete categories. In responsibility *to*, the source of authority is more external and the emphasis may be on meeting others' demands; whereas responsibility *for* is a positive concept which emphasises internal authority and man's responsibility for his own self-realising and affirmation. The distinction is reminiscent of that suggested by Fromm (1942) between the concepts of freedom *from* and freedom *to*, the former implying absence of negative restrictions, and the latter implying presence of positive potential for self-realising.

## ULTIMATE AND MEDIATING GOALS

Parloff (1967) suggests that the goals of therapy can be better understood if they are divided into two categories: mediating and ultimate. A similar classification for differentiating between goals is the distinction between specific and general goals. For instance, behaviourists focus on very specific goals, whereas client-centred counsellors focus on the general goal of facilitating client self-actualising. Thus it might be said that the behaviourists do not have a vision of ultimate goals, whereas client-centred therapists do not see the need for specifying mediating goals. In a comprehensive approach to counselling, there seems merit in retaining both ideas. The concept of responsibility is viewed as an integrating link which operates both vertically (between the ultimate and mediating goals) and horizontally (among the various mediating goals). Especially where the individual is not highly vulnerable, progress toward the ultimate goals may be facilitated by paying attention to mediating goals. Indeed, any full definition of the former would mention adequate functioning on all the latter.

The paramount objective of counselling for responsibility is to increase people's effective conscious control over themselves and their environment so that they may best meet the four basic needs or the four R's of psychological well-being: realism, relatedness, rewarding activity, and right-and-wrong (an ongoing process of ethical living), all of which are mediating goals. The ultimate goal of counselling for responsibility is self-realising, which involves a high level of responsible functioning in the areas of the four mediating goals. An individual so functioning might rightly be termed a 'responsible person'.

Figure 1 shows the ultimate and mediating goals of counselling for responsibility, which are goals for ourselves as well as for our clients. In sense, all these goals pertain to various forms of relatedness: to ourselves, to others, to work, to nature, and to the species and the universe. Self-realising and the mediating goals and sub-goals, are not static events but have a process quality about them.

## ULTIMATE GOAL: SELF-REALISING

The responsible person who engages in a high level of self-realising is the goal of counselling and of living. Self-realising is used in the psychological literature with two different meanings: as a motivating drive, and as a criterion of psychological functioning.

There are three important and interrelated issues in regard to self-realising as a motivating drive: whether there is such a motivating drive; whether such a drive is pro-social; and whether the absence of an assumption of self-realising is likely to lead to irresponsible individuals, totalitarian societies and mechanistic therapies. On the first issue, we will

*Figure 1:* **Ultimate and mediating goals of counselling for responsibility**

| *Ultimate goal* | *Mediating goals and sub-goals* | |
|---|---|---|
| | 1.Realism | Openness to experience |
| | | Realistic conceptual framework |
| | | Realistic attribution |
| | | Realistic evaluation |
| | | Realistic anticipation |
| | 2. Relatedness | Appropriate self-disclosure |
| | | Empathic listening |
| Self-realising | | Integration of sexuality |
| (the responsible person) | | |
| | 3. Rewarding | Identification of interests |
| | activity | Sense of competence |
| | | Actual competence |
| | | Appropriate activity level |
| | 4. Right-and- | Humane valuing process |
| | wrong | Effective philosophy of life |
| | | Social empathy and commitment |

assume that man does have an ongoing drive to express his humanity. On the second, we will assume that truly humanised values are pro-social in terms of the individual, his environment and the species; also that, in the absence of conclusive evidence either way, arguments about the inherent goodness or badness of man are less important than acknowledging that man has the potential for both good and evil, so that the task is to help set in motion an irreversible process of humanisation, developing the potential for good. On the third issue, we will assume that there are risks in both under- and over-emphasising self-realising as a motivating drive, in that both extremes may erode individual responsibility. Those who feel they are totally controlled by external stimuli, and those who misunderstand the concept of self-realising and feel that they just should wait for the drive to emerge rather than do something about it, share a common impediment. They both fail to assume adequate responsibility for attaining happiness and fulfilment in their lives.

In the following sections, mediating goals and sub-goals are described in a way which attempts a definition of self-realising as a criterion of psychological functioning. There are a number of ways of assessing an individual's level of self-realising: judgments by some external criteria; judgments which take into account his genetic endowment, social environment and learning history; and helping him to assess himself in such a way that he may, if necessary, make constructive changes. The last emphasis is most important in an counselling relationship.

Responsibly functioning people demonstrate a fusion of the two meanings of self-realising in that they demonstrate both the means and ends of truly effective living. As Maslow (1970) has observed, such people are rare, and the majority of us self-realise well below our potential.

## MEDIATING GOALS: (1) REALISM

The word 'realism' often refers to two interrelated aspects of human functioning: feeling and thinking. An attempt will now be made to indicate what it means to feel, to think, and to jointly feel and think, realistically or responsibly.

Realistic feeling, *openness to experience*, or the capacity to listen to our own valuing processes, is a basic form of responsiveness. It is a kind of inner empathy which helps us to be genuinely self-realising. A woman in late nineteenth-century Vienna who loves her husband but is afraid to have sex with him, or a British college student who is depressed and has the feeling of always being a spectator rather than a participant in life, may both be incapable of being truly responsive to their feelings. Sometimes it will seem as though a person has lost his or her capacity to feel anything. It is often the positive and caring parts of themselves to which people become deaf. As they become more highly self-realising, their capacity to experience and recognise their feelings increases (Walker *et al.*, 1960). Responsible feeling or openness to experience is more popularly expressed as: 'To thine own self be true'. It requires that the individual know himself and be aware of the reality both of himself and of the external environment. It also requires that the individual have an adequate sense of worth or of self-esteem.

Of all animals, man is unique in his capacity for symbolic language and for thinking, yet much of this potential goes unrealised. Realistic thinking involves a number of different and frequently interrelated elements. A *realistic conceptual framework* is central to thinking effectively, since each person needs a realistic set of concepts or a set of working hypotheses about human behaviour to govern his approach to life. It may be difficult to be responsible if the individual does not possess adequate concepts and, for instance, simplistically labels as 'lazy' an able, academically anxious and underachieving student.

It also may be difficult to think and act effectively if people are incapable of *realistic attribution*. The term 'attribution' is used in social psychology to refer to the ways and processes by which people attribute causes and meanings to their own behaviour, to others' behaviour, and to environmental events (Shaver, 1975). Accurate attribution is essential for effective living, and often the road to feelings of worthlessness and impotence is littered with misattributions. One way of avoiding responsibility is to attribute current behaviour and feelings to causes outside our control. Here are some illustrations of misattribution:

❖ Joan 'it's my childhood' is an attractive 24-year-old girl who recently had plastic surgery on her nose because she felt she was insufficiently beautiful. Much of the time she feels empty, as though she has nothing to offer. She feels that she grew up in an emotionally inclement atmosphere in which a younger brother was favoured and in which she was squashed by parents whom she perceives as punitively domineering. She now bitterly resents her parents, whom she blames for her present unhappiness.

❖ Philip 'it's my social-class background' is a 45-year-old engineer, married with three children. Despite all outward appearances of being happy and successful, inwardly he feels somewhat of a failure in both his business and personal relationships. His father was the gardener and his mother the cook to a wealthy family, and he blames his humble social origins for his present feelings of worthlessness.

❖ Bill 'you make me feel this way' is a young married executive who is having difficulties in both his job and his marriage. Despite his erratic behaviour, he feels that neither his boss nor his wife understands him. When his boss questions his work, Bill gets sullen and inwardly resentful. When his wife makes even the mildest criticism, Bill gets openly aggressive. He blames both his wife and his boss for his aggressive feelings and actions.

Running throughout these vignettes is the theme of inappropriate external attribution, in that they all represent belief systems which perpetuate inability to improve the situation. For instance, while there may be some truth in the assertion that childhood rejection may be associated with later unhappiness, a partial truth has been converted into a whole truth, with the effect of blocking motivation for change.

Inappropriate internal attribution is also a possibility, in that the wrong sort of personal responsibility may be assumed, thus again curtailing effective responsibility. For example, a student who has been brought up in a family where both parents presented highly idealised versions of themselves, while overtly and subtly disparaging their son for his real or imagined misdeeds, may attribute all his present misfortunes to his intrinsic badness. This 'it's all my fault' attitude may hinder motivation for change, since it may lower self-confidence and is based on only-partially-accurate perceptions.

Accurate attribution is not only relevant to the past, but even more important to the future. Glasser (1965) stresses it is not enough to help a patient face reality: he must also learn to fulfil his needs. Thus accurate attribution sooner or later must be oriented toward the future. Glasser defines responsibility as 'the ability to fulfil one's needs, and to do so in a way that does not deprive others of the ability to fulfil their needs'. Like reality therapy, counselling for responsibility involves a *responsibility principle*: namely, that no matter what my past and current emotional and social deprivations may be, I alone am responsible for meeting my needs in the present and the future. Questions of attribution thus become more questions of 'whither' than questions of 'whence'.

Caution needs to be exercised to ensure that the responsibility principle itself does not engender inappropriate internal attributions. The principle needs to be learned. It is a standard to which people should aspire rather than one with which to devalue themselves if they fall short. It does not deny that there may be adverse personal, social and environmental influences, but encourages people, for the sake of their fulfilment, to cope with these as effectively as possible. Kelly (1967) has observed that, 'to put it simply, it is not what the past has done to a man that counts so much as it is what the man does with his past'. Similarly, it is not what the future may do to a man that counts so much as it is what the man does with his future.

Another way in which responsibility may be encouraged is by *realistic evaluation*. A set of evaluations which is particularly influential concerns positive and negative assessments of our personal characteristics. People tend to have internal rules or self-standards, and it is important that these rules are helpful rather than harmful to self-realising. Many harmful internal rules cause self-derogation. For example, a girl student had academic and social concerns which were not helped by her thinking that, while it was all right for others to have problems, she should not have them herself. She repeatedly reminded herself that she was 'so stupid' for having problems, thus further lowering her confidence and perpetuating her situation. A more responsible rule would be that it was inconvenient, rather than wrong, to have problems, thus relieving her of the need for self-derogation.

As well as needing realistic evaluation, man also needs *realistic anticipation*. In fact the two tend to be heavily intertwined, since evaluations form the basis for anticipations. Allport (1955) was very aware of man's future reference when he wrote: 'People, it seems, are busy leading their lives into the future, whereas psychology, for the most part, is busy tracing them into the past'. Perhaps Kelly (1955) is the psychologist who has most stressed man's future orientation, since the fundamental postulate of his psychology of personal constructs is that 'a person's processes are psychologically channelised by the ways in which he anticipates events'. Anticipations affect action. A person who evaluates others as basically threatening is likely to anticipate and behave in personal relationships in a quite different way from a person who views others as basically welcoming. A person who feels he is under the control of some powerful others is likely to anticipate and behave very differently from the person who feels that what happens to him is to a large extent under his control.

The need for people to be responsive to their own feelings or valuing processes and to listen accurately to themselves has been discussed, as has the importance of using our potential for thinking in such areas as attribution, evaluation and anticipation. As Ellis (1962) stresses, the ways in which we think and the ways in which we feel are interrelated. For instance, the ways in which we think about others can alter our feelings bout them: a college student who sees his father as a rigid and authoritarian person may feel differently about him if he perceives him as someone who, like himself, is struggling to maintain his feelings of worth. Also, the way in which we think about ourselves can alter our feelings about others: another college student who devalued herself for not having a boyfriend might experience her mother as cold and rejecting, yet the same student, with the confidence gained from a good heterosexual relationship, might experience the same mother as less of a threat and possibly even as a friend. Realistic perception involves using the potential for both feeling and thinking. In fact our self-realising drive needs support from realistic thinking. Effective action is based on accurate perception, and accordingly realism is a vital mediating goal for the responsible person.

## MEDIATING GOALS: (2) RELATEDNESS

Another important mediating goal is the capacity for relatedness. Relatedness refers to man's need to belong, to love and be loved, and to give and receive friendship. It encompasses his sexual activity, his relationships with his workmates, and having satisfying parent–child relationships. Relatedness acknowledges that man is a social creature who needs other people so that he may psychologically exist. He needs to be known as he really is so as to fully experience his being, though he may be discriminating in how and to whom he reveals himself.

Two central features of our capacity for relatedness are the ways in which we receive information about ourselves. Indeed the two are inter-related, since the way in which we reveal ourselves creates an emotional climate which may make it easier or more difficult for others to send us information about themselves, and this, in turn, may further affect the extent and way in which we reveal ourselves. Similarly, the way in which we receive information about others may affect the way they send their information and receive our information, both of which may again affect our subsequent communications.

Sullivan (1954), in his work with schizophrenic patients, observed that their speech served to keep people at a distance, thus protecting an already vulnerable self-esteem. As with Sullivan's schizophrenics, re-latedness requires us to be good senders and receivers of verbal, para-verbal and non-verbal information – or, more simply, good communicators. This involves realistic feeling and thinking. It also requires us to possess the basic sender and receiver skills of appropriate self-disclosure and of empathic listening.

*Appropriate self-disclosure* requires us to take responsibility for the way we talk about ourselves to others, not only meeting our needs but helping them to meet theirs. Maslow's (1970) self-actualising people 'have deeper and more profound interpersonal relations than any other adults . . . .' One of the strands of Rogers and his colleagues' (Walker *et al.*, 1960) scale to measure process changes in psychotherapy is that of communication of self. At low stages of the scale communication of self is lacking whilst in the high stages rich self-awareness is communicated when desired. Also, Mowrer (1964) sees psychological pain arising from a devious *private* life style, and asserts that the individual has allowed himself to be alienated from his fellow humans and, consequently, needs to open himself to change through *public* transparency. The three fundamental rules of his integrity therapy are honesty, responsibility, and involvement (Mowrer, 1972; Mowrer and Vattano, 1975).

Appropriate self-disclosure includes paying attention to the extent to which positive and negative aspects of self are revealed or concealed, the degree to which people communicate their own thoughts and feelings directly, the ways and accuracy with which risks and gains in self-disclosure are assessed, and the nature and effect of various kinds of para-verbal and non-verbal communication. It assumes that individuals know themselves moderately well, but for some, 'consciousness raising' also may be necessary to achieve awareness of the effects their disclosures are having on themselves and others.

*Empathic listening* involves the ability to be sensitive to and to understand the message that the sender is communicating from his viewpoint or frame of reference, as well as the ability to communicate these understandings and awarenesses when the sender is ready and in a language attuned to his needs. Empathic listening also involves tentatively checking out understandings of the sender's messages and, if inaccurate, reformulating these understandings. It is as much a matter of attitude and emotional climate as of technique. Rogers (1975) uses the word 'companionship' to describe empathy, and indeed at its higher levels it is a caring, sensitive, perceptive way of being with other people and of helping them accept and affirm themselves.

Responsibility for empathic listening can be assumed or avoided. Frequently, a by-product of counselling is that the client becomes a much better listener in his outside relationships. This is both because he becomes better at listening to his own feelings, and because he has learned – in part by imitation – the skill of listening to others and of allowing others to help him understand their personal world. Empathic listening is an attitude and skill which non-clients would do well to learn, be they marital partners, parents, teachers, management or workers. There is some evidence that untrained people are very deficient in this skill (Nelson-Jones and Patterson, 1974). Indeed, trained counsellors also are in danger of becoming unempathic in everyday situations where their own needs are involved.

*Integration of sexuality* may involve a number of different elements. For some, this may involve what Sanford (1962) terms 'freeing of impulse' or the ability to accept, experience and enjoy libidinous impulses and feelings. Sexual self-realising entails a capacity to listen to inner sexual experiencing and to appropriately disclose this experiencing to a partner. Furthermore, it entails the capacity to listen empathically to a partner's sexual experiencing and to act as a good companion in facilitating its expression. A recent study of the sexual experiences of American women (Hite, 1976), albeit methodologically deficient, indicated the following: fairly widespread misunderstanding of the physiology of female sexual responsiveness by both sexes; poor body image for a number of women, including disparagement of their genital area; the inability of many men adequately to listen to and to facilitate their partner's sexual experiencing; and the difficulty many women had in understanding constructively their sexual and emotional needs. There seems little reason to believe that the situation is very different in Britain.

For many, integration of sexuality involves the need to develop out of superficial and compulsive sexual patterns into a capacity for real intimacy. Furthermore, the exclusively homosexually-oriented may need to learn to accept their sexual orientation and find appropriate relationships in which to express their needs for relatedness. Also, persons with bisexual feelings may need both to accept these feelings and also to make decisions concerning what dimensions of their sexual potential they wish to actualise. In all of the above instances, there is the opportunity for assuming or avoiding responsibility for sexual and emotional self-realising.

## MEDIATING GOALS: (3) REWARDING ACTIVITY

The third mediating goal is rewarding activity, which acknowledges that man needs to find outlets for his energies and time not only for psychological satisfaction but also for his physiological well-being (Selye, 1974). The term 'activity' is used to cover both work and non-work activities. Rewarding activity is inter-related with the earlier mediating goal of realism, since both choosing and carrying out the activity involve realistic feeling and thinking. Additionally, activity is often rewarding because of the quality of the relationships involved: hence there is also a connection with the mediating goal of relatedness.

Rewarding activity may be expressive of self-realising in terms of both direction and use of powers. People tend to like to do things in which they are interested, and they obtain a sense of achievement and competence if they do well. The direction of our activities, while in part circumscribed by external factors, is also heavily dependent on our capacity for internal empathy – our ability to listen to ourselves and to identify what interests us and not just other people. Thus accurate *identification of interests*, both work and recreational, is one of the means to rewarding activity.

Almost a definition of rewarding activity is its capacity to generate absorption. The combination of interest and use of powers helps the individual both to lose self-awareness and to find himself in the fulfilment of the activity. A characteristic of people who get absorbed is that they enjoy the process of the activity and not just the product. Accordingly, Fromm (1976) distinguishes between those who relate to their work in a 'being' rather than a 'having' way. Counsellors would agree that numerous clients who have difficulty in performing in various situations are more involved with other people's reactions to the product of their performance than they are with the task in hand.

A further means to rewarding activity, then, is to have the confidence to perform adequately. White's (1959; 1973) concept of sense of competence and Bandura's (1977) idea of self-efficacy both emphasise the importance of an appropriate *sense of competence*. While it is important to feel competent, however, people also have a responsibility for affirming themselves by developing *actual competence*, or the ability for environmental mastery.

Another area where responsibility can be assumed or avoided is the maintenance of health. For some, this may be a matter of regulating pleasurable activities such as eating, drinking and smoking. For others, the maintenance of health may require a careful look at the stresses in their lives and at their constructive and destructive coping patterns. It may also require recognising that much stress is internally generated and that there may be a need for a change in attitude to work, achievement, or whatever is proving stressful. An *appropriate activity level* seems essential for self-realising (Selye, 1974; McQuade and Aikman, 1974), yet rarely does this seem to be stressed in the counselling and psychology literature. Each individual needs to work towards his own best activity level, which may be a matter of acknowledging both strengths and limitations, and also of achieving the right balance between work, family, and recreational activities.

A final point is once again to stress the inter-related nature of mediating goals. Success in work or leisure activities may generate confidence for more successful relationships, and vice-versa. Also, achievement in one area may make it easier to cope with lack of achievement in another area. For instance, interest in a job or sport may help stabilise someone who is otherwise very isolated.

### MEDIATING GOALS: (4) RIGHT-AND-WRONG

'Right-and-wrong' refers to the nature of our responsibilities to each other, our community and our species. It deals with questions of values and ethics, and how they can best represent and facilitate our own and others' self-realising. It seems that in recent years many have tended to focus on rights rather than responsibilities, leading to bitterness and anger when rights are felt to be violated (Strong, 1975). While a focus on appropriate attainment of rights can be constructive, it can – if overdone – be egocentric and destructive. What is needed is a psychology of ethics which focuses on others' needs and rights as well as on our own. Within the mediating goal of right-and-wrong there appear to be three inter-related sub-goals: a humane valuing process, an effective philosophy of life, and social empathy and commitment.

Regarding a *humane valuing process*, a number of writers on children's moral development have observed a shift with age from external responsibility (or respect and submission to authority) to internal responsibility (or self-government and control). Piaget (1932) notes that children move from 'moral realism', or a morality of constraint by external rules, to a morality of co-operation or of individual principles of conscience (Hoffman, 1970). Again, Allport (1961) talks of the movement from a child's 'must' conscience, evolved out of tribal and parental control, to a mature adult's 'ought' conscience, based on individual control. Fromm (1949), likewise, makes a distinction between 'authoritarian conscience', which is the voice of an internalised external authority, and 'humanistic conscience', which he defines as 'the reaction of our total personality to its proper functioning or dysfunctioning' or 'the voice of our loving care for ourselves'.

Attainment of a truly autonomous and internal conscience is rare in our culture, yet it is an important criterion of the highly self-realising person. A valuing process seems inherent in the human organism, and we need to learn to listen empathically to it. For this process is both part of and guardian of our self-realising potential. Gendlin (1967) writes of an experiential process leading to value-conclusions, and indicates that what we term 'values' may only be conclusions to this process of experiencing. It is possible for us both to be in touch with our basic process of experiencing and also to use our powers of thought to let our meanings unfold. What was earlier termed 'realism', a combination of openness to experience and realistic thinking, leads to a humane valuing process. Such a valuing process has an internal referent which provides a basis for judging external situations. Thus, with the highly self-realising person, ethics are both generated by, and validated in terms of, this inner voice.

There are several reasons why it is important to listen to our internal valuing processes. First, when we are true to ourselves we tend to feel fulfilled, gratified and psychologically well. Second, when we are untrue to ourselves we tend to feel, however subtly, unfulfilled, ungratified and psychologically unwell. Third, our valuing processes reflect our basic nature which, if anything, is positive and social. Fourth, the study of highly self-actualising persons suggests that they have a firm foundation for their value system supplied by their 'intrinsic dynamics' (Maslow, 1970). Fifth, counselling and psychotherapy may, to a large extent, be seen as unfolding, uncovering and strengthening the individual's own valuing process. The more this unfolding and strengthening is achieved, the more clients and patients tend to become effective in living. Also, once they are better at listening to their valuing processes, clients become reluctant to revert to their former ways.

Another area of responsibility is the development of an *effective philosophy of life*, involving assumptions about life's purposes, and reflecting long-range goals and strivings. These goals tend to be more strongly and clearly formulated in self-realising people. Reasons for this include their greater capacity to be in touch with their self-realising drive, which is interrelated with their greater capacity to think autonomously and, where appropriate, to be independent of their culture (Riesman, 1950).

A number of points may be made relating to the sub-goal of an effective philosophy of life. First, philosophical concerns are a legitimate area for, if not part of, counselling psychology. The task of counselling psychology appears to be, where possible, to state philosophical positions and predicaments in easily comprehensible terms and thus, where appropriate, to help clients and others in their philosophical and spiritual self-exploration and also, where necessary, to refer clients on to people specialising in facilitating such self-exploration.

Second, many philosophical and spiritual concerns may be spurious in that they reflect *lack* of self-affirmation as being almost a prerequisite of genuine spiritual self-affirmation. Also, Maslow (1970) observes 'that much else of what passes for morals, ethics and values may be simple by-products of the pervasive psychopathology of the average', and that given a basic acceptance of self and of human nature 'many conflicts, frustrations and threats (which force the kind of choice in which value is expressed) evaporate or resolve for the self-actualising person'. For example, the antagonistic interests of sex and age differences might not appear so antagonistic for self-realising people.

Third, the philosophy of life of self-realising people may be seen as strongly representing values which are universal, probably because their philosophy represents the values inherent in man's self-realising drive. Rogers (1967) has observed:

> 'Stated in older terms, individuals who are thus in touch with their experiencing come to value such directions as sincerity, indepen-dence, self-direction, self-knowledge, social responsivity, social responsibility, and loving interpersonal relationships'.

Fourth, the attainment of an effective philosophy of life may require much effort, much spiritual development and, possibly, much pain and suffering. Looking at Maslow's criterion group of self-actualising people, they are people who are likely to have thought very deeply about life and their relatedness to the universe (Maslow, 1970).

Fifth, it may well be that attainment of a philosophy of life representative of universal values implies a religious sense which represents the underlying spirit of religion without what Tillich (1952) calls 'the theistic objectivation of a God'. More recently, Fromm (1976) has called for a humanistic 'religiosity' without dogmas and institutions and based on the idea of being.

*Social empathy and commitment* seems especially apparent in people whose relationships are not constricted by learned fears and suspicions. Those whose affections are undistorted appear to have some innate feeling for their species being capable of a wide identification with others. For highly self-realising people, three levels of empathy are apparent: they are able sensitively to understand themselves and also other people in their immediate environment, as well as to have a much wider identification with their species.

The term 'social empathy' is used here to refer to a broader identification than that required to meet our needs for friendship and intimate relatedness. It seems that at the higher levels of self-realising the identification with the community and species may be so strong that self-interest and social interest are synonymous. Adler (Adler, 1927; Ansbacher and Ansbacher, 1956) used the term *Gemeinschafsegefühl* – social feeling or social interest – to describe the individual's innate potentiality to develop a 'deep sense of his fellowship in humanity'. He used it to refer both to our capacity for identification with those in our immediate community and to a striving for an ideal human community, and saw it as an innate potentiality which had to be consciously developed.

Responsibility for developing social empathy may be assumed or avoided. While the early development of such empathy relies on such people as parents and teachers, ultimately we ourselves need to take responsibility for its development. It is hard to see how social empathy can be highly developed without some form of social commitment. Maslow (1970) observed that for self-actualising people there did not seem to be a gap between thought and action apart from that caused by realistic problems. When such people knew what was the right thing to do, they did it. It is likely that this behaviour represented a higher stage of their development, and that many of these people earlier in their lives had to struggle to develop genuine social empathy and commitment. Probably all people have to strive if they wish to develop this weak but good part of themselves. Client-centred writers such as Rogers (1951) are over-optimistic if they consider a strong sense of social empathy and commitment to be a frequent outcome of their counselling. What tends to happen is that clients develop a level of social interest similar to the norm in individualistic Western culture. It is the exceptional person – client or otherwise – who develops a strong sense of social empathy manifested in active commitment.

### CONCLUDING COMMENTS

The above goals represent an ideal toward which counsellors might strive in their professional and personal lives. These goals of counselling for responsibility have implications for practice, involving helping clients not only to acknowledge and explore feelings, but also to think, communicate and act more effectively. Furthermore, counselling for responsibility may involve dealing with central issues of values, motivation and commitment.

A major implication of the goals cited is that none of the existing counselling schools, such as the behavioural or the client-centred, is conceptualised comprehensively enough to be able to attain all of them. A further implication is that these goals are relevant to a psychology of wellness for the less disturbed majority as well as toward helping the more severely disturbed minority with their problems. Super (1977) observes that the main feature distinguishing counselling from clinical psychology is the emphasis on developmental help rather than on pathology. If, however, counselling psychology is to come of age, both intellectually and in practice, it requires the development of a comprehensive body of theory which takes into account the needs of reasonably functioning people. Furthermore, as reflected in the current interest in psychological education in the USA (Ivey, 1976), it requires models for counselling practice which meet these needs. A later paper will deal with some of the practical concerns in implementing the suggested goals.

A number of pertinent issues arise from this paper. For instance, how might a spastic, a blind man or a terminal cancer patient responsibly self-realise? Much unavoidable pain and suffering exists. Nevertheless, even in concentration camps, as Frankl has shown (Frankl, 1946; Frankl, 1959), people's attitude toward and behaviour in their predicament may save them from compounding unavoidable suffering with the added burden of much self-inflicted suffering. For the sick and the disabled, the goals of counselling for responsibility include working on attitudes and behaviours which help diminish the elements of pain which are potentially avoidable. In regard to delinquency, the critical psychological issues may resolve less around concepts like diminished responsibility and more around preventive and remedial counselling, psychological education, and environmental change strategies focused on increasing pro-social behaviours which help potential or actual delinquents meet their human needs. Counselling for responsibility, however, is not just about the needs of special groups, but about the needs, suffering and self-realising of all of us. In the final analysis, the primary method of such counselling must be *effective self-help*.

## REFERENCES

Adler, A.: *Understanding Human Nature*. New York: Premier, 1927.
Allport, G.W.: *Becoming*. New Haven: Yale University Press, 1955.
Allport, G.W.: *Pattern and Growth in Personality*. New York: Holt, Rinehart & Winston, 1961.
Ansbacher, H., and Ansbacher, R.: *The Individual Psychology of Alfred Adler*. New York: Harper Colophon, 1956.
Bandura, A.: 'Self-Efficacy: Toward a Unifying Theory of Behavioral Change'. *Psychological Review*, Volume 84, 1977, pp. 191–215.
Bonhoeffer, D.: *Letters and Papers from Prison*. London: SCM, 1953.
Combs, A.W., and Snygg, D.: *Individual Behavior* (revised edition). New York: Harper & Row, 1959.
Ellis, A.: *Reason and Emotion in Psychotherapy*. New York: Lyle Stuart, 1962.
Frankl, V.E.: *The Doctor and the Soul*. Harmondsworth: Penguin, 1946.
Frankl, V.E.: *Man's Search for Meaning*. New York: Washington Square Press, 1959.
Fromm, E.: *The Fear of Freedom*. London: Routledge & Kegan Paul, 1942.
Fromm, E.: *Man for Himself*. London: Routledge & Kegan Paul, 1949.
Fromm, E.: *To Have or to Be?* London: Cape, 1976.
Gendlin, E.T.: 'Values and the Process of Experiencing'. In Mahrer, A.R. (ed.).: *The Goals of Psychotherapy*, pp. 180–205. New York: Appleton Century Crofts, 1967.
Glasser, W.: *Reality Therapy*. New York: Harper & Row, 1965.
Hite, S.: *The Hite Report*. London: Summit Books, 1976.
Hoffman, M.L.: 'Moral Development'. In P.H. Mussen (ed.): *Carmichael's Manual of Child Psychology*, Volume 2 (3rd edition), pp. 261–349. New York: Wiley, 1970.
Ivey, A.E.: 'Counseling Psychology, the Psychoeducator Model and the Future'. *The Counseling Psychologist*, Volume 6 No. 3, 1976, pp. 72–75.
Jahoda, M.: *Current Concepts of Positive Mental Health*. New York: Basic Books, 1958.
Kelly, G.A.: *A Theory of Personality: the Psychology of Personal Constructs*. New York: Norton, 1955.
Kelly, G.A.: 'A Psychology of the Optimal Man'. In Mahrer, A.R. (ed.): *The Goals of Psychotherapy*, pp. 238–258. New York: Appleton Century Crofts, 1967.
McQuade, W., and Aikman, A.: *Stress: How to Stop Your Mind Killing Your Body*. London: Hutchinson, 1974.
Mahrer, A.R. (ed.): *The Goals of Psychotherapy*. New York: Appleton Century Crofts, 1967.
Maslow, A.H.: *Motivation and Personality* (2nd edition). New York: Harper & Row, 1970.
Mowrer, O.H.: *The New Group Therapy*. Princeton, NJ: Van Nostrand, 1964.

Mowrer, O.H.: 'Integrity Groups: Principles and Procedures'. *The Counseling Psychologist*, Volume 3 No. 3, 1972, pp. 7–33.

Mowrer, O.H., and Vattano, A.J.: *Integrity Groups – the Loss and Recovery of Community*. Urbana, Illinois: Integrity Groups, 1975.

Nelson-Jones, R., and Patterson, C.H.: 'Some Effects of Counsellor Training'. *British Journal of Guidance and Counselling*, Volume 2, 1974, pp. 191–199.

Parloff, M.D.: 'Goals in Psychotherapy: Mediating and Ultimate'. In Mahrer, A.H. (ed.): *The Goals of Psychotherapy*, pp. 5–19. New York: Appleton Century Crofts, 1967.

Paton, A.: *Instrument of Thy Peace*. Glasgow: Fontana, 1968.

Piaget, J.: *The Moral Judgment of the Child*. London: Routledge & Kegan Paul, 1932.

Riesman, D.: *The Lonely Crowd*. New Haven: Yale University Press, 1950.

Rogers, C.R.: *Client-Centred Therapy*. Boston: Houghton Mifflin, 1951.

Rogers, C.R.: *On Becoming a Person*. Boston: Houghton Mifflin, 1961.

Rogers, C.R.: 'Toward a Modern Approach to Values: the Valuing Process in the Mature Person'. In Rogers, C.R., and Stevens, B. (eds.): *Person to Person*, pp. 13–28. London: Souvenir Press, 1967.

Rogers, C.R.: 'Empathy: an Unappreciated Way of Being'. *The Counseling Psychologist*, Volume 5, 1975, pp. 2–10.

Sanford, R.N.: 'Developmental Status of the Entering Freshman'. In Sanford, R.N. (ed.): *The American College*, pp. 253–282. New York: Wiley, 1962.

Selye, H.: *Stress Without Distress*. Sevenoaks: Hodder & Stoughton, 1974.

Shaver, K.G.: *An Introduction to Attribution Processes*. Cambridge, Mass.: Winthrop, 1975.

Strong, S.R.: 'Christian Counseling'. Unpublished manuscript, University of Minnesota, 1975.

Sullivan, H.S.: *The Psychiatric Interview*. New York: Norton, 1954.

Super, D.E.: 'The Identity Crisis of Counseling Psychologists'. *The Counseling Psychologist*, Volume 7 No. 2, 1977, pp. 13–15.

Thoresen, C.E., and Coates, T.J.: 'What Does it Mean to be a Behavior Therapist?' *The Counseling Psychologist*, Volume 7 No. 3, 1978, pp. 3–21.

Tillich, P.: *The Courage to Be*. New Haven: Yale University Press, 1952.

Walker, A.M., Rablen, R.A., and Rogers, C.R.: 'Development of a Scale to Measure Process Changes in Psychotherapy'. *Journal of Clinical Psychology*, Volume 16, 1960, pp. 79–85.

White, R.W.: 'Motivation Reconsidered: the Concept of Competence'. *Psychological Review*, Volume 66, 1959, pp. 297–333.

White, R.W.: 'The Concept of Healthy Personality: What Do We Really Mean?' *The Counseling Psychologist*, Volume 4 No. 2, 1973, pp. 3–12.

# GOALS FOR COUNSELLING, PSYCHOTHERAPY AND PSYCHOLOGICAL EDUCATION: RESPONSIBILITY AS AN INTEGRATING CONCEPT
## RICHARD NELSON-JONES

## POSTSCRIPT

If psychologists write about their problem areas, I must have had a personal responsibility problem. I still do! Being personally responsible and making the choices that work for rather than against our affirmation is a life-long struggle.

### ORIGINS: FROM PERSONAL RESPONSIBILITY

Whence did my paper on counselling goals come? What was its context? In 1976, I wrote a 60-page paper called 'Personal Responsibility Therapy' that was later developed into a book called *Personal Responsibility Counselling and Therapy* (Nelson-Jones, 1984). From 1976 to 1978, I approached about ten British publishers to get my *Personal Responsibility* manuscript developed and published. There was unanimity: all publishers declined it! However, Holt, Rinehart and Winston suggested that I write a counselling textbook. Seeing this as a way to increase my credibility with publishers, I placed the *Personal Responsibility* book on hold. Instead, from 1978 to 1981, I wrote *The Theory and Practice of Counselling Psychology* (Nelson-Jones, 1982). However, not wishing to lose the idea of my personal responsibility book, I put a mental down-payment on it by writing 'Goals for Counselling, Psychotherapy and Psychological Education: Responsibility as an Integrating Concept'.

My interest in broader approaches to counselling than that offered by single theoretical positions stemmed partly from my 50 or so hours of individual psychotherapy in the early 1960s with Dr John Black, then Director of Stanford University's Counselling and Testing Center. John Black was a pure client-centred therapist who helped immensely to free me from the shackles of an oversocialised upbringing. Also, during this period, I attended some groups at the Stanford Medical Center, one co-led by the now famous doyen of group psychotherapy, Irvin Yalom. In retrospect, I might have gained even more from these individual and group experiences if some specific self-defeating patterns of thinking and acting had been addressed more directly. My subsequent work as a counsellor was another influence for breadth. Here to be maximally effective I needed to draw on the theoretical and practical insights from more than one counselling approach. My work as a counsellor trainer at the University of Aston was a further influence for breadth. Each year I set the students an essay in which they were to state the theory and practice of how they would counsel. Having read numerous attempts by students to develop integrative approaches, I decided to have a go myself.

Why focus on personal responsibility as an integrating concept? When teaching counselling theory I observed it as a consistent theme, varying in explicitness, in all major theories. In the early 1970s, I was influenced by Mowrer's work on Integrity Group Therapy in which the concept of responsibility featured prominently (Mowrer, 1964; 1966; 1972; Mowrer and Vattano, 1975). I noticed the centrality of personal responsibility in my counselling practice and personal life. The challenge was to break the concept of personal responsibility down into its component parts. One way to do this was operationalise personal responsibility into a statement of counselling goals and sub-goals. Hence my goals paper.

### DEVELOPMENTS: TO LIFESKILLS HELPING

My goals paper formed part of my 1984 *Personal Responsibility Counselling and Therapy* book. Here I (**1**) explored personal responsibility in existing theoretical positions, (**2**) stated a theoretical position using personal responsibility as an integrating concept, and (**3**) discussed interventions for attaining each of what had then become the mediating goals of responsiveness, realism, relatedness and rewarding activity. The concluding statement of my 1979 paper was that the primary focus of counselling for responsibility must be on effective self-help. Writing *Personal Responsibility Counselling and Therapy* further convinced me that effective helping was mainly about imparting the skills of effective self-help. Consequently, personal responsibility therapy needed to become a people-centred and not just a helper-centred approach.

My next challenge was how to turn the relatively intellectual content of my personal responsibility book into a people-centred approach. My route to this was to incorporate the concept of skills. To attain the mediating goals of personal responsibility, people require skills. However, to retain the emphasis on personal responsibility, each skills area needed to be viewed as an area in which people choose. For instance, to be a good listener, people need to make the choices entailed in good listening. In 1984 and 1985 I wrote *Human Relationship Skills* (Nelson-Jones, 1986), my first psychological education book. Here I explored skills for attaining the mediating goal of relatedness. A few years later, I wrote *Effective Thinking Skills* (Nelson-Jones, 1989), in which I explored skills for attaining the mediating goal of realism, and the second edition of *Human Relationship Skills* (Nelson-Jones, 1990). During this period, I wrote the second edition of *Practical Counselling and Helping Skills* (Nelson-Jones, 1988). This book contained a model for managing problems. I was moving toward a counselling and helping model using personal responsibility as a central concept. However, I had still not arrived at a helping model clearly focused on developing clients' lifeskills.

By 1989, I had decided to state both an individual and a group approach to personal responsibility in skills language. In 1989 and 1990, I wrote *Lifeskills: a Handbook* (Nelson-Jones, 1991) about how to lead lifeskills training groups. Recently I completed a book called *Lifeskills Helping*, its American title, published in Britain as the third edition of *Practical Counselling and Helping Skills* (Nelson-Jones, 1993). *Lifeskills Helping* presents DASIE, a five-stage model for helping:

D ~*Develop* the relationship, identify and clarify problem(s).
A ~*Assess* problem(s) and redefine in skills terms.
S ~*State* working goals and plan interventions.
I ~ *Intervene* and develop client self-helping skills.
E ~*End* and consolidate self-helping skills.

DASIE goes beyond an Egan-style problem-management model (Egan, 1990) to become a problematic skills model. A problematic skills model focuses not only on managing immediate problems, but on assisting clients to alter the underlying patterns of skills weaknesses that sustain problems. Clients' problems are redefined into the skills required for assuming more responsibility for their lives. Helpers then offer a range of interventions to assist clients in attaining self-helping goals. After helping, clients still need to assume responsibility for using, maintaining and developing their skills. Ideally, former clients become their own best helpers.

### REFERENCES

Egan, G.: *The Skilled Helper: a Systematic Approach to Effective Helping* (4th edition). Pacific Grove, CA.: Brooks/Cole, 1990.
Mowrer, O.H.: *The New Group Therapy*. Princeton, NJ: Van Nostrand, 1964.
Mowrer, O.H.: *Abnormal Reactions or Actions?* Dubuque, Iowa: Brown, 1966.
Mowrer, O.H., Vattano, A.J., and others: *Integrity Groups: the Loss and Recovery of Community*. Urbana, IL: Integrity Groups, 1973.
Mowrer, O.H.: 'Integrity Groups: Principles and Procedures'. *The Counseling Psychologist*, Volume 3 No. 2, 1972, pp. 17–33.
Nelson-Jones, R.: *The Theory and Practice of Counselling Psychology*. London: Cassell, 1982.
Nelson-Jones, R.: *Personal Responsibility Counselling and Therapy: An Integrative Approach*. Milton Keynes: Open University Press, 1984.

Nelson-Jones, R.: *Human Relationship Skills: Training and Self-Help* (1st edition). London: Cassell, 1986.

Nelson-Jones, R.: *Practical Counselling and Helping Skills: Helping Clients to Help Themselves* (2nd edition). London: Cassell, 1988.

Nelson-Jones, R.: *Effective Thinking Skills: Preventing and Managing Personal Problems.* London: Cassell, 1989.

Nelson-Jones, R.: *Human Relationship Skills* (2nd edition). London: Cassell, 1990.

Nelson-Jones, R.: *Lifeskills: a Handbook.* London: Cassell, 1991.

Nelson-Jones, R.: *Practical Counselling and Helping Skills: How to use the Lifeskills Helping Model* (3rd edition). London: Cassell, 1993.

# THE RELEVANCE OF RESEARCH IN COUNSELLING AND PSYCHOTHERAPY FOR THE COUNSELLING PRACTITIONER

## WINDY DRYDEN

*Current research paradigms are outlined and appraised to enable counsellors to see more clearly the practical relevance of counselling research. The standpoint taken is that although it is possible to criticise current research paradigms on a number of grounds, practitioners who know their own biases and the limitations of these paradigms can successfully experiment with interventions suggested by research in their own practice. An example is presented from the research on paralinguistic variables in client-centred therapy.*

## THE DOMINANT RESEARCH PARADIGM: ITS SCOPE AND LIMITATIONS

Current research in counselling and psychotherapy is carried out either in actual clinical settings or, more often, in experimental laboratory settings. While the latter enquiry is often called 'analogue' research, Kazdin (1978) has pointed out that all counselling research is analogous in so far as a situation is constructed which allows for the more-or-less controlled study of particular phenomena. Thus even such a study as Sloane *et al.* (1975), which compared psychoanalytically-oriented therapy and behaviour therapy by employing 'real' clients and experienced therapists, was an analogue of the clinical situation in that clients were told they were participating in a research study and were required to complete an extensive assessment battery on several occasions; this situation clearly differs from the normal clinical context where clients are *not* informed that they are participating in a research investigation and do *not* have to complete frequent assessment forms (Kazdin and Rogers, 1978).

Viewing all counselling research as analogous leads to the identification of dimensions along which a study can be evaluated in terms of the extent to which it is an analogue of the counsellor's normal working context. These dimensions include: client population, areas of client concern, treatment employed, client recruitment, and length of treatment. Kazdin (1978) has argued that 'the relation between an analogue study and generality to clinical situations for a given dimension itself is an area of research' (p. 684). Such research is badly needed to enable

First published in the *British Journal of Guidance and Counselling*, Volume 8 No.2, July 1980.

counsellors to assess the degree of external validity of results gained from analogue studies (i.e. the extent to which results can be generalised to clinical situations). The existing evidence suggests that the relationship will be complex. Kushner (1978) found that the utility of an analogue as a predictor of real therapy behaviour depended on: (1) therapist experience level; (2) how therapist performance was measured; and (3) which dependent variables were employed in the analysis. If the complexity of Kushner's findings is widely replicated, then counsellors can be excused if they throw their hands up in despair. I believe, however, that such a reaction would be precipitate and would – as will be suggested below – deprive counsellors of a source of helpful guidelines for counselling practice.

The emphasis in the dominant research paradigm is on maximising internal validity, i.e. 'the extent to which a given set of procedures allows one to draw valid conclusions about what actually happened in an experiment' (Mahoney, 1978). The aim is to control as many factors as possible so that if an effect occurs it can be attributed to the independent variable(s). The issue of control is important here. Practitioners are often more concerned with *why* an effect occurs than *that* an effect occurs. Thus it is not enough for the counsellor to know that in a given experiment, systematic desensitisation helps students reduce their examination anxiety more than client-centred therapy. The question is 'why?'.

To show that systematic desensitisation itself has greater therapeutic efficacy than the competing treatment, the researcher must show that the results cannot be attributed to such factors as: (1) differences in counsellors' expertise, experience and enthusiasm; (2) differences in clients' expectations and preferences regarding treatment; and (3) differences in perceived treatment credibility. In order to do this, the researcher must employ the relevant control groups. Even if these control groups are not employed, however, counsellors can still employ systematic desensitisation in the treatment of examination anxiety in a spirit of open-minded enquiry, particularly if they pay attention to and deal therapeutically with clients' expectations, preferences and perceptions of treatment credibility. In addition, it is incumbent on the counsellor to gain expertise and experience in the procedure and to carry it out with appropriate enthusiasm. If the counsellor ignores clients' expectations, preferences and perceptions of treatment credibility, and carries out the procedure in an uninspired, inept fashion, it is unlikely that the procedure of systematic desensitisation will have enough specific therapeutic potency to negate these other negative factors (Kazdin and

Wilcoxon, 1976). Thus although counsellors should be sensitive to the quality of a given research study or group of studies, they can try out treatment interventions suggested as effective by poorly-designed re-search studies.

Lazarus (1978) suggests that the dominant research paradigm has distinct limitations when it comes to tailoring systematic desnsitisation for use with individual clients. He argues that research can help to determine *when* to use the procedure but not *how* to use it with a given client. He claims that its efficacy depends on 'the different ways in which I explain its rationale to specific clients, the individual pace, manner and structure I employ with different people, the variety of ways in which I introduce scenes, embroider images and embellish tailor-made themes . . .' (p. 24). It remains to be seen to what extent studies carried out within the dominant research paradigm can answer the 'specificity' question: in which ways can different counsellors effectively employ systematic desensitisation with different clients? It is doubtful, however, whether Lazarus will get from such studies the information he requires to employ systematic desensitisation effectively with a given client.

One barrier to the application of findings derived from the dominant research paradigm stems from the fact that research reports in general do not indicate clearly enough *how* treatments are carried out. Thus in a study comparing cognitive therapy and behaviour therapy in the treatment of depression, it is not sufficient for the researcher to provide independent evidence that treatment guidelines were followed (Shaw, 1977): he must also provide independent evidence with respect to how well the treatment was carried out. A somewhat different and interesting point of view has been expressed by Kazdin (1978) regarding treatment. He points out if good results can be attributed to a treatment carried out by inexperienced counsellors in a standard fashion (which the dominant research paradigm requires), then greater confidence can be placed in the treatment's therapeutic potency than if the results were obtained by experienced therapists skilled in the treatment. He raises the possibility that the analogue situation may provide 'a more conservative test of a relation between treatment and therapeutic change than that provided in the clinical situation'.

It is hazardous, although not necessarily foolhardy, to make changes in one's counselling work on the basis of results from a single study. Garfield (1978) has argued that it is wise to view unreplicated findings as basically suggestive and to withhold final judgment until the findings have been replicated. Strict replications are, however, relatively rare in counselling and psychotherapy research: a recent survey of contributors to the *Journal of Consulting and Clinical Psychology* revealed that replication of past research was viewed as a low priority (Kendall and Ford, 1979). Consequently counsellors should be tentative in putting into practice the findings from any one study. Results of the counsellor's attempts to put into practice the researcher's findings could, though, be fed back to the researcher, perhaps using a single-case experimental design (Hersen and Barlow, 1976), thus initiating a much-needed dialogue between researchers and practitioners.

A more reliable procedure would be for practitioners to look at a group of studies on a relevant issue rather than extrapolating from isolated studies. But what if individual studies in a series or group of studies are seriously flawed? Are counsellors justified in dismissing the area as having poor external validity because of poor internal validity? Strictly speaking yes, but practically they had better not. Orlinsky and Howard (1978) concur:

> 'If study after flawed study seemed to point significantly in the same direction we could not help believing that somewhere in all that variance there must be a reliable real effect' (pp. 288–289).

An example follows.

### IMPLICATIONS OF RESEARCH FOR PRACTICE: AN EXAMPLE FROM DOMINANT PARADIGM RESEARCH

A series of studies has been carried out within the client-centred framework on counsellor and client paralinguistic behaviour (Rice, 1965; Rice and Wagstaff, 1967; Duncan *et al.*, 1968; Rice and Gaylin, 1973; Rice, 1973; Wexler, 1975; Wexler and Butler, 1976). The results of these studies indicate that (1) client expressiveness (expressive voice quality and connotative language) is significantly and positively related to counselling outcome and to level of client's psychological functioning; (2) in productive therapy sessions, counsellors focus on the client's inner experience, using fresh connotative language in an expressive fashion, speaking with normal stress, oversoft intensity and overlow pitch, and using open vocal cord control with unfilled pauses (i.e. they sound serious, warm, relaxed and concerned); and (3) a counsellor can improve the poor prognosis of an inexpressive client by stimulating the client's expressive participation with the counsellor's own expressive interventions.

These studies, however, had flaws which threaten both their internal and external validity. Firstly, therapy outcome assessment was problematic. Change was not measured multi-dimensionally, nor were change criteria individualised. Changes in both behaviour and internal states were not assessed, and evaluation was too dependent on counsellor and client perspectives, i.e. changes were not assessed from the perspective of relevant others in the client's life or from the perspective of trained raters of outcomes. Secondly, the counsellors employed in the studies were not blind to the purposes of the studies. The series was originated and carried out at the University of Chicago Counselling Centre, and it may be that the counsellors there were particularly sensitive to the therapeutic potency of paralinguistic features and of expressiveness of communications since they would have been more aware of the research group's focus than most other client-centred practitioners. Thirdly, the studies were done within a client-centred framework 'in which the primary task of the therapist is to help the client to engage in a process of self-exploration with as much freshness and immediacy as possible' (Rice and Wagstaff, 1967). Thus the results may not be generalisable to other therapies which emphasise different therapist primary tasks. In addition, the change process may not be the same for all counselling systems.

However flawed this set of studies may be, reliable effects were found which may well have implications for practising client-centred counsellors. They could well lead such counsellors to pay close attention to the paralinguistic style of their interventions and to experiment with making their interventions more expressive, particularly with inexpressive clients, while still remaining within the client's frame of reference. The effects of therapeutic procedures are, however, mediated by other factors as outlined earlier, e.g. client expectations. An important and often neglected mediating variable between a procedure and its effect is the counsellor-as-person.

One facet will be explored here. It may be that client-centred counsellors who deliberately try to make their interventions more expressive may be perceived as non-genuine in so doing. Schoeninger (1966) found that therapists who were rated as genuine in their use of self-disclosure were more effective in making such interventions than therapists rated as non-genuine in their use of self-disclosure. Thus there are hidden problems in applying even consistent research findings, since counsellors who attempt to put into practice such findings vary across many dimensions, some of which may interact negatively with counsellor expressiveness. An additional problem with the research literature in this respect is that we know very little about the counsellors who carry out the treatments. More information is necessary here for counsellors to make sense of the impact of counsellor-as-person variables on treatment efficacy.

As a result, 'cautious experimentation' with research findings is necessary, although this very attitude may affect the therapeutic value of interventions. This paradox should be accepted rather than lamented. One possible solution to the paradox would be for counsellors to form 'research application' groups where the implications of research findings are discussed and new ways of intervening with clients tried out first in role-play and co-counselling situations.

## SOME ALTERNATIVE RESEARCH PARADIGMS

The dominant paradigm in counselling and psychotherapy research has recently been subjected to scrutiny from critics advocating alternative paradigms. Smail (1978), for example, has criticised counselling and psychotherapy researchers for the overemphasis they place on scientific control. The implicit assumption here is that subjects are static, and that this results in an alienating relationship between researchers and their subjects. Again, Goldman (1976) argues that counselling researchers should give up their scientific models which, while perhaps appropriate for use in the physical sciences, are not appropriate in the study of the counselling process. He argues for a contractual relationship between researcher and subjects where researchers share with each subject, 'as much as possible, the goals of the study and what is going to happen, and seek an open and collaborative relationship with the subject before data are collected and before experimental interventions begin' (p. 549).

The paradigm which Goldman and Smail advocate can, of course, itself be criticised on a number of grounds. Internal validity might be threatened, since it may be difficult to attribute effects to a given source due to lack of control of interfering variables. The paradigm would be more concerned with identifying associations than causal relationships. But the point is that we will not find an infallible research paradigm: each one has its strengths and weaknesses. There is room for several paradigms, and if researchers discover similar findings from different paradigms, then they will be in a much stronger position to make practical recommendations to counsellors.

One variant of the 'contractual' research paradigm would be to focus on the unique features of an ongoing relationship and on the 'negotiated meanings' which emerge between the participants. As Smail (1978) has put it:

'What happens to one person in psychotherapy cannot be generalised (except with the greatest caution) to others because one person's psychotherapy involves a unique combination of two people's sets of meanings (his own and his therapist's)' (p. 57).

It is possible, however, that such unique relationships may share common features. The study of sets of meanings shared between counsellor and client and how these change over time is known as *process* research. The dominant research paradigm has so far failed to reveal much of value in its attempts to study process, since investigators have endeavoured to *impose* a meaningful structure on the raw data. An alternative paradigm approach would involve *eliciting* meanings from the participants themselves. Kagan *et al.* (1967) have suggested that researchers adopt an 'inquirer' role, in which they would help the counsellor and client reflect on the counselling process and would help them to identify, for example, episodes which were important in initiating change, i.e. critical incidents and the impact of these incidents on both participants from their own perspectives. It would be possible to chart the progress of counselling relationships in this way, so as to determine the unique and shared features of such relationships.

Another approach to the study of elicited meaning would be for both participants to keep diaries. Evans and Robinson (1978) report on the diary of a client who received nineteen sessions of behaviour therapy. The authors concluded that 'the diary exposed us to the limitations of therapy and the crudity of our working model. . .'. Comparing clients' diaries and counsellors' accounts could yield interesting discrepancies from which counsellors could re-evaluate their work. The results of such studies could be then compared with process studies based on the dominant research paradigm with its emphasis on clarification by imposed meaning. Again there is room for both paradigms.

## THE BIAS OF RESEARCH CONSUMERS

It is possibly a truism to say that counsellors do not read research reports without bias. It is probable that counsellors' views of what is important in counselling affect their interpretation of research more often than research affects their views of what is important. Cohen and Suchy (1979) found that psychoanalytically-oriented practitioners rated an outcome study as less methodologically adequate when the results of the study demonstrated the superiority of behaviour therapy than when the outcome favoured psychoanalytically-oriented therapy. Although the study (which unbeknown to therapist raters was fictitious) involved short-term treatment (5 months) and was thus biased against psychoanalytically-oriented therapy, therapists of that persuasion were not affected by this bias in general, but may have focused on it when the results did not support the efficacy of their therapeutic orientation. I, myself, have to closely monitor my adeptness at criticising studies not demonstrating the superiority of RET while remaining relatively uncritical of research favouring my preferred approach. Mahoney (1977) and Meichenbaum (1977) have similarly criticised Ellis (1977) in this respect.

Thus it is important for counsellors to be aware of their own biases and of how these might influence their reading of – and consequently their attempts at applying – research findings.

## CONCLUDING STATEMENT

A recent survey of members of the British Association for Counselling (Nelson-Jones and Coxhead, 1978) showed that the membership viewed research as a low priority for BAC attention. While it is not possible to determine the reasons for this opinion from the survey, it may be that counsellors question the relevance of research in counselling for their practical work. The present article was written with this possibility in mind. If counsellors have doubts concerning the relevance of research studies which they read, it is incumbent on them to speak up and indicate what type of research would be more credible to them. At the same time, researchers have a responsibility to encourage practitioners to disclose their concerns with respect to counselling practice and to modify their activities accordingly. Perhaps BAC can provide a forum for such an interchange.

### REFERENCES

Cohen, L.H., and Suchy, K.R.: 'The Bias in Psychotherapy Research Evaluation'. *Journal of Clinical Psychology*, Volume 35 No. 1, 1979, pp. 184–187.

Duncan, S., Jr., Rice, L.N., and Butler, J.M.: 'Therapists' Paralanguage in Peak and Poor Psychotherapy Hours'. *Journal of Abnormal Psychology*, Volume 73 No. 6, 1968, pp. 566–570.

Ellis, A.: 'Rational-Emotive Therapy: Research Data that Supports the Clinical and Personality Hypotheses of RET and Other Modes of Cognitive-Behavior Therapy'. *The Counseling Psychologist*, Volume 7 No. 1, 1977, pp. 2–41.

Evans, I.M., and Robinson, C.H.: 'Behavior Therapy Observed: the Diary of a Client'. *Cognitive Therapy and Research*, Volume 2 No. 4, 1978, pp. 335–355.

Garfield, S.L.: 'Research on Client Variables in Psychotherapy'. In S.L. Garfield and A.E. Bergin (eds.): *Handbook of Psychotherapy and Behavior Change: an Empirical Approach* (2nd edition). New York: Wiley, 1978.

Goldman, L.: 'A Revolution in Counseling Research'. *Journal of Counseling Psychology*, Volume 23 No. 6, 1976, pp. 543–552.

Hersen, M., and Barlow, D.H.: *Single Case Experimental Designs*. New York: Pergamon, 1976.

Kagan, N., Krathwohl, D.R., Goldberg, A.D., Campbell, R.J., Shauble, P.G., Greenberg, B.S., Danish, S.J., Resnikoff, A., Bowes, J., and Bondy, S.B.: *Studies in Human Interaction: Interpersonal Process Recall Simulated by Videotape*. East Lansing: Educational Publication Services, Michigan State University, 1967.

Kazdin, A.E.: 'Evaluating the Generality of Findings in Analogue Therapy Research'. *Journal of Consulting and Clinical Psychology*, Volume 46 No. 4, 1978, pp. 673–686.

Kazdin, A.E., and Rogers, T.: 'On Paradigms and Recycled Ideologies: Analogue Research Revisited'. *Cognitive Therapy and Research*, Volume 2 No. 1, 1978, pp. 105–117.

Kazdin, A.E., and Wilcoxon, L.A.: 'Systematic Desensitization and Nonspecific Treatment Effects: a Methodological Evaluation'. *Psychological Bulletin*, Volume 83 No. 5, 1976, pp. 729–758.

Kendall, P.C., and Ford, J.D.: 'Reasons for Clinical Research: Characteristics of Contributors and Their Contributions to the *Journal of Consulting and Clinical Psychology*'. *Journal of Consulting and Clinical Psychology*, Volume 47 No. 1, 1979, pp. 99–105.

Kushner, K.: 'On the External Validity of Two Psychotherapy Analogues'. *Journal of Consulting and Clinical Psychology*, Volume 46 No. 6, 1978, pp. 1394–1402.

Lazarus, A.A.: 'Science and Beyond'. *The Counseling Psychologist*, Volume 7 No. 3, 1978, pp. 24–25.

Mahoney, M.J.: 'A Critical Analysis of Rational-Emotive Theory and Therapy'. *The Counseling Psychologist*, Volume 7 No. 1, 1977, pp. 44–46.

Mahoney, M.J.: 'Experimental Methods and Outcome Evaluation'. *Journal of Consulting and Clinical Psychology*, Volume 46 No. 4, 1978, pp. 660–672.

Meichenbaum, D.H.: 'Dr Ellis, Please Stand Up'. *The Counseling Psychologist*, Volume 7 No. 1, 1977, pp. 43–44.

Nelson-Jones, R., and Coxhead, P.: 'Whither BAC: A Survey of Members' Views on Policy and Priorities'. *Counselling News*, No. 21, June 1978, pp. 2–5.

Orlinsky, D.E., and Howard, K.I.: 'The Relation of Process to Outcome in Psychotherapy'. In S.L. Garfield and A.E. Bergin (eds.): *Handbook of Psychotherapy and Behavior Change: an Empirical Approach* (2nd edition). New York: Wiley, 1978.

Rice, L.N.: 'Therapist's Style of Participation and Case Outcome'. *Journal of Consulting Psychology*, Volume 29 No. 2, 1965, pp. 155–160.

Rice, L.N.: 'Client Behavior as a Function of Therapist Style and Client Resources'. *Journal of Counseling Psychology*, Volume 20 No. 4, 1973, pp. 306–311.

Rice, L.N., and Gaylin, N.L.: 'Personality Processes Reflected in Client and Vocal Style and Rorschach Processes'. *Journal of Consulting and Clinical Psychology*, Volume 40 No. 1, 1973, pp. 133–138.

Rice, L.N., and Wagstaff, A.K.: 'Client Voice Quality and Expressive Style as Indexes of Productive Psychotherapy'. *Journal of Consulting Psychology*, Volume 31 No. 6, 1967, pp. 557–563.

Schoeninger, D.W.: 'Client Experiencing as a Function of Therapist Self-Disclosure and Pre-Therapy Training in Experiencing'. *Dissertation Abstracts International*, Volume 26, 1966, p. 5551.

Shaw, B.F.: 'Comparison of Cognitive Therapy and Behavior Therapy in the Treatment of Depression'. *Journal of Consulting and Clinical Psychology*, Volume 45 No. 4, 1977, pp. 543–551.

Sloane, R.B., Staples, F.R., Cristol, A.H., Yorkston, N.J., and Whipple, K.: *Psychotherapy Versus Behavior Therapy*. Cambridge, Mass.: Harvard University Press, 1975.

Smail, D.J.: *Psychotherapy: a Personal Approach*. London: Dent, 1978.

Wexler, D.A.: 'A Scale for the Measurement of Client and Therapist Expressiveness'. *Journal of Clinical Psychology*, Volume 31, 1975, pp. 486–489.

Wexler, D.A., and Butler, J.M.: 'Therapist Modification of Client Expressiveness in Client-Centred Therapy'. *Journal of Consulting and Clinical Psychology*, Volume 44 No. 2, 1976, pp. 261–265.

# THE RELEVANCE OF RESEARCH IN COUNSELLING AND PSYCHOTHERAPY FOR THE COUNSELLING PRACTITIONER

## WINDY DRYDEN

### POSTSCRIPT

Just before the above paper was published, but after it was written and submitted to the *BJGC*, Gelso (1979) published a lengthy major contribution in *The Counseling Psychologist* which reviewed current (at that time) methodological and professional issues in counselling research. In that paper, Gelso put forward and expanded on the view that every attempt at solving methodological problems in counselling research created further problems of its own (the so-called 'bubble' hypothesis). While advocating paradigmatic diversity in research into counselling, Gelso cautioned that quantitative and qualitative methodologies each have their strengths and weaknesses and that we need to understand the trade-offs that are being made when appraising research studies. In short, we need to recognise that in the same way that we cannot eliminate a bubble that appears when we cover a book with clear film, we cannot eliminate the bubble from counselling research. We can move it around, but we cannot get rid of it.

I find it gratifying that such an eminent researcher as Gelso was articulating a position very similar to my own, roughly at the same time (albeit more fully and far more eloquently). I also find it interesting that more than a decade later I still agree with the basic thesis of my paper – namely, that if as practising counsellors we take care to appreciate the strengths and weaknesses of research emanating from different paradigms, we can cautiously explore the relevance of findings from such research to our own practice.

Since that time, the status of counselling research and its relevance for practising and trainee counsellors has continued to be debated in the professional counselling journals. Such has been the interest in this topic that several special issues of journals and journal symposia have been devoted to the issue of counselling research and its utility. In this postscript I will briefly review some of this published work.

In 1982, *The Counseling Psychologist* published a second special issue on research in counselling psychology (the first was published in 1979 and was based on the article by Gelso mentioned above). Two papers in that second special issue stand out in that they reflect current concerns with making research increasingly relevant for counselling practitioners. The first, by Clara Hill (1982) on what is now known as change process research, showed that the field is increasingly interested not in the question 'Does counselling work?', but in the question 'How does counselling work?' The second, by Neimeyer and Resnikoff (1982) on qualitative strategies in counselling research, argues for the use of convergent methodology and in so doing echoes a position that I took in my own paper: 'By combining qualitative and quantitative methods, a researcher maximizes an investigation's internal and external validity. Where similar results are obtained across methods, the validity of the experimental conjecture is reinforced. Where results diverge, new information becomes available' (p. 84).

Seven years later, in a third special issue on counselling research published in *The Counseling Psychologist*, Hoshmand (1989) argues more forcefully against the use of what she calls 'the positivistic research tradition of reductive-experimentation' in counselling (i.e. the traditional quantitative paradigm), and discusses three alternative paradigms: (**i**) the naturalistic-ethnographic; (**ii**) the phenomenological; and (**iii**) the cybernetic. Nine years after my paper was published, the debate on the relative merits of traditional and non-traditional research paradigms in counselling is still continuing.

In 1985, the *Journal of Counseling and Development* published a small symposium on the relevance of counselling research for practitioners. In the lead article, George Howard (1985) drew on the work of Joseph Rychlak who had distinguished among four different types of causal explanation: (**i**) material causes, emanating from the substance of which a thing is made (e.g. the effect of serotonin on human behaviour); (**ii**) efficient causes – the impetus or force in events (e.g. the impact of level of counsellor empathy on client self-disclosure); (**iii**) formal causes – the recognisable organisation in the flow of events (e.g. the efficacy of different problem-solving stategies on student learning); and (**iv**) final causes – the reason, intention or goal of an action (e.g. the effect of intentionally chosen goals on eating behaviour). Howard contended that most counsellors are interested in final causes, while much counselling research neglects this type of causation, a situation which helps to explain the oft-heard cry of lack of relevance from practitioners about counselling research. Howard argued for a greater emphasis on multi-level counselling research – i.e. research which assesses the impact of causes across Rychlak's causation spectrum. In particular, he proposed increased attention on final causes in research studies.

In the following year, the *American Psychologist* published a special issue on psychotherapy research. Morrow-Bradley and Elliott (1986) reported the results of a mail survey of practising psychotherapists which showed, amongst other things, that the utilisation of therapy research by their sample was low, with therapists preferring to learn about therapy from other non-research sources. However, the sample of therapists did state that they would like to make more use of research. The authors closed by making the usual plea for researchers to place greater value on the external validity of their studies and, in particular, to focus more on typical populations, settings and orientations. However, what makes this plea more compelling is that it was made by their sample of practising therapists.

Many writers have made the point that one way of encouraging counsellors to develop more positive views about research is through educational efforts when they are still in training. A short symposium published in the *Journal of Counseling and Development* dealt with this issue from the North American perspective (see Heppner *et al.*, 1987). From this side of the Atlantic, Dimmock (1988), in an unpublished Masters thesis using qualitative research methods (with understandably small numbers of 'subjects'), showed how important it is for Masters-level counselling trainees to follow their own interests if they are to develop a positive view of counselling research. Dimmock also showed how easy it is for these students to become discouraged in the face of learning statistics and quantitative research design. We need more studies on trainees' experiences of learning how to appraise the research of others and how to carry out their own research. It would be particularly gratifying if some of these studies could emanate from Britain.

It will come as no surprise to learn that virtually all the sources I have quoted above are American. My main regret about my article is that while it reflected ongoing concerns about the relevance of counselling research for practitioners, it seemingly failed to stimulate a similar debate on this side of the Atlantic. Maybe I need to try again?

### REFERENCES

Dimmock, M.: *Student Attitudes to the Research Component of a Postgraduate Course in Counselling*. Unpublished MSc thesis, Roehampton Institute of Higher Education, London, 1988.
Gelso, C.J.: 'Research in Counseling: Methodological and Professional Issues'. *The Counseling Psychologist*, Volume 8 No. 3, 1979, pp. 7–36.
Heppner, P.P., Gelso, C.J., and Dolliver, R.H.: 'Three Approaches to Research Training in Counseling'. *Journal of Counseling and Development*, Volume 66, 1987, pp. 45–49.
Hill, C.E.: 'Counseling Process Research: Philosophical and Methodological Dilemmas'. *The Counseling Psychologist*, Volume 10 No. 4, 1982, pp. 7–19.

Hoshmand, L.L.S.T.: 'Alternate Research Paradigms: a Review and Teaching Proposal'. *The Counseling Psychologist*, Volume 17 No. 1, 1989, pp. 3–79.

Howard, G.S.: 'Can Research in the Human Sciences Become More Relevant to Practice?' *Journal of Counseling and Development*, Volume 63, 1985, pp. 539–544.

Morrow-Bradley, C., and Elliott, R.: 'Utilization of Psychotherapy Research by Practising Psychotherapists'. *American Psychologist*, Volume 41, 1986, pp. 188 197.

Neimeyer, G., and Resnikoff, A.: 'Qualitative Strategies in Counseling Research'. *The Counseling Psychologist*, Volume 10 No. 4, 1982, pp. 75–85.

# HUMOUR AS A TOOL IN COUNSELLING AND PSYCHOTHERAPY: A REVERSAL ~ THEORY PERSPECTIVE

## STEPHEN J. MURGATROYD

*Humour has occasionally been regarded as a valuable tool in counselling and psychotherapy. The specific uses of humour and its potential as a coping tactic are rarely described. The therapeutic use of humour is accordingly examined in the light of reversal theory (Apter, 1982a). It is suggested that the use of humour needs to be related to the motivational task implicit in the therapeutic interaction.*

Norman Cousins has claimed that his recovery from a serious collagen illness, which was regarded by his doctors as incurable, was due to taking massive doses of both vitamin C and humour (Cousins, 1979). Like other writers (e.g. Dixon, 1980), Cousins suggests that the use of humour significantly reduced his overall stress and anxiety levels, facilitated active coping (Lazarus, 1966) and enabled the body to deal better with 'its' disease. This case encouraged many to re-examine the relationship between humour and coping, and the place of humour in therapeutic processes. This paper is the result of one such re-examination.

### HUMOUR AND COPING

Both Janis (1958) and Lazarus (1966) have given emphasis to the importance of cognitive and personality factors and previous experience in coping with life stress. In an earlier review of the literature on coping (Murgatroyd, 1982), a variety of coping strategies and tactics useful in the context of crisis intervention and crisis counselling were identified. In none of the papers reviewed was much attention paid to humour as a coping tactic. Instead the available literature gives emphasis to the locus of control (Johnson and Sarason, 1978), social support (Medalic and Goldbourt, 1976) and sensation seeking (Johnson *et al.*, 1978) as stress-buffering devices. A more recent review of the literature on coping and adaptation by Howard (1984) only mentions humour in passing, and the *Handbook of Stress* (Goldberger and Breznitz, 1982) does not mention humour as a coping device in any of its 800 pages. Why have psychologists paid so little attention to humour as a coping tactic?

Much of the responsibility for this situation is perhaps due to Freud's suggestion that humour (not simply joke telling) is 'the highest of the

First published in the *British Journal of Guidance and Counselling*, Volume 15 No.3, Sept., 1987.

defensive processes' (Freud, 1960), since it aims at significant savings in psychic energy by permitting the super-ego to comfort and console the ego when the latter is distressed. Humour *as* defence became translated in the mind of some psychologists as humour as a symbol of repression. In consequence, humour has been regarded by some (within the psychoanalytic tradition at least) as a maladaptive coping tactic – not to be encouraged. But Freud did not see humour in this way. On the contrary, he regarded humour in coping as 'a rare and precious gift' (Freud, 1959). He saw it as having 'a particularly liberating effect and elevating effect' which enables the person to refuse 'to undergo suffering, asseverates the invincibility of one's ego against the real world and victoriously upholds the pleasure principle, *yet all without quitting the ground of mental sanity*' (Freud, 1959, p. 217 [my emphasis]). For Freud, then, humour was a valuable tool for the maintenance of sanity. Some of his followers do not share this view, especially in the context of the therapeutic process, as we shall later see.

Freud is not alone in regarding humour as an important coping tactic. Allport (1950) observed that 'the neurotic who learns to laugh at himself may be on the way to self management, perhaps to cure' – a view that would find support in the writings of May (1969), O'Connel (1976) and Dixon (1980). Frankl, the founder of logotherapy, also regards humour as a valuable device for the recognition of incongruity, enabling people to see themselves with irony (Frankl, 1969). Indeed, this use of humour for the recognition of ambiguity and the construction of irony lies at the root of the process of paradoxical intention – a central process in both logotherapy and Adlerian psychotherapy (Adler, cited in Ansbacher and Ansbacher, 1956, p. 346).

A list of the functions of humour evidenced in the psychological literature would include the following: (**a**) the exercise of superiority; (**b**) the use of surprise; (**c**) a safe statement of some ambivalence about the 'self'; (**d**) a device for recognition, release and relief; (**e**) a means by which seemingly unconnected thoughts, ideas or objects are brought together in some synergistic way; (**f**) a means by which fantasy can be more directly related to reality for a person; and (**g**) a device for the accurate perception of incongruity, sometimes enabling unwanted incongruity to be resolved. All of these functions could be regarded as active coping functions: they better enable people to relate to the environment in which they live and work, taking full account of their motives and psychobiographies. In short, humour provides an opportunity for active coping and has many different tactical components aimed at enhancing and extending 'person-environment fit'. Given this observation, it is even more surprising that coping theorists pay such scant attention to humour.

To be fair, Mechanic (1957) does observe the use of humour as an ego-defence amongst students experiencing test-anxiety, but is dismissive of its importance. Again Janis (1958) documents humour as a coping tactic amongst air pilots in combat, but does not integrate it into any structure for coping. Lazarus (1966) is aware of these and other studies, but appears dismissive of them. What is lacking is a motivational theory of coping that takes full account of humour: ego-defence (Freud's model) is inadequate in its account of humour as a coping device.

## HUMOUR IN COUNSELLING AND PSYCHOTHERAPY

Most of the writing about humour in counselling and psychotherapy relates to the use of jokes by the therapist. Little has been written about situational comedy within therapy or about non-verbal humour, and even less has been said about client-initiated humour.

Kubie (1971) has argued strongly against the use of therapist-centred (i.e. therapist-initiated) or client-centred (i.e. client-initiated) humour. Writing from a psychoanalytic tradition, he argues that humour can be damaging in the following ways:

**1.** Therapist use of humour may block or arrest free association.

**2.** Therapist use of humour may confuse the client by creating unnecessary concerns as to whether the therapist is serious or not.

**3.** Therapist use of humour may cause the client to accept that which *is* serious as being less serious than it actually is.

**4.** Client use of humour may increase ego-defence and thus extend the period of therapy unnecessarily.

**5.** Client use of humour masks pain and thus makes therapy more, rather than less, difficult.

**6.** Excessive use of therapist humour may unduly restrict the client's expression of fear, anger, remorse or pain – he or she may not wish to spoil the therapist's 'fun'.

**7.** Humour makes the therapist more visible than he or she ought to be, since it impairs 'necessary incognito'.

Mindess (1976) has countered these seven assertions by suggesting that they could well be applied to many other processes, such as paradoxical intention (Frankl, 1969), cognitive restructuring (Meichenbaum, 1977) or rational-emotive therapy (Ellis, 1962). Rather than being a rejection of humour, they may more usefully be regarded as a defence of a particular model of therapy which seeks to minimise the levels and frequency of affective contact between client and therapist. In contrast to Kubie's pessimistic rejection of humour as a therapeutic tool, Vintis (1980) has documented some uses of humour in behavioural therapy, especially in relation to systematic desensitisation processes. He particularly highlights the importance of client-centred humour, reinforcing Allport's (1968) observation that: '. . . so many tangles in life are ultimately hopeless that we have no appropriate sword other than laughter. I venture to say that no person is in good health unless he can laugh at himself quietly and privately, noting where he is over-reached or when his pretentions have been overblown or pedantic' (p. 134). Vintis notes that this remark supports the view that humour is both an indicator of mental health and a vehicle by which mental health can be both preserved and promoted.

Klein (1976), reflecting on his Canadian counselling experiences, notes that 'humour will advance rapport more quickly than empathy, but unlike empathy some social rapport is a pre-requisite' for appropriate uses of humour in counselling. Though he cites a number of inappropriate and potentially damaging misuses of humour, Klein regards humour as 'central to counselling processes – it dulls criticism and suspends judgements, leaving reason impotent to restore our former opinions'.

Indeed a variety of therapists have begun to locate humour in their skills repertoire. Novaco (1978), working from a cognitive-behavioural perspective, uses humour as a device in his psycho-education programme aimed at anger-reduction; Mindess (1976), like Frankl (1969), regards humour as a therapeutic tool that can 'expose hidden truths and articulate philosophic positions of no little moment'; Dixon (1980) strongly supports the use of humour in stress-reduction programmes; while Martin and Lefcourt (1983) note the value of humour as a mediator of life-stress and have developed some instrumentation valuable in counselling processes; Nevo (1986) provides insights into the way in which humour can be used in career counselling.

Reading accounts of the therapeutic uses of humour and discussing the issues associated with such use with some of those mentioned here, it becomes clear that a theoretical understanding of why humour is an effective therapeutic tool is lacking in many of these studies and reports. Dixon (1980) gets near to proposing a process-outcome theory when he suggests that the beneficial effects of humour are produced by means of the 'cognitive shifts' which it entails and the changes in affective quality which accompany it. This view is supported by O'Connel (1976), who suggests that it is the therapist's skilled use of 'rapid perceptional-cognitive switches in frames of reference' which facilitates the productive use of humour in therapy. Unbeknown to Dixon and O'Connel, this 'perspective shifting' lies at the heart of a reversal theory of humour.

## REVERSAL THEORY OF HUMOUR

The theory of psychological reversals, developed by Smith and Apter (1975), and elaborated by Apter (1982a), first offered an explanation of humour processes in 1976, reinforcing this with a case-study analysis of a comedy television series – *Fawlty Towers* (Apter, 1982b). A study by Wicker *et al.* (1982) offers data supporting the explanatory value of reversal theory against other theories of humour, while Svebak's research at the University of Bergen offers substantial psychological *and* physiological support to the reversal explanation of the humour process (Svebak, 1980).

An earlier paper (Murgatroyd, 1981) offered a basic description of reversal theory relevant in a counselling context, and a full description of the theory and its relevance to the humour process can be found in Apter (1982a). The following points are offered in summary:

**1.** Humour depends crucially on identity synergies – situations which contain contrasts between appearance and reality or between make-believe and reality. Humour occurs when one suddenly realises the difference between appearance and reality (transition humour) or when one comes to see some amusing incongruity between these two components of the synergy (non-transition humour).

**2.** To be humorous, an identity synergy needs to be experienced both emotionally and cognitively: the person needs to be able to evaluate and weigh the components of the humour situation *as well as* being able to experience their own emotional and intellectual reaction to that situation. Such an evaluation will lead to higher arousal.

**3.** Humour is always experienced in a paratelic mode (playful, arousal-seeking, spontaneous) rather than a telic mode (serious, arousal-avoiding, future-oriented). This often means that the person has to switch from the telic to the paratelic mode in order to experience humour – the switching process identified by O'Connel (1976) and Dixon (1980).

**4.** The full expression of humour or mirth will relate to the environmental context in which people find themselves – inappropriate environments may lead to the experience of arousal as anxiety rather than 'fun'.

From experience (see also Apter, 1982a, p. 187), environmental cues and social expectations can facilitate the processes outlined here, especially in relation to switching the person from the telic to the paratelic mode. This observation has some importance when considering the role of the counsellor in the creation of environmental cues for humour in therapy: to use humour effectively, the counsellor needs to 'cue' this reversal.

### THERAPEUTIC 'NEEDS' IN REVERSAL-THEORY TERMS

Whereas clinical models of psychopathology use the medical model to clarify the problems experienced by clients, reversal theory essentially uses a process model to create a taxonomy of clients' presenting problems. This taxonomy is briefly examined by Murgatroyd (1981) and Apter (1982a), and has been more fully documented by Murgatroyd and Apter (1984; 1986). In essence, four major types of presenting problems are recognised within the theory. These are:

**1.** *Reversal inhibition* ~ when a person is unable to reverse between two related states (i.e. telic/paratelic), even when it would be appropriate to do so.

**2.** *Inappropriate reversal* ~ the person reverses from one state to another (e.g. telic or paratelic, negativistic or conforming) despite the inappropriateness of such reversals.

**3.** *Temporally inappropriate behaviour* ~ when the achievement of satisfaction in one state makes reversal more difficult or makes the achievement of satisfaction in the same or alternative state less likely in the future.

**4.** *Socially inappropriate behaviour* ~ when the person's behaviour is compatible with the state they are experiencing, but the behaviour is harmful to them or not socially sanctioned.

The point to note here is that these four major categories of clients' presenting problems direct counsellors to underlying personality and motivational processes within which current emotional, behavioural and cognitive difficulties can be evaluated.

### HUMOUR AND CLIENTS' PRESENTING PROBLEMS

The taxonomy of clients' presenting problems offered above provides a framework within which it is possible to review the place of humour in therapeutic practice. Using this taxonomy, it also becomes possible to identify certain situations in which humour processes are *not* appropriate for counselling.

**1. Reversal failure**. The underlying feature of this presenting problem is that the person is unable to reverse between one metamotivational mode and another: they are 'trapped' in one mode (e.g. telic) for relatively long periods of time. For clients 'trapped' in the paratelic mode (i.e. actively seeking to increase their arousal, to experience pleasure, to live in the 'here and now', to avoid planning ahead, to be spontaneous), humour is an inappropriate therapeutic tactic. For although, as we have seen, humour involves the person being in the paratelic mode, the fact is that if the aim of therapy is to facilitate reversal into the telic mode, maintenance of the paratelic mode for the purposes of humour is *not* going to be effective.

In contrast, for clients who find themselves 'locked' into the telic mode and seeking reversal into the the paratelic mode, humour is a useful and dynamic tactic for achieving this. Indeed, for humour to be successful, reversal *must* be achieved. In order to make this possible, the therapist can use three specific tactics. These are:

(**a**) To create (via verbal, audio-visual and drama-therapy techniques) identity synergies which act to encourage the perception of personal incongruity. Especially useful here are the hot-seat techniques developed by Perls (1969) and refined by Zinker (1977), and paradox (Frankl, 1969). The aim is to highlight incongruities at which the person can laugh or smile. It may also be useful to engage in physical activities which increase physiological arousal (i.e. dynamic mediation), especially if the therapist interprets any signs of fatigue in a humorous way.

(**b**) To encourage the client to review existing identity synergies and to enable them to see more clearly their meta-interpretation. This requires the therapist to engage in some confrontation so as to highlight the synergy recognised or implied by the client, and to enable the therapist to review and examine the way in which the client interprets his or her recognition of an incongruous identity synergy.

(**c**) To create a paratelic climate in therapy so that the perception of identity synergies is experienced in a paratelic way. Frequent use of smiles by the therapist, encouragement of client smiling, some use of self-directed jokes (i.e. jokes directed at the person telling the joke) by the therapist, and encouragement of such jokes on the part of the client: all of these techniques can contribute significantly to the creation of a paratelic climate. In group counselling situations, many of the warm-up games typically used to create group cohesion and identity can be regarded as being aimed at creating a paratelic climate within which some work on identity synergy could be conducted.

These three tactical features of therapy provide a framework for the eclectic use of a variety of 'standard' therapeutic techniques. For example, synergies can be constructed by highlighting opposing 'games' used by the person, where the game strategies are derived from transactional analysis: alternatively, the use of systematic desensitisation can be achieved in humorous ways (Vintis, 1980). Reversal theory provides a structural understanding of the process by which a person experiences a situation, thought or feeling as humorous. What the therapist needs to work at is the structured use of both synergy and reversal in a way that is personally meaningful to each individual engaged in therapy.

**2. Inappropriate reversal**. This presenting problem involves the person, often despite their desire to do otherwise, reversing in an inappropriate way. The therapeutic task may have two components, depending upon the person's stated needs. These are: (**a**) to reduce the extent to which the person experiences their thoughts, feelings and actions as increasing the intensity of their experience of a given mode; and (**b**) to facilitate a reversal into the opposite (more appropriate) mode.

When reversals to the paratelic mode occur, the therapist needs to exercise caution about the use of humour. There is a danger that the excessive use of humour or the use of inappropriate forms of humour may increase rather than decrease the person's paratelic experience. Two particular humour strategies do, however, seem appropriate for this presenting problem. The first of these is paradoxical intention (Dowd and Milne, 1986); the second is the use of 'black' humour.

Paradoxical intention involves the therapist in the deliberate exaggeration of the person's belief-defence tactic. For example, a person who has a fear of confined spaces and who believes they will have a heart attack in such an environment is encouraged to go into an elevator and have a really epic seizure, making sure the elevator is full of people so that they can all observe the person's distress, pain and discomfort. Again suicide threats are matched by therapist demands that the person actively makes sure that there will be no mistakes and that the attempt will be successful. Though some may regard these devices as callous, Frankl (1969) sets their use in the context of creating a climate in which the person rebels at the logical extension of their own beliefs. A similar strategy lies at the heart of EST (Rhinehart, 1977) and is also the framework for much of the process work in rational-emotive therapy (Ellis, 1962).

Clearly, therapists need to exercise some care in their use of paradox. They need to ensure: (**a**) that their understanding of the belief system is accurate; (**b**) that the client is in a state of 'paradox-readiness'; (**c**) that the paradox used is perceived as a logical extension of their own belief system, but will be unacceptable to the person; and (**d**) that the confrontation process involved in the presentation of the paradox to the person contains an element of humour. If these conditions can be met, the paradox serves as a mirror which confronts them with an absurd view of themselves.

Similar cautions apply to the use of 'black' humour – what here may be regarded as the cynical confrontation of the person in a way that is derogatory, using some feature of that person for the focal point of that humour. Once again, the process aim of this tactic is to encourage clients to recognise the absurdity of their own position within a paratelic frame and to react to that recognition by becoming more telic in their response.

When the inappropriate reversal is to the telic state, the therapist's task may be regarded as having two components: (**a**) to enable the person to recognise their presenting problem in terms of their inappropriate reversal; and (**b**) to enable the person to become less intensely telic or to reverse into the paratelic. Humour can play a part in this process, but it is a part of an overall strategy aimed at restoring appropriate reversals for the person. In particular, the use of paradox or the use of humorous drama therapy to highlight the incongruities of the person's life are likely to prove effective in so far as they confront the person with the logical extension of themselves if they continue to increase the intensity of their telic experience. From experience, the enactment of a comic fantasy is also useful in this circumstance.

Whilst the use of paradox may be common to both the paratelic and telic versions of this presenting problem, the focus for the paradox is likely to be different. In the paratelic mode, the paradox is likely to focus upon the here-and-now, pleasureful experiences of the person (the key characteristics of this state); whereas in the telic state, the paradox is likely to focus on the goals the person is pursuing and their future consequences. In both cases, the paradox will be most effective if the humour component of the paradox is gradually developed rather than 'exploded' upon the person. In both states, the humour will do much to relieve the tension of the confrontation that paradox necessarily involves.

**3. Temporally inappropriate behaviour**. Here, people behave in a way appropriate to their current state, but doing so has unwanted consequences for the future. In a telic state of mind, a person seeks to avoid anxiety by avoiding the problem which is causing the anxiety. Whilst this may temporarily alleviate the anxiety, it could lead to greater anxiety at a later date. A concrete example of this is the woman who, noticing a breast growth, chooses not to have a medical examination in the hope that the growth will subside: doing so alleviates her immediate anxiety, but the subsequent anxiety may be greater if the tumour is cancerous and its growth could have been prevented with early intervention.

A second example concerns the paratelic state. In order to satisfy the need for excitement, an individual may perform an action (e.g. driving a car at a very fast speed), only to find that the long-term consequences are serious (e.g. when he or she is caught speeding). Or an individual may engage in extra-marital sex in order to satisfy an immediate and temporary need, and in so doing may endanger his or her marriage.

Humour can be used to highlight the tension and contradiction between immediate and future needs in two ways. First, it can be used as a means of highlighting and exaggerating this tension. Second, it can be used to address the more general patterns of behaviour in which the individual is engaged.

Some drama-therapy and role-play techniques (Johnstone, 1981) can be powerful ways of exaggerating such tensions. In particular, the absurdity of not taking into account the future but only focusing on the present is a classic feature of farce. With some clients (especially those who are paratelic-dominant), drama can be a powerful tool in showing them why they need to 'stop and think'. For others, a more effective technique can be to seek to perfect avoidance strategies – another form of paradoxical intention. Both of these methods address the tension of a particular action.

Ordeal therapy, described by Haley (1984), is a way of ensuring that individuals give time to the consequences of their behaviour. Through a variety of means, the individuals are required to make up for time lost or to behave in a way that looks to the future, and are asked to review their ordeal in a humorous way.

Those who do not respond well to these and other tactics appear to have two features in common: (a) they are highly telic-dominant and actively appear to resist reversals to the paratelic mode; and (b) they regard counselling and psychotherapy as very serious processes and have well-developed and fixed views of what constitutes 'good' therapy. If these features characterise the person in need, then humour is not advisable.

**4. Socially inappropriate behaviour**. Here clients experience one of two consequences of their behaviour. First, they may be engaging in behaviour which, whilst appropriate to the mode in which they are operating (e.g. telic or paratelic), nonetheless has harmful physical, emotional, interpersonal or cognitive consequences for them. Whilst they may be aware of these consequences (especially if they are in the telic mode) they do not feel able to disengage from the mode and the behaviour. Alternatively, they may be engaging in mode-appropriate behaviour which they do not see as being harmful to them but which is socially regarded as unacceptable.

Humour is useful in highlighting the nature of the presenting problem and in identifying the specific feature of the behaviour which is giving rise to the difficulty. In several cases, the use of humour as a flooding device – using grossly amusing images of the consequences of the client's behaviour repeatedly so that the behaviour is always associated with these gross images – has proven to be effective.

Three other techniques involving humour appear especially effective for this problem. These are:

**1.** *Comic literal description:* the client or the counsellor offers a description of current behaviour or thinking which seeks to be a literal description but which is in fact a comic near-literal description which maximises the use of identity (real/apparent) synergies.

**2.** *Comic monodrama:* the client uses the hot-seat technique developed in gestalt counselling (Perls, 1969) and refined in co-counselling (Heron, 1973); one of the seats requires the client to speak of themselves in amusing terms or to examine their behaviour or attitudes from a humorous but safe vantage point.

**3.** *Comic fantasy:* the client is encouraged and enabled to engage in a projective self-fantasy in which humour is intended to play an important part in the sharing of the fantasy – a humorous guided fantasy may be a useful precursor to this process.

With each of these processes it is most helpful to encourage the person to generate the synergies that may give rise to humour. Some valuable suggestions for achieving this are offered by Johnstone (1981).

## CONCLUSION

This paper has examined the place of humour in counselling and psychotherapy and has used the theory of psychological reversals to provide a theoretical and practical framework for understanding both the role of humour in therapy and the structure of humour. It should be clear from the descriptions provided that humour is *not* always an appropriate therapeutic tactic. Reversal theory helps to identify some of the conditions in which humour is appropriate.

Implicit in the paper is the idea that humour is a valuable resource for the task of coping, both for the person seeking help and for the therapist. Humour is clearly a resource which some are willing to embrace and use, while for others it is anxiety-provoking. The role of humour in active coping has yet to be explored.

## REFERENCES

Allport, G.W.: *The Individual and His Religion.* New York: Macmillan, 1950.

Allport, G.W.: *The Person in Psychology: Selected Essays.* Boston: Beacon Press, 1968.

Ansbacher, H.L.L., and Ansbacher, R.R.: *The Individual Psychology of Alfred Adler.* New York: Basic Books, 1956.

Apter, M.J.: *The Experience of Motivation: the Theory of Psychological Reversals.* London: Academic Press. 1982(a).

Apter, M.J.: 'Fawlty Towers – a Reversal Theory Analysis of a Popular Television Comedy Series'. *Journal of Popular Culture*, Volume 6, 1982(b), pp. 128–138.

Cousins, N.: *Anatomy of an Illness.* New York: Norton, 1979.

Dixon, N.F.: 'Humor – a Cognitive Alternative to Stress'. In Sarason, I.G., and Spielberger, C.D. (eds.): *Stress and Anxiety*, Volume 7. Washington, DC: Hemisphere, 1980.

Dowd, E.T., and Milne, C.R.: 'Paradoxical Interventions in Counseling Psychology'. *Counseling Psychologist*, Volume 4, 1986, pp. 237–282.

Ellis, A.: *Reason and Emotion in Psychotherapy.* New York: Lyle Stuart, 1962.

Frankl, V.: *The Doctor and the Soul: an Introduction to Logotherapy.* New York: Knopf, 1969.

Freud, S.: 'Humour'. In Jones, E., Riviere, J., and Strachey, J.A. (eds.): *Collected Papers of Sigmund Freud*, Volume 5. New York: Basic Books, 1959.

Frued, S.: *Jokes and their Relation to the Unconscious.* New York: Norton, 1960.

Goldberger, L., and Breznitz, S. (eds.): *Handbook of Stress: Theoretical and Clinical Aspects.* New York: Free Press, 1982.

Haley, J.: *Ordeal Therapy: Unusual Ways to Change Behavior.* San Francisco: Jossey-Bass, 1984.

Heron, J.: 'Re-Evaluation Counselling: Personal Growth through Mutual Aid'. *British Journal of Guidance and Counselling*, Volume 1, 1973, pp. 22–36.

Howard, R.W.: *Coping and Adapting.* London: Robertson, 1984.

Janis, I.: *Psychological Stress.* New York: Wiley, 1958.

Johnson, J.H., and Sarason, I.G.: 'Moderator Variables in Life Stress Research'. In Sarason, I.G., and Spielberger, C.D. (eds.): *Stress and Anxiety*, Volume 6. Washington, DC: Hemisphere, 1978.

Johnson, J.H., Sarason, I.G., and Siegel, J.M.: 'Arousal Seeking as a Moderator of Life Stress'. *Perceptual and Motor Skills*, Volume 49, 1979, pp. 665–666.

Johnstone, K.: *Impro-Improvisation and the Theatre.* London: Methuen, 1981.

Klein, J.: 'Rationality and Humour in Counselling'. *Canadian Counsellor*, Volume 11, 1976, pp. 28–32.

Kubie, L.: 'The Destructive Potential of Humor in Psychotherapy'. *American Journal of Psychiatry*, Volume 127, 1971, pp. 861–866.

Lazarus, R.S.: *Psychological Stress and the Coping Process.* New York: McGraw-Hill, 1966.

Martin, R.A., and Lefcourt, H.M.: 'The Sense of Humor as a Moderator Between Stress and Moods'. *Journal of Personality and Social Psychology*, Volume 45, 1983, pp. 1313–1324.

May, R.: *Man's Search for Himself*. New York: Random House, 1969.

Mechanic, D.: *Students Under Stress*. *New York: Free Press, 1957*.

Medalic, J.H., and Goldbourt, U.: 'Angina among 10,000 Men – Psychosocial and Other Risk Factors'. *American Journal of Medicine*, Volume 60, 1976, pp. 910–921.

Meichenbaum, D.: *Cognitive Behavior Modification: an Integrative Approach*. New York: Plenum, 1977.

Mindess, H.: 'The Uses and Abuses of Humor in Psychotherapy'. In Chapman, A., and Foot, H.C. (eds.): *It's a Funny Thing, Humour*. Oxford: Pergamon, 1976.

Murgatroyd, S.: 'Coping and the Crisis Counsellor'. *British Journal of Guidance and Counselling*, Volume 10, 1982, pp. 151–166.

Murgatroyd, S.: 'Reversal Theory: a New Perspective on Crisis Counselling'. *British Journal of Guidance and Counselling*, Volume 9, 1981, pp. 180–193.

Murgatroyd, S., and Apter, M.J.: 'Eclectic Psychotherapy: a Structural Phenomenological Approach'. In Dryden, W. (ed.): *Individual Therapy in Britain*. London: Harper & Row, 1984.

Murgatroyd, S., and Apter, M.J.: 'A Structural Phenomenological Approach to Eclectic Psychotherapy'. In Norcross, J. (ed.): *Handbook of Eclectic Psychotherapy*. New York: Brunner-Mazel, 1986.

Nevo, O.: 'Uses of Humor in Careers Counseling'. *Vocational Guidance Quarterly*, Volume 34, 1986, pp. 188–196.

Novaco, R.W.: 'Anger and Coping with Stress – Cognitive Behavioural Interventions'. In Foreyt, J.P., and Ratljen, D.P. (eds.): *Cognitive Behaviour Therapy: Research and Applications*. New York: Plenum, 1978.

O'Connel, W.: 'Freudian Humour – the Eupsychia of Everyday Life'. In Chapman, A.J., and Foot, H.C. (eds.): *It's a Funny Thing, Humour*. Oxford: Pergamon, 1976.

Perls, F.: *Gestalt Therapy Verbatim*. Moab, Utah: Real People Press, 1969.

Rhinehart, L.: *The Book of EST*. New York: Holt, Rinehart and Winston, 1977.

Smith, K.C.P., and Apter, M.J.: *A Theory of Psychological Reversal*. Chippenham: Picton, 1975.

Sveback, S.: 'Effects of Self-Induced Respiratory Changes Upon Parietal EEG in Seriousminded versus Playful Subjects'. *Biofeedback and Self Regulation*, Volume 7, 1980, pp. 592–593.

Vintis, L.: 'Humor in Behavior Therapy'. In Mindess, H., and Turek, J. (eds.): *The Study of Humor*. Los Angeles: Antioch University, 1980 (mimeo).

Wicker, W.F., Thorelli, I.M., Barron, W.L., and Willis, A.C.: 'Studies of Mood and Humor Appreciation'. *Motivation and Emotion*, Volume 5, 1981, pp. 47–59.

Zinker, J.: *Creative Process in Gestalt Therapy*. New York: Vintage Books, 1977.

# HUMOUR AS A TOOL IN COUNSELLING AND PSYCHOTHERAPY: A REVERSAL ~ THEORY PERSPECTIVE

## STEPHEN J. MURGATROYD

### POSTSCRIPT

Humour in counselling and psychotherapy is not a feature of many texts designed for helping professionals. Indeed, counsellor education and training is, most often, a serious business. After all, the thinking goes, depression and sadness, anxiety and stress, job-loss and grief are all serious things. What is more, counsellors and therapists earn their living by persuading people that their needs and concerns are serious enough to warrant help from a professional.

Yet these same things – stress, anxiety, depression, grief, job-loss, sadness – often have humourful components. Certainly, the helpers I have worked with have found humour in these topics – we needed to find some sort of relief or else we would have been in deep trouble ourselves.

Humour as a defence mechanism or release-of-anxiety mechanism has been well understood. What interested me in writing the piece above was 'what else do we use humour for in therapy?'. I also wanted to challenge the idea that the primary function of humour was defence. Linked to this, I wanted to show a construction of humour from within reversal theory which would help practitioners better choose a humour strategy.

Part of the motivation for this paper was something else. I had been in New York working at Columbia Hospital and had discovered a great deal of humour amongst those who were socially and seriously economically deprived because of their birthplace and colour. This matched Victor Frankl's account of humour in the concentration camps amongst those who were survivors – it was one of the tools of hope and friendship. I had also attended an international conference on the psychology of humour and had been disturbed by how constricted the views of North American psychologists were with respect to humour and how serious their presentations had been. I wanted to make a contribution to thinking differently about humour as a helping tool.

### DEVELOPMENTS IN STUDYING AND USING HUMOUR

I have continued to find the topic of humour and helping interesting. Indeed, I have recently offered a paper on the nature and social functions of humour in a text on adult play (Murgatroyd, 1991). I have also examined some aspects of humour in the study of organisational behaviour (Mills and Murgatroyd, 1991). What is more interesting, at least to me, is that I have become more adept at using humour – having earned money doing so in stand-up work and in after-dinner speaking, as well as in training, consulting and public presentations.

Humour has become recognised as an opportunity for healing in several hospitals in Canada. In those which specialise in cancer treatment and hospice care, for example, it would not be unusual to see a Comedy Centre within the hospital where patients could watch comic videos, listen to audio cassettes of their favourite comedians, leaf through books of cartoons, read books of jokes or have a one-man show from a visiting comedian. These have been seen as having value as part of a comprehensive programme of patient care.

Humour has also become strongly recognised as an area for psychological study. In addition to the now annual conferences on the nature of humour (the first was in Cardiff – my former base – in 1976), there is also an international journal devoted to the study of humour. Articles on humour now appear more frequently in the cited psychological journals.

### DEVELOPMENTS IN THE UNDERSTANDING OF HUMOUR

The theoretical models associated with the explanation of humour have not advanced significantly since the piece above was written. Despite considerable developments in the field of cognitive psychology, especially in relation to thinking processes and their effects on social action, humour remains a 'sidelines' issue. Even in the two volumes of *Lines of Thinking* (Gilhooly *et al.*, 1990), humour receives but a small mention.

Reversal theory, however, continues to extend its understanding of humour both in terms of humour as a psychological process (Apter, 1989) and in terms of its place in adult development (Kerr and Apter, 1991). I have suggested ways in which the reversals model of humour can be extended, notably by looking at the impact of the transactional states (both the mastery and sympathy states and the autocentric and allocentric states) on the character of humour (Murgatroyd, 1991). Since humour produces both a cognitive and emotional response, reversal theory is ideally placed to provide a thorough phenomenological and scientific explanation of these two processes (Apter, 1988).

While the theory has become more robust and comprehensive in its understanding of humour, it has also become much more widely accepted, with 58 papers appearing in internationally recognised journals between 1979 and 1991 offering validation of key constructs. Books summarising developments appeared in 1982, 1985, 1988 and 1989, and others are planned. Five international conferences have been held in Wales, Ontario, the Netherlands, Alberta and Kansas City. Future conferences are planned for Norway (1993) and Melbourne (1995). As one of the founding fathers of the theory, these developments are gratifying. In this context, the paper above has been much cited.

### DEVELOPMENTS IN THE USE OF HUMOUR IN HELPING

Humour is a valuable tool in the use of paradoxical intervention and in some aspects of cognitive restructuring. It can also be helpful in gestalt work and in drama therapy.

In training counsellors, I have often made considerable use of humour and creative activity. An insightful student once observed to me that counselling was like writing a script for an interesting drama. Using this as a text, I developed a course on focusing skills for counsellors at the University of Saskatchewan in 1985 which was built upon improvisation drama and a jumbo bag of comedy. Using Keith Johnstone's (1981) text *IMPRO – Improvisation and the Theatre* as a basis for a great deal of this work, I sought to develop the skills of attending in the 'here and now', dealing with power in helping relationships, spontaneity, supporting and developing narrative and finally, wearing masks and inducing 'as if'. I supplemented these pieces with ideas from my more conventional text (Murgatroyd, 1985). These processes were full of humour and enjoyment – something graduate students at a Canadian University do not normally experience. More importantly, the learning that developed from this creative work was substantial and very visible.

What I learned from this, and this went into the thinking about the original paper, is that using humour in all aspects of life can be rewarding in terms of personal learning.

### REFERENCES

Apter, J.: 'Reversal Theory as a Theory of the Emotions'. In Apter, M.J., Kerr, J.H., and Cowles, M.P. (eds.): *Progress in Reversal Theory – Advances in Psychology (Volume 51)*. Amsterdam: North Holland, 1988.

Apter, M.J.: *Reversal Theory: Motivation, Emotion and Personality*. London: Routledge, 1989.

Gilhooly, K.J., Eane, M.T.G., Logie, R.H., and Erdos, G. (eds.): *Lines of Thinking* (2 volumes). Chichester: Wiley, 1990.

Johnstone, K.: *IMPRO – Improvisation and the Theatre*. London: Methuen, 1981.

Kerr, J.H., and Apter, M.J.: *Adult Play: a Reversal Theory Perspective*. Amsterdam: Swets & Zeitlinger, 1991.

Mills, A.J., and Murgatroyd, S.: *Organizational Rules – a Framework for Understanding Organizational Action*. Milton Keynes: Open University Press, 1991.

Murgatroyd, S.: *Counselling and Helping*. London: Routledge, 1985.

Murgatroyd, S.: 'The Nature and Social Functional of Humour'. In Kerr, J., and Apter, M.J. (eds.): *Adult Play – a Reversal Theory Perspective*, pp. 119–129. Amsterdam: Swets & Zeitlinger, 1991.

# ECLECTICISM AND INTEGRATION IN COUNSELLING AND PSYCHOTHERAPY: MAJOR THEMES AND OBSTACLES

## JOHN C. NORCROSS AND LISA M. GRENCAVAGE

*The movement to integrate the psychotherapies has experienced dramatic and unprecedented growth in the past decade. This article overviews the integration movement, beginning with a confluence of mutually reinforcing factors which have fostered its development. The three main modes of the movement – technical eclecticism, theoretical integration, and common factors – are critically reviewed. Recurrent obstacles to psychotherapy integration are then considered, including territorial interest of 'pure systems' therapists, the paucity of empirical research, and absence of a common language. Finally, six emerging themes that characterise eclecticism and integration are presented: complementarity; convergence; systematic practice; prescriptive matching; an empirical base; and the long view.*

A metamorphosis is occurring in mental health (London, 1988; Moultrup, 1986): the integration of the psychotherapies. This movement has experienced dramatic and unprecedented growth in the past decade (Beitman *et al.*, 1989). Consider the following pieces of evidence – like exhibits introduced into a court of law – to support the assertion that eclecticism and integration are here to stay and merit our attention:

**Exhibit A:** Between one-third and one-half of all American psychotherapists now identify themselves as eclectics (e.g. Beitman *et al.*, 1984; Garfield and Kurtz, 1974; Jayaratne, 1982; Norcross *et al.*, 1989; Perlman, 1985; Peterson *et al.*, 1982; Prochaska and Norcross, 1983; Smith, 1982; Watkins *et al.*, 1986), making it the modal theoretical orientation of clinicians. If you are forced to guess a colleague's persuasion, then guess eclecticism.

**Exhibit B:** Several interdisciplinary psychotherapy organisations devoted to rapprochement and integration have been formed in the past ten years. Prominent among these are the Society for the Exploration of Psychotherapy Integration (SEPI) and the International Academy of Eclectic Psychotherapists (IAEP).[1]

**Exhibit C:** The National Institute of Mental Health (NIMH) sponsored a workshop on research in psychotherapy integration (Wolfe and

---

First published in the *British Journal of Guidance and Counselling*, Volume 17 No.3, Sept. 1989.

Goldfried, 1988), because of their belief 'that treatments of greater efficacy, efficiency, and safety will result from efforts to integrate the best elements from different schools of psychotherapy. In addition, research on integrated treatment models may lead to the development of a comprehensive model of psychotherapy process that will have solid empirical backing.'

**Exhibit D:**  The founding of an international quarterly – the *Journal of Integrative and Eclectic Psychotherapy* – explicitly devoted, for the first time, to the systematic synthesis of therapeutic methods, theories, and/or formats.[2]

**Exhibit E:**  The publication of at least 50 books, by our count, on synthesising various counselling concepts and techniques. These volumes range from attempts to meld two theories of psychotherapy – such as Wachtel's (1977) benchmark *Psychoanalysis and Behavior Therapy* – through acclaimed systems of eclectic practice – such as Lazarus's (1976; 1981; 1985) *Multimodal Therapy* – to compilations of prescriptive treatments – such as Frances *et al.*'s (1984) *Differential Therapeutics in Psychiatry*.

**Exhibit F:**  Examination of a number of leading counselling textbooks (Brabeck and Welfel, 1985) reveals a growing trend to identify their theoretical perspective as eclectic. Authors explicitly state that counsellors must adopt an eclectic stance based on mounting research, a relativistic perspective to 'truth', the individuality of the practitioner, and the uniqueness of the client.

**Exhibit G:**  As one final piece of evidence, a recent panel of psychotherapy experts predicted that eclecticism would increase in popularity more than any therapy system in the forthcoming decade (Prochaska and Norcross, 1982).

In this article we overview the burgeoning movement to integrate the psychotherapies. We will begin with the historical origins of the movement and consider the modes of integration. Recurrent obstacles to, and emerging themes of, the movement are then reviewed. Our focus is primarily on synthesising counselling methods and theories; neither the combination of psychotherapy and psychopharmacology, nor the synthesis of therapeutic formats (e.g. individual, family, group), are addressed here.

## ORIGINS OF THE MOVEMENT

Eclecticism as a point of view has probably existed as long as philosophy and psychotherapy. The third-century biographer, Diogenes Laertius, referred to an eclectic school which flourished in Alexandria in the second century AD (Lunde, 1974). In psychotherapy, Freud consciously struggled with the selection and integration of diverse methods (Frances, 1988). More formal ideas on synthesising the psychotherapies appeared in the literature as early as the 1930s (French, 1933).

Although the notion of integrating various therapeutic approaches has intrigued mental health professionals for some time (Goldfried, 1982; Goldfried and Newman, 1986), it has been only within the past 15 years that integration has developed into a clearly delineated area of interest. The last decade, in particular, has witnessed both a general decline in ideological struggle and the stirrings of rapprochement. The debates across theoretical systems appear to be less polemical, or at least more issue-specific. The theoretical substratum of each system is undergoing intensive reappraisal, as psychotherapists acknowledge the inadequacies of any one system and the potential value of others.

A confluence of scientific, professional, and socio-economic circumstances produced the recent preoccupation with psychotherapy integration. Five intertwined, mutually reinforcing factors have fostered the movement in the past decade (Beitman *et al.*, 1989; Goldfried and Newman, 1986; London, 1983; 1988; Norcross, 1986).

**1. Proliferation of therapies**. Psychotherapy systems appear and vanish with bewildering rapidity on the diffuse, heterodox scene. In the late 1950s, Harper (1959) identified 36 distinct systems of psychotherapy. In the mid-1970s, Parloff (1976) discovered over 130 therapies on the marketplace, or more appropriately, the 'therapeutic jungleplace'. In the mid-1980s, Karasu (1986) reported a count of more than 400 presumably different 'schools' of psychotherapy. The proliferation of therapies has been accompanied by a deafening cacophony of rival claims. The result has been variously characterised as confusion, fragmentation, and discontent (Norcross, 1986).

In describing the genesis of scientific revolutions, Kuhn (1970) found that the abandonment of any given paradigm is ordinarily preceded by a period of 'crisis'. This crisis is characterised by the open expression of discontent about the current state of affairs and by the proliferation of different orientations. The field of psychotherapy, it would appear, is currently experiencing such a pre-paradigmatic crisis (Goldfried and Padawer, 1982).

The field has been staggered by over-choice and fragmented by future shock. Which of 400 plus therapies should be studied, taught, or bought?

No single theory has been able to corner the market on validity or utility. London (1988, pp. 5–6) wryly observed that the hyperinflation of brand name therapies has produced narcissistic fatigue. 'With so many brand names around that no one can recognize, let alone remember, and so many competitors doing psychotherapy, it is becoming too arduous to launch still another new brand.'

**2. Inadequacy of single theories.** A related factor is the growing consensus that no one approach is clinically adequate for all problems, patients, and situations. Beutler (1983) suggests that the proliferation of theories is both a cause and symptom of the problem – that neither the theories nor the techniques are adequate to deal with the complexity of psychological problems. Clinical realities have come to demand a more flexible, if not integrative, perspective.

Psychotherapy has entered a period of intense self-examination in which the failures of our pet theories are reappraised and their limitations realised. The grand systems era has been undermined by a wave of scepticism in which leading figures of each school have criticised their own theories and assumptions. Omer and London (1988) trace scepticism within psychoanalysis (e.g. implausibility of truly 'free associations', doubts about Freud's archaeology metaphor), behaviour therapy (e.g. questions on presumed derivation from learning theory, over-reliance on observed behaviours), and cognitive therapy (e.g. doubts on the precedence of cognition over affect and behaviour, difficulty of dispelling dysfunctional thinking). Obviously, no clinical theory has a monopoly on truth or utility.

The integration movement, to some extent, reflects dissatisfaction with single approaches. Surveys of self-designated eclectic and integrative clinicians have revealed that their alignment is motivated in part by disillusionment with single therapy systems (Garfield and Kurtz, 1977; Norcross and Prochaska, 1988). Indeed, very few counsellors adhere tenaciously to a single therapeutic tradition (Larson, 1980; Smith, 1982).

**3. Equality of outcomes.** Despite a noticeable increase in the quantity and quality of psychotherapy research, it has not been possible to show that one therapeutic approach is clearly superior to another (see e.g. Bergin and Lambert, 1978; Frank, 1979; Landsman and Dawes, 1982; Smith *et al.*, 1980). There are few conditions in which the therapy system leads to differential success in outcome, and with few exceptions, there is little compelling evidence to recommend the use of one type over another in the treatment of specific problems. Luborsky *et al.* (1975), borrowing a phrase from the Dodo bird in *Alice in Wonderland*, concluded that 'everybody has won and all must have prizes'. Or, in the words of London (1988, p. 7): 'Meta-analytic research shows charity for all treatments and malice towards none'.

A paradox has emerged from the equivalence conclusion: no differential effectiveness despite technical diversity (Stiles *et al.*, 1986). A number of resolutions to this paradox have been advanced, including the unspecificity of outcome measurement, the poor integrity of treatments, and the elucidation of common core factors in the therapist, client, or alliance. The two most common responses seem to be a specification of factors common to successful treatments and a synthesis of useful concepts and methods from disparate therapeutic traditions.

**4. Search for common components**. The identification of common change processes or therapeutic factors has been called the most important psychotherapy trend in the 1980s (Bergin, 1982). Strupp (1973; 1982) has noted that the significant advances in psychotherapy research have resulted from better conceptual analyses of basic processes operating in all forms of therapy rather than from premature comparisons of techniques. This observation stems from the emerging view that the commonalities in all forms of therapy are far more impressive than their apparent differences. A transtheoretical analysis of prominent psychotherapy systems demonstrated how much therapeutic systems agree on the processes producing change while disagreeing on the content to be changed (Prochaska, 1984).

Frank (1973; 1982) posited that all psychotherapeutic methods are elaborations and variations of age-old procedures of psychological healing. The features that distinguish psychotherapies from each other, however, receive special emphasis in our pluralistic and competitive society. Since the prestige and financial security of counsellors hinge on their particular approach being more successful than that of their rivals, little attention has traditionally been accorded to the identification of shared components.

Frank, among others, has argued that therapeutic change is predominantly a function of factors common to all approaches: an emotionally charged, confiding relationship; a healing setting; a rationale or conceptual scheme; and a therapeutic ritual. For Garfield (1980), these common factors entail the relationship, catharsis, explanation, reinforcement, desensitisation, information, and time. Similarly, Karasu (1986) identified three non-specific change agents that all therapy schools share:

affective experiencing, cognitive mastery, and behavioural regulation. These authors have noted that features shared by all therapies account for an appreciable proportion of clinical improvement, and psychotherapy outcome research has generally substantiated this claim (Lambert, 1986). Ironically, 80% of the psychotherapy literature is devoted to specific technologies and procedures, which account for only 10%–12% of change (Beutler, 1986).

**5. Socio-economic contingencies**. A fifth and final reason for integrating the psychotherapies is a matrix of social, political, and economic influences. The total therapy industry continues to grow: invasion of non-doctoral and non-medical counsellors, the boom in professional practice, the mushrooming of training institutes, and the outpouring of third-party funding in the States (London, 1988).

Meanwhile, pressures are mounting in the United States from insurance companies, government policy-makers, consumer groups, and judicial officials for accountability. Third parties and the public are demanding crisp and informative answers regarding the quality, durability, and efficiency of psychosocial treatments (Parloff, 1979). Until recently the field has had the luxury of functioning within a culture of individual professional freedom. Clinical services had been in steady demand in the marketplace, generally oblivious to economic forces and socio-political realities. However, the shrinking job market, increased competition, and diminishing public support portend a future discontinuous with our expansive past (Fishman and Neigher, 1982).

Without some change from the field, psychotherapists stand to lose prestige, customers, and money. These socio-political considerations have Americans increasingly pulling together rather than apart. Mental health professionals report that the impact of political and economic changes have led them to work harder, to be more creative, and to adjust their treatments to meet the needs of their clients (Brown, 1983). Intertheoretical co-operation and a more unified psychotherapy community represent attempts to respond to these socio-political forces. As the external demands escalate, so too will the spirit of open inquiry and therapeutic integration.

## MODES

Three main thrusts have become evident in the contemporary movement to integrate the psychotherapies: (**1**) technical eclecticism; (**2**) theoretical integration; and (**3**) common factors (Arkowitz, 1989). The common factors approach, as previously mentioned, seeks to determine the core ingredients different therapies might share in common, with the eventual goal of developing more efficacious treatments based on these components. The long considered 'noise' in psychotherapy research is being reconsidered by some as the main 'signal' elements of treatment (Omer and London, 1988).

One way of determining common therapeutic principles is by focusing on a level of abstraction somewhere between theory and technique. This intermediate level of abstraction, known as a clinical strategy, may be thought of as a heuristic that implicitly guides the efforts of experienced therapists. Goldfried (1980, p. 996) argues:

'To the extent that clinicians of varying orientations are able to arrive at a common set of strategies, it is likely that what emerges will consist of robust phenomena, as they have managed to survive the distortions imposed by the therapists' varying theoretical biases.'

Common factors may, in fact, be the curative factors.

Some observers have argued that the concentrated study of commonalities across theoretical orientations may prove premature or unproductive (cf. Allport, 1968; Haaga, 1986; Henle, 1986; Messer, 1983; 1986a; Messer and Winokur, 1980; 1984; Norcross, 1981; Wilson, 1982). For one, different therapies embody alternative visions of life with different basic possibilities of human existence and growth. These are not easily subjected to integration or consensus. For another, the common factors – or non-specific – approach is a way of thinking, not a way of conducting therapy. One cannot do 'nothing specific' in therapy or training. For still another, commonalities identified to date may be so superficial – radically different in substance, structure, and intent – as to make clinical strategies analogous to broad descriptive classification. The category of 'fruit' is surely a superordinate category of both apples and oranges, but their comparisons might not be particularly useful. As such, commonalities not only fail to provide much direction for training and therapy but also provide inadequate guidelines for research. Messer expounds on these and other trade-offs in his article in this symposium on 'Integration and Eclecticism in Counselling and Psychotherapy: Cautionary Notes'.

The preponderance of clinical practice and professional contention resides, however, in the distinctions between eclecticism and integration.

*Table 1:* **Eclecticism v. integration**

| Eclecticism | Integration |
| --- | --- |
| Technical | Theoretical |
| Divergent (differences) | Convergent (commonalities) |
| Choosing from many | Combining many |
| Applying what is | Creating something new |
| Collection | Blend |
| Selection | Synthesis |
| Applying the parts | Unifying the parts |
| Atheoretical but empirical | More theoretical than empirical |
| Sum of parts | More than sum of parts |
| Realistic | Idealistic |

How do they differ? Which is the more fruitful strategy for knowledge acquisition and clinical practice?

The NIMH Workshop (Wolfe and Goldfried, 1988) and two recent studies (Norcross and Napolitano, 1986; Norcross and Prochaska, 1988) have clarified this question. Table 1 summarises the consensual distinctions between eclecticism and integration.

The definition of eclecticism parallels the dictionary meaning: 'choosing what is best from diverse sources, styles, and systems'; 'using techniques and rationales based on more than one orientation to meet the needs of the individual case'; 'the systematic use of a variety of therapeutic interventions in the treatment of a single patient'; and 'the pragmatics of selecting a variety of procedures and wider interventions for specific problems'. The common thread is that technical eclecticism is relatively atheoretical, pragmatic, and empirical.

Lazarus (1967; 1977; 1984), the most eloquent proponent of technical eclecticism, uses procedures drawn from different sources without necessarily subscribing to the theories that spawned them, whereas the theoretical integrationist draws from diverse systems which may be epistemologically or ontologically incompatible. For Lazarus and other technical eclectics, no necessary connection exists between metabeliefs and techniques. It is not necessary to build a composite from divergent theories, on the one hand, nor to accept divergent conceptions, on the other, in order to utilise their technical procedures. 'To attempt a theoretical rapprochement is as futile as trying to picture the edge of the universe. But to read through the vast amount of literature on psychotherapy, *in search of techniques*, can be clinically enriching and therapeutically rewarding' (Lazarus, 1967, p. 416). Lazarus advances this argument in more detail in his article 'Why I am an Eclectic (Not an Integrationist)' in this symposium.

Theoretical integration, by small contrast, refers to a commitment to a conceptual or theoretical creation beyond a technical blend of methods. This creation is described as 'an articulated framework or roadmap', 'superordinate umbrella', 'new, conceptually superior theory', and 'a coherent and continually evolving theoretical framework'. It is theoretical, idealistic, and, for now at least, less empirical. In his article elsewhere in this issue, 'Why I am an Integrationist (Not an Eclectic)', Beitman advances a synthetic perspective based on theoretical integration and common factors.

To reiterate: the primary distinction is that between empirical pragmatism and theoretical flexibility. Or to take a culinary metaphor (cited in Norcross and Napolitano, 1986, p. 253): 'The eclectic selects among several dishes to constitute a meal, the integrationist creates new dishes by combining different ingredients.'

The net result of this differentiation is that the term 'eclecticism' is restricted in use to the technical, atheoretical combination of methods. The term 'integration' denotes the conceptual synthesis of diverse theoretical systems. We hasten to add that the goals of both eclectics and integrationists are similar indeed, although their means may diverge. In clinical practice, however, the distinction is largely semantic and conceptual, not particularly functional. Moreover, the two strategies are not as distinct as they may appear: no technical eclectic can totally disregard theory and no theoretical integrationist can totally ignore technique.

Recent research demonstrates an emerging preference for both the term 'integration' and the practice of theoretical integration, as opposed to technical eclecticism. Results of these two studies (Norcross and Napolitano, 1986; Norcross and Prochaska, 1983) show clinicians preferring the self-identification of integrative over eclectic by almost a two to one margin. That is, they like the ring of 'integrative' better than 'eclectic'. In similar fashion, when instructed to select the type of integration they practise, the majority of eclectics – 61% and 65% – chose theoretical integration.

The preference for integration over eclecticism probably represents a historical shift. In a 1975 investigation (Garfield and Kurtz, 1977), most favoured eclecticism; in our 1986 study (Norcross and Prochaska, 1988), most favoured integration. This may reflect a theoretical progression analogous to a social progression: one that proceeds from segregation to desegregation to integration. Eclecticism has represented desegregation, in which ideas, methods, and people from diverse theoretical backgrounds mix and intermingle. Currently we appear to be in transition from desegregation to integration, with increasing efforts directed at discovering viable integrative principles for assimilating and accommodating the best that different systems have to offer.

This, then, summarises *how* counsellors are integrating – the method. Let us now turn to *what* they integrate – the content.

The short and simple answer is 'everything' – counsellors are mixing and mingling techniques, theories, and formats from every theory ever promulgated. The longer and more complex answer is shown in table 2. Here, eclectic psychologists rated their frequency of use of six theories in clinical practice. The ratings formed a matrix of 15 possible, nonredundant combinations; the nine most frequent are presented in table 2. *All* possible combinations were selected by at least one respondent. A cognitive behavioural integration was the most common, followed closely by humanistic-cognitive and psychoanalytic-cognitive syntheses. Interestingly, the cognitive revolution in psychotherapy is making its impact known here: the three most popular combinations all involve cognitive theory.

The synthesis of theories and techniques is assuredly part of the integration movement. But what about the combination of therapy formats – individual, family, group – and the combination of medication

*Table 2:* **Most frequent combinations of theoretical orientations**

| Combination | 1986 | | 1976* | |
|---|---|---|---|---|
| | % | Rank | % | Rank |
| Cognitive and behavioural | 12 | 1 | 5 | 4 |
| Humanistic and cognitive | 11 | 2 | | |
| Psychoanalytic and cognitive | 10 | 3 | | |
| Behavioural and humanistic | 8 | 4 | 11 | 3 |
| Interpersonal and humanistic | 8 | 4 | 3 | 6 |
| Humanistic and systems | 6 | 6 | | |
| Psychoanalytic and interpersonal | 5 | 7 | | |
| Systems and behavioural | 5 | 7 | | |
| Behavioural and psychoanalytic | 4 | 9 | 25 | 1 |

*Percentages and ranks were not reported for all combinations in the 1976 study (Garfield and Kurtz, 1997).

and psychotherapy? In both cases, a strong majority of clinicians – 80% plus – considered these to be within the legitimate boundaries of integration (Norcross and Napolitano, 1986). Of course, the inclusion of psychopharmacology enlarges the scope to integrative treatment, rather than integrative psychotherapy *per se*.

These findings underscore the obvious: eclecticism comes in many guises and manifestations. It is clearly not a monolithic entity or a single operationalised system. To refer to *the* eclectic or integrative approach falls prey to the 'uniformity myth' (Dryden, 1984; Kiesler, 1966).

Conspicuously absent from our discussions are the more conventional, pure-form (or brand name) therapy systems, such as behavioural and psychoanalytic therapy. Do these contribute to the integrative and eclectic movements? No, in the narrow sense of not creating a paradigm for synthesising various interventions and conceptualisations. But yes, in the broader and more important sense of adding to our therapeutic armamentarium and enriching our understanding of the clinical process. One cannot integrate what one does not know.

## RECURRENT OBSTACLES

The accelerated development of eclectic and integrative psychotherapies has not been paralleled by serious consideration of their potential obstacles and trade-offs (Arkowitz and Messer, 1984; Dryden, 1986). If we are to avoid uncritical growth or fleeting interest in eclectic/integrative psychotherapy, then some honest recognition of the barriers we are likely to encounter is sorely needed (Goldfried and Safran, 1986). Caught up in the excitement and possibilities of the movement, we have neglected the problems – the 'X-rated topics' of integration. Healthy maturation, be it for individuals or for movements, requires self-awareness and constructive criticism.

What's stopping psychotherapy integration now? Norcross and Thomas (1988) conducted a survey of the Society for the Exploration of Psychotherapy Integration (SEPI) membership to answer this question. Fifty-eight prominent integrationists rated, in terms of severity, twelve potential obstacles using a five-point, Likert-type scale. The top five obstacles and their mean scores are presented in table 3.

The most severely rated obstruction centred around the partisan zealotry and territorial interests of 'pure'-form psychotherapists. Representative responses here were: 'egocentric, self-centered colleagues'; 'the institutionalisation of schools'; and 'ideological warfare, factional rivalry'. In examining the history of different therapy methods, Goldfried

*Table 3:* **Obstacles to psychotherapy integration**

| Obstacle | Severity rating | |
|---|---|---|
| | Mean | Rank |
| Intrinsic investment of individuals in their private perceptions and theories | 3.97 | 1 |
| Inadequate commitment to training in more than one psychotherapy system | 3.74 | 2 |
| Approaches have divergent assumptions about psychopathology and health | 3.67 | 3 |
| Inadequate empirical research on the integration of psychotherapies | 3.58 | 4 |
| Absence of a 'common' language for psychotherapists | 3.47 | 5 |

1 = not an obstacle; 3 = moderate obstacle; 5 = severe obstacle.

(1980, p. 991) notes that, traditionally, therapists have been guided by a particular theoretical framework, 'often to the point of being completely blind to alternative conceptualizations and potentially effective intervention procedures'.

Unfortunately, professional reputations are made by emphasising the new and different, not the basic and similar. In the field of psychotherapy, as well as in other scientific disciplines, the ownership of ideas secures far too much emphasis. Although the idea of naturally-occurring, co-operative efforts among professionals is engaging, their behaviour, realistically, may be expected to reflect the competition so characteristic of our society at large (Goldfried, 1980).

Inadequate training in eclectic/integrative therapy was the second-ranked impediment. The reasons are multiple and explicable. Training students to competence in multiple theories and interventions is unprecedented in the history of psychotherapy. Understandable in the light of its exacting and novel nature, the acquisition of integrative perspectives has occurred quite idiosyncratically and perhaps serendipitously to date.

The critical training question is how to facilitate adequate knowledge of and competence in the various psychotherapeutic systems. On the one hand, intense concentration on a single theoretical system, though possibly myopic and misleading, is often secure and complete. Cursory exposure to multiple therapeutic systems, on the other hand, leaves students with a few clichés and disunited techniques, though it does encourage integration (Norcross, 1986; Robertson, 1986). Three special sections of the JIEP have addressed integrative training and supervision (Beutler *et al.*, 1987; Halgin, 1988; Norcross *et al.*, 1986).

The third-ranked obstacle concerned differences in ontological and epistemological issues. These entail basic and sometimes contradictory assumptions about human nature, determinants of personality development, and the origins of psychopathology. For instance, are people innately good, evil, both, neither? Do phobias represent learned maladaptive habits or intrapsychic conflicts? But it may be precisely these diverse world views that make psychotherapy integration interesting, in that it brings together the individual strengths of these complementary orientations (Beitman *et al.*, 1989).

We have not conducted sufficient research on psychotherapy integration – the fourth obstacle to be addressed here. Comparative outcome research has been a limited source of direction with regard to selection of method and articulation of prescriptive guidelines. If our empirical research has little to say, and if collective clinical experience has divergent things to say, then why should we do A, not B? We may again be guided by selective perception and personal preference, a situation the integrative movement seeks to avoid.

A seemingly intractable obstacle to the establishment of clinically sophisticated and consensually validated integrative psychotherapies is the absence of a common language (Norcross, 1987). This was rated the fifth most serious impediment to progress. Each psychotherapeutic tradition has its own jargon, a clinical shorthand among its adherents, which widens the precipice across differing orientations (Goldfried and Newman, 1986).

The 'language problem', as it has become known, confounds understanding of each other's constructs and, in some cases, leads to active avoidance of those constructs. Many a behaviourist's mind has wandered when case discussions turn to 'transference issues' and 'warded-off conflicts'. Similarly, psychodynamic therapists typically tune out buzz words like 'conditioning procedures' and 'discriminative stimuli'. Isolated language systems encourage clinicians to wrap themselves in semantic cocoons from which they cannot escape and which others cannot penetrate. As Lazarus (1986) concluded: 'Basically, integration or rapprochement is impossible when a person speaks and understands only Chinese and another converses only in Greek!' (p. 241).

A common language thus offers the promise of increased communication between clinicians and researchers, on the one hand, and among practitioners of diverse persuasions, on the other. Meaningful trans-theoretical dialogue may allow us to enrich each other's clinical practices, access the empirical literature, and discover robust therapeutic phenomena cutting across varying orientations (Norcross, 1987).

The purpose of a common language is to facilitate communication, comprehension, and research. It is not intended to establish consensus. Before an agreement or a disagreement can be reached on a given matter, it is necessary to ensure that the same phenomenon is in fact being discussed. Punitive super-ego, negative self-statements, and poor self-image may indeed be similar phenomena, but that cannot be known with certainty until the constructs are defined operationally and consensually (Stricker, 1986).

To be sure, this is a demanding task (Messer, 1987). In the short run, using the vernacular – descriptive, ordinary, natural language – might suffice (Driscoll, 1987). In the long run, a common language may profit from being linked to a superordinate theory of personality or derived from an empirical data base (e.g. Ryle, 1987; Strong, 1987).

### EMERGING THEMES

**1. Complementarity**. Clinical experience and research findings alike lead us to the conclusion that each therapeutic orientation has its share of failures, and that none is consistently superior to any other. These observations have stimulated many workers in the field to suggest that contributions from orientations other than their own might be fruitfully employed. The weakness of any one perspective might be complemented by another's strength. Pinsof (1983, p. 20), for example, describes his integrative problem-centred therapy as one that 'rests upon the twin assumptions that each modality and orientation has its particular domain of expertise, and that these domains can be interrelated to maximize their assets and minimize their deficits'.

In considering the potential strengths and liabilities of an integrative approach, patient variables will probably play the central role in determining the most appropriate therapeutic intervention (Beitman *et al.*, 1989). Treatment decision rules have been advanced for a number of patient variables: verbal and introspection skills, stage of change, reactance and defensive style, and breadth of psychopathology (e.g. Beitman, 1987; Beutler, 1983; Fensterheim, 1983; Prochaska and DiClemente, 1984; Wachtel, 1987).

This, then is the important first step: to view rival systems not as an adversary, but as a healthy diversity (Landsman, 1974); not as contradictory, but as complementary (Norcross, 1986). We can begin to build rather than burn the bridges which span chasms separating theories. At long last, perhaps we can temper our splitting propensities and reject our puerile claims of 'We are good – they are bad' (Miller, 1985) and proudly exclaim 'We are good – they are also good' (Norcross, 1988).

**2. Convergence**. There is a pernicious misconception in our field that certain processes and outcomes are the exclusive property of particular therapy systems. Norcross (1988) labelled this fallacy the 'exclusivity myth'. Cases in point are the behaviourist's contention of exclusive ownership of behaviour change, the experientialist's presumed monopoly on intense affective expression, and the psychoanalyst's assertion of unique genetic insights. The exclusivity myth is part and parcel of the hostile, ideological cold war. The profession has encountered a proliferating number of therapies – each purportedly superior with regard to some disorder or clientele.

Fortunately, amid the strife and bewilderment, a therapeutic 'underground' has slowly emerged (Wachtel, 1977). Though not associated with any particular school and not detailed in the literature, the underground reflects an unofficial consensus of what experienced clinicians believe to be true.

Many observers (Goldfried, 1982; Karasu, 1977; Marmor, 1980; Messer, 1986b) have noted increasing confluence of attitudes and practices amongst the psychotherapies. Moreover, recent studies of clinical practitioners point to many areas of convergence as well as remaining points of contention. In one study (Mahoney *et al.*, 1989), 486 clinical psychologists representing five major theoretical orientations responded to 40 standardised questions about optimal practices in psychotherapy. The results indicated considerable transtheoretical convergence on the importance of novel exploratory activity, self-examination, and self-development in psychotherapy. Behaviourists rated psychological change as significantly less difficult than did their colleagues of other persuasions unless they had been in psychotherapy themselves. In another study (Friedling *et al.*, 1984), 85 psychodynamic and 110 behavioural psychologists reported on their use of operationally-defined therapy activities. Over one-half of these methods were used by both groups, 15% were mutually rejected, and only 29% were employed exclusively by members of either orientation.

Unfortunately, the early research is based on what counsellors *say* they do rather than on direct observations of what they *actually* do or, more importantly, what their clients experience them as doing. Nonetheless, there does appear to be a contemporary tendency to grow alike, to develop similarities in form. These areas of convergence, moreover, may well reflect robust phenomena that stand a good chance of being related ultimately to successful therapy outcome (Goldfried and Safran, 1986; Lambert, 1986).

**3. Systematic practice**. The term 'eclecticism' has acquired an emotionally ambivalent, if not negative, connotation for some clinicians due to its alleged disorganised and indecisive nature. In some corners, eclecticism still connotes undisciplined subjectivity, 'muddle-headedness', the 'last refuge for mediocrity, the seal of incompetency', or 'a classic case of professional anomie' (quoted in Robertson, 1979). Dryden (1984) observes that many of these psychotherapists wander around in a daze of professional nihilism experimenting with new 'fad' methods indiscriminately. Indeed, it is surprising that so many clinicians admit to being eclectic in their work, given the negative valence the term has acquired (Garfield, 1980).

This unsystematic eclecticism is primarily an outgrowth of pet techniques and inadequate training. It is eclecticism 'by default', lacking sufficient competence for an integrated approach and selecting interventions on the basis of subjective appeal. Eysenck (1970, p. 145) characterises this haphazard form of eclecticism as a 'mish-mash of theories, a hugger-mugger of procedures, a gallimaufry of therapies', having no proper rationale or empirical evaluation.

The emergent trend is to view integration in its many guises as systematic (Norcross and Prochaska, 1988). A product of painstaking clinical research and theoretical work, systematic integration is necessarily 'by design': that is, clinicians competent in several therapeutic systems who select interventions based on clinical experience and research findings. The strengths of systematic integration lie in its ability to be taught, replicated, and evaluated. Rotter (1954, p. 14), years ago, summarised the matter as follows: 'All systematic thinking involves the synthesis of pre-existing points of view. It is not a question of whether or not to be eclectic but of whether or not to be consistent and systematic.'

**4. Prescriptive matching.** Maslow once remarked that if you only have a hammer you treat everything like a nail. The history of psychotherapy has repeatedly confirmed this observation. Sad to say, the preponderance of contemporary clinicians probably still reach for their favourite tool when confronted with puzzling or unsettling cases. It is not uncommon for our inveterate colleagues to recommend the identical treatment – their treasured proficiency – to virtually every patient who crosses their paths (Norcross, 1985).

The integration movement asks clinicians to become discriminating craftworkers who selectively draw on experience and research to meet the multivaried challenges of clinical reality. Discriminating clinicians go beyond subjective preference, institutional custom, and immediate availability to predicate their treatment selection on patient need and comparative outcome research. That is, they develop and employ an expanded toolbox instead of senselessly 'hammering away' at anything remotely similar to a nail.

The challenge is to enhance the optimal match between patient and treatment. This process has been assigned various names – differential therapeutics (Frances *et al.*, 1984), treatment matching (Beutler, 1983), dispositional assignment (Beutler and Clarkin, in press), prescriptive psychotherapy (Goldstein and Stein, 1976). But the goal is identical: to improve the efficacy, applicability, and efficiency of psychotherapy by tailoring it to the unique needs of the client. The question is no longer 'Does it work?' Rather, the question has become 'Does it work best for this client?' Answers to this query will probably place the client's welfare above the counsellor's theoretical narcissism.

Prescriptionism is concerned with that elusive, empirically driven match among patient, disorder, and treatment. With increasing refinement in the categorisation of disorders and more precise delineation of change strategies, further advantages of prescriptive treatments may be found. At that point, effective therapy will be 'defined not by its brand name, but by how well it meets the need of the patient' (Weiner, 1975, p. 44).

**5. Empirical base**. The reader may understandably protest: how do we consensually determine 'what works best' given our divergent ontological and epistemological assumptions? The question is less problematic for technical eclectics who meld techniques separate from their 'theoretical baggage', but it remains a thorny issue for integrationists trying to synthesise entire theories. Adams (1984, p. 92) pointedly inquires how clinicians settle their differences: 'by negotiation, kissing and making up, taking a vote, or gathering data?'.

Our preference is for gathering empirical data. Clinicians and researchers alike have long called for the development of psychotherapies with a strong empirical base. An empirical base for practice has at least two meanings (Fischer, 1986). The first is the use of research to inform practice, as in the selection of clinical techniques and interpersonal stances; the second is in the careful, objective evaluation of the effects of the psychotherapies. The latter is particularly urgent as there is little unambiguous evidence of the clinical superiority of an integrative approach over existing systems (Yates, 1983). It is important to note, though, that the reverse is true as well (Wachtel, 1983).

We need to discover, in functional terms, which therapist behaviours and treatment strategies are more effective with which types of clients (Cross and Sheehan, 1981; Paul, 1967). In this respect, a natural affinity exists between process research and psychotherapy integration (Beutler and Clarkin, 1989; Goldfried and Safran, 1986; Wolfe and Goldfried, 1988). 'Bottom up' research strategies (i.e. descriptive and exploratory investigations, both clinical and empirical, at the level of actual therapeutic practice), especially those which investigate process-outcome linkages, can unearth the mechanisms of therapeutic change and develop a cumulative body of knowledge regarding the process of change. Process-outcome linkages can thereby contribute to all three of the current thrusts of the integrative movement – by stimulating theory (theoretical integration), by identifying effective methods for that disorder and that client (technical eclecticism), and by delineating transtheoretical elements (common factors).

Several years ago the senior author and a colleague (Norcross and Prochaska, 1983) examined how hundreds of clinical psychologists, the plurality (31%) of whom were eclectic, selected their theoretical orientations. Of a list of 14 possible influences on this selection process, outcome research ranked a disappointing tenth. The average rating fell between 'weak influence' and 'some influence'. Our hope for a future replication study is that, as a result of the emerging empirical base in psychotherapy, the influence of outcome research will rank much higher.

**6. The long view.** Sibling rivalry among theoretical orientations has a long and undistinguished history in psychotherapy, dating back to Freud. In the infancy of the field, therapy systems, like battling siblings, competed for attention and affection in a 'dogma eat dogma' environment (Larson, 1980). Mutual antipathy and exchange of insults between adherents of rival persuasions were very much the order of the day.

These conflicts are probably a necessary developmental stage to mature synthesis. Kuhn (1970) has described this period as a pre-paradigmatic crisis. Feyerabend (1970), another philosopher of science, has concluded that the interplay between tenacity and proliferation is an essential feature in the actual development of science. The upshot is that the road to sophisticated integration is long, circuitous, and filled with obstacles. An arduous journey is to be expected; steady progress and the long view are to be encouraged.

To use a psychotherapy metaphor, resistance to psychotherapy integration is more chronic and severe than generally recognised. If Kuhn and other philosophers of science are correct in their analyses, most psychotherapists cannot be expected to explore integration naturally or easily. Casual support alone is inadequate to disrupt the historically ingrained and continuously reinforced 'my system, the right system, the only system' attitude which pervades psychotherapy.

In concluding, let us share a quote from Arthur Houts (from Norcross and Thomas, 1988): 'We need to wait for whatever it is that will follow the post-modern era. We are in the post-modern era, but we do not yet know what comes next. There is an old Middle Eastern proverb that applies: "He who plants dates does not live to eat dates." We need to be careful to plant dates rather than pumpkins.'

While eclecticism and integration in psychotherapy have experienced, and will continue to experience, meaningful progress in our lifetimes, the greater legacy of the integrative movement may lie in the future. This legacy, for us, entails the promotion of open inquiry, informed pluralism, empirical research, and intellectual relativism. As with the clinical enterprise itself, the seeds we sow now may produce enticing flowers quickly, but may not bear the sustaining fruit for years to come. Our fervent hope is that we all work diligently enough and live long enough to partake of that fruit together.

### NOTES

[1] Membership applications for SEPI may be obtained from Dr George Stricker, Derner Institute of Advanced Psychological Studies, Adelphi University, Garden City, NY 11530, USA.

[2] Correspondence regarding JIEP subscriptions and back issues should be addressed to Subscription Department, Brunner/Mazel, 19 Union Square West, New York, NY 10013, USA.

### REFERENCES

Adams, H.E.: 'The Pernicious Effects of Theoretical Orientations in Clinical Psychology'. *The Clinical Psychologist*, Volume 37, 1984, pp. 90–93.

Allport, G.W.: 'The Fruits of Eclecticism: Bitter or Sweet?' In Allport, G.W. (ed.): *The Person in Psychology*. Boston: Beacon, 1968.

Arkowitz, H.: 'The Role of Theory in Psychotherapy Integration'. *Journal of Integrative and Eclectic Psychotherapy*, Volume 8 No. 1, 1989.

Arkowitz, H., and Messer, S.B. (eds.): *Psychoanalytic and Behavior Therapy: Is Integration Possible?* New York: Plenum, 1984.

Beitman, B.D.: 'Commentary: the Teenage Prosecutor as an Example of Systematic Eclecticism'. In Norcross, J.C. (ed.): *Casebook of Eclectic Psychotherapy*. New York: Brunner/Mazel, 1987.

Beitman, B.D., Chiles, J., and Carlin, A.: 'The Pharmacotherapy-Psychotherapy Triangle: Psychiatrist, Nonmedical Psychotherapist, and Patient'. *Journal of Clinical Psychiatry*, Volume 45, 1984, pp. 458–459.

Beitman, B.D., Goldfried, M.R., and Norcross, J.C.: 'The Movement toward Integrating the Psychotherapies: an Overview'. *American Journal of Psychiatry*, Volume 146, 1989, pp. 138–147.

Bergin, A.E.: 'Comment on *Converging Themes in Psychotherapy*'. New York: Springer, 1982.

Bergin, A.E., and Lambert, M.J.: 'The Evaluation of Therapeutic Outcomes'. In Garfield, S.L., and Bergin, A.E. (eds.): *Handbook of Psychotherapy and Behavior Change* (2nd edition). New York: Wiley, 1978.

Beutler, L.E.: *Eclectic Psychotherapy: a Systematic Approach*. New York: Pergamon, 1983.

Beutler, L.E.: 'Systematic Eclectic Psychotherapy. In Norcross, J.C. (ed.): *Handbook of Eclectic Psychotherapy*. New York: Brunner/Mazel, 1986.

Beutler, L.E., and Clarkin, J.: *Differential Treatment Assignment: Toward Prescriptive Psychological Treatments*. New York: Brunner/Mazel, 1989.

Beutler, L.E., Mahoney, M.J., Norcross, J.C., Prochaska, J.O., Collod, R.M., and Robertson, M.: 'Training Integrative/Eclectic Psychotherapists II'. *Journal of Integrative and Eclectic Psychotherapy*, Volume 6, 1987, pp. 296–332.

Brabeck, M.M., and Welfel, E.R.: 'Counseling Theory: Understanding the Trend toward Eclecticism from a Developmental Perspective'. *Journal of Counseling and Development*, Volume 63, 1985, pp. 343–349.

Brown, B.S.: 'The Impact of Political and Economic Changes upon Mental Health'. *American Journal of Orthopsychiatry*, Volume 53, 1983, pp. 583–592.

Cross, D.G., and Sheehan, P.W.: 'Classification of Variables in Psychotherapy Research: Therapeutic Change and the Concept of Artifact'. *Psychotherapy: Theory, Research, and Practice*, Volume 18, 1981, pp. 345–355.

Driscoll, R.: 'Ordinary Language as a Common Language for Psychotherapy'. *Journal of Integrative and Eclectic Psychotherapy*, Volume 6, 1987, pp. 184–194.

Dryden, W.: 'Issues in the Eclectic Practice of Individual Therapy'. In Dryden, W. (ed.): *Individual Therapy in Britain*. London: Harper & Row, 1984.

Dryden, W.: 'Eclectic Psychotherapies: a Critique of Leading Approaches'. In Norcross, J.C. (ed.): *Handbook of Eclectic Psychotherapy*, pp. 353–375. New York: Brunner/Mazel, 1986.

Eysenck, H.J.: 'A Mish-Mash of Theories'. *International Journal of Psychiatry*, Volume 9, 1970, pp. 140–146.

Fensterheim, H.: 'Introduction to Behavioral Psychotherapy'. In Fensterheim, H., and Glazer, H.I. (eds.): *Behavioral Psychotherapy: Basic Principles and Case Studies*. New York: Brunner/Mazel, 1983.

Feyerabend, P.: 'Consolations for the Specialist'. In Lakatos, I., and Musgrave, A.E. (eds.): *Criticism and the Growth of Knowledge*. Cambridge: Cambridge University Press, 1970.

Fischer, J.: 'Eclectic Casework'. In Norcross, J.C. (ed.): *Handbook of Eclectic Psychotherapy*. New York: Brunner/Mazel, 1986.

Fishman, D.B., and Neigher, W.D.: 'American Psychology in the Eighties: Who Will Buy?' *American Psychologist*, Volume 37, 1982, pp. 533–546.

Frances, A.: 'Sigmund Freud: The First Integrative Therapist'. Invited address to the

Fourth Annual Convention of the Society for the Exploration of Psychotherapy Integration, Boston, Mass., May 1988.

Frances, A., Clarkin, J., and Perry, S.: *Differential Therapeutics in Psychiatry*. New York: Brunner/Mazel, 1984.

Frank, J.D.: *Persuasion and Healing* (2nd edition). Baltimore: John Hopkins University Press, 1973.

Frank, J.D.: 'The Present Status of Outcome Studies'. *Journal of Consulting and Clinical Psychology*, Volume 47, 1979, pp. 310–316.

Frank, J.D.: 'Therapeutic Components Shared by All Psychotherapies'. In Harvey, J.H., and Parks, M.M. (eds.): *Psychotherapy Research and Behavior Change: 1981 Master Lecture Series*. Washington, DC: American Psychological Association, 1982.

French, T.M.: 'Interrelations between Psychoanalysis and the Experimental Work of Pavlov'. *American Journal of Psychiatry*, Volume 89, 1933, pp. 1165–1203.

Friedling, C., Goldfried, M.R., and Stricker, G.: *Convergence in Psychodynamic and Behavior Therapy*. Paper presented at the annual convention of the Eastern Psychological Association, Baltimore, Maryland, April 1984.

Garfield, S.L.: *Psychotherapy: an Eclectic Approach*. New York: Wiley, 1980.

Garfield, S.L., and Kurtz, R.: 'A Survey of Clinical Psychologists: Characteristics, Activities, and Orientations'. *The Clinical Psychologist*, Volume 28, 1974, pp. 7–10.

Garfield, S.L., and Kurtz, R.: 'A Study of Eclectic Views'. *Journal of Clinical and Consulting Psychology*, Volume 45, 1977, pp. 78–83.

Goldfried, M.R.: 'Toward the Delineation of Therapeutic Change Principles'. *American Psychologist*, Volume 35, 1980, pp. 991–999.

Goldfried, M.R.: 'On the History of Therapeutic Integration'. *Behavior Therapy*, Volume 13, 1982. pp. 572–593.

Goldfried, M.R., and Newman, C.: 'Psychotherapy Integration: an Historical Perspective'. In Norcross, J.C. (ed.): *Handbook of Eclectic Psychotherapy*. New York: Brunner/Mazel, 1986.

Goldfried, M.R., and Padawer, W.: 'Current Status and Future Directions in Psychotherapy'. In Goldfried, M.R. (ed.): *Converging Themes in Psychotherapy: Trends in Psychodynamic, Humanistic, and Behavioral Practice*. New York: Springer, 1982.

Goldfried, M.R., and Safran, J.D.: 'Future Directions in Psychotherapy Integration'. In Norcross, J.C. (ed.): *Handbook of Eclectic Psychotherapy*. New York: Brunner/Mazel, 1986.

Goldstein, A.P., and Stein, N.: *Prescriptive Psychotherapies*. New York: Pergamon, 1976.

Haaga, D.A.: 'A Review of the Common Principles Approach to Integration of Psychotherapies'. *Cognitive Therapy and Research*, Volume 10, 1986, p. 527–538.

Halgin, R.P. (ed.): 'Special Section: Issues in the Supervision of Integrative Psychotherapy'. *Journal of Integrative and Eclectic Psychotherapy*, Volume 7, 1988, pp. 152–180.

Harper, R.A.: *Psychoanalysis and Psychotherapy: 36 Systems*. Englewood Cliffs, NJ: Prentice-Hall, 1959.

Henle, M.: 'Some Problems of Eclecticism'. In *1879 and All That: Essays in the Theory and History of Psychology*. New York: Columbia University Press, 1986.

Jayaratne, S.: 'Characteristics and Theoretical Orientations of Clinical Social Workers: a National Survey'. *Journal of Social Service Research*, Volume 20, 1982, pp. 476–485.

Karasu, T.B.: 'Psychotherapies: an Overview'. *American Journal of Psychiatry*, Volume 134, 1977, pp. 851–863.

Karasu, T.B.: 'The Specificity versus Nonspecificity Dilemma: Toward Identifying Therapeutic Change Agents'. *American Journal of Psychiatry*, Volume 143, 1986, pp. 687–695.

Kiesler, D.J.: 'Some Myths of Psychotherapy Research and the Search for a Paradigm'. *Psychological Bulletin*, Volume 65, 1966, pp. 110–136.

Kuhn, T.S.: *The Structure of Scientific Revolutions* (2nd edition). Chicago: University of Chicago Press, 1970.

Lambert, M.J.: 'Implications of Psychotherapy Outcome Research for Eclectic Psychotherapy'. In Norcross, J.C. (ed.): *Handbook of Eclectic Psychotherapy*. New York: Brunner/Mazel, 1986.

Landsman, J.T., and Dawes, R.M.: 'Smith and Glass' Conclusions Stand Up Under Scrutiny'. *American Psychologist*, Volume 37, 1982, p. 504–516.

Landsman, J.T.: 'Not an Adversity but a Welcome Diversity.' Paper presented at the meeting of the American Psychological Association, New Orleans, August 1974.

Larson, D.: 'Therapeutic Schools, Styles, and Schoolism: a National Survey'. *Journal of Humanistic Psychology*, Volume 20, 1980, pp. 3–20.

Lazarus, A.A.: 'In Support of Technical Eclecticism'. *Psychological Reports*, Volume 21, 1967, pp. 415–416.

Lazarus, A.A.: *Multimodal Behavior Therapy*. New York: Springer, 1976.

Lazarus, A.A.: 'Has Behavior Therapy Outlived its Usefulness?' *American Psychologist*, Volume 32, 1977, pp. 550–554.

Lazarus, A.A.: *The Practice of Multimodal Therapy*. New York: McGraw-Hill, 1981.

Lazarus, A.A.: 'Multimodal Therapy'. In Corsini, R.J. (ed.): *Current Psychotherapies* (3rd edition). Itasca, Illinois: Peacock, 1984.

Lazarus, A.A. (ed.): *Casebook of Multimodal Therapy*. New York: Guilford, 1985.

Lazarus, A.A.: 'From the Ashes'. *International Journal of Eclectic Psychotherapy*, Volume 5, 1986, pp. 241–242.

London, P.: 'Ecumenism in Psychotherapy'. *Contemporary Psychology*, Volume 28, 1983, pp. 507–508.

London, P.: 'Metamorphosis in Psychotherapy: Slouching toward Integration'. *Journal of Integrative and Eclectic Psychotherapy*, Volume 7, 1988, pp. 3–12.

Luborsky, L., Singer, B., and Luborsky, L.: 'Comparative Studies of Psychotherapies: Is it True that "Everybody has Won and All Must Have Prizes?"'. *Archives of General Psychiatry*, Volume 32, 1975, pp. 995–1008.

Lunde, D.T.: 'Eclectic and Integrated Theory: Gordon Allport and Others'. In Burton, A. (ed.): *Operational Theories of Personality*, pp. 381–404. New York: Brunner/Mazel, 1974.

Mahoney, M.J., Norcross, J.C., Prochaska, J.O., and Missar, C.D.: 'Psychological Development and Optimal Psychotherapy: Converging Perspectives among Clinical Psychologists'. *Journal of Integrative and Eclectic Psychotherapy*, Volume 8, 1989.

Marmor, J.: 'Recent Trends in Psychotherapy'. *American Journal of Psychiatry*, Volume 137, 1980, pp. 409–416.

Messer, S.B.: 'Integrating Psychoanalytic and Behaviour Therapy: Limitations, Possibilities and Trade-Offs'. *British Journal of Clinical Psychology*, Volume 22, 1983, pp. 131–132.

Messer, S.B.: 'Eclecticism in Psychotherapy: Underlying Assumptions, Problems, and Trade-Offs'. In Norcross, J.C. (ed.): *Handbook of Eclectic Psychotherapy*. New York: Brunner/Mazel, 1986(a).

Messer, S.B.: 'Behavioral and Psychoanalytic Perspectives at Therapeutic Choice Points'. *American Psychologist*, Volume 41, 1986(b), pp. 1261–1272.

Messer, S.B.: 'Can the Tower of Babel be Completed? A Critique of the Common Language Proposal'. *Journal of Integrative and Eclectic Psychotherapy*, Volume 6, 1987, pp. 195–199.

Messer, S.B., and Winokur, M.: 'Some Limits to the Integration of Psychoanalytic and Behavior Therapy'. *American Psychologist*, Volume 35, 1980, pp. 818–827.

Messer, S.B., and Winokur, M.: 'Ways of Knowing and Visions of Reality in Psychoanalytic Therapy and Behavior Therapy'. In Arkowitz, H., and Messer, S.B. (eds.): *Psychoanalytic Therapy and Behavior Therapy: Is Integration Possible?* New York:

Plenum, 1984.

Miller, M.H.: 'We are Good – They are Bad'. *Journal of Nervous and Mental Disease*, Volume 173, 1985, pp. 279–281.

Moultrup, D.: 'Integration: a Coming of Age'. *Contemporary Family Therapy*, Volume 8, 1986, pp. 157–167.

Norcross, J.C.: 'All in the Family? On Therapeutic Commonalities'. *American Psychologist*, Volume 36, 1981, pp. 1544–1545.

Norcross, J.C.: 'For Discriminating Clinicians Only'. *Contemporary Psychology*, Volume 30, 1985, pp. 757–758.

Norcross, J.C. (ed.): *Handbook of Eclectic Psychotherapy*. New York: Brunner/Mazel, 1986.

Norcross, J.C. (ed.): 'Special Section: Toward a Common Language for Psychotherapy'. *Journal of Integrative and Eclectic Psychotherapy*, Volume 4, 1987, pp. 165–205.

Norcross, J.C.: 'The Exclusivity Myth and Equifinality Principle in Psychotherapy'. *Journal of Integrative and Eclectic Psychotherapy*, Volume 7, !988, pp. 415–421.

Norcross, J.C., and Napolitano, G.: 'Defining our Journal and Ourselves'. *International Journal of Eclectic Psychotherapy*, Volume 5, 1986, p. 249–255.

Norcross, J.C., and Prochaska, J.O.: 'Clinicians' Theoretical Orientations: Selection, Utilization, and Efficacy'. *Professional Psychology*, Volume 14, 1983, pp. 197–208.

Norcross, J.C., and Prochaska, J.O.: 'A Study of Eclectic (and Integrative) Views Revisited. *Professional Psychology: Research and Practice*, Volume 19, 1988, pp. 170–174.

Norcross, J.C., and Thomas, B.L.: 'What's Stopping Us Now? Obstacles to Psychotherapy Integration'. *Journal of Integrative and Eclectic Psychotherapy*, Volume 7, 1988, pp. 74–80.

Norcross, J.C., Beutler, L.E., Clarkin, J.F., DiClemente, C.C., Halgin, R.P., Frances, A., Prochaska, J.O., Robertson, M., and Suedfeld, P.: 'Training Integrative/Eclectic Psychotherapists'. *International Journal of Eclectic Psychotherapy*, Volume 5, 1986, pp. 71–94.

Norcross, J.C., Prochaska, J.O., and Gallagher, K.M.: 'Clinical Psychologists in the 1980's: I. Demographics, Affiliations, and Satisfactions'. *The Clinical Psychologist*, Volume 42 No. 2, 1989.

Omer, H., and London, P.: 'Metamorphosis in Psychotherapy: End of the Systems Era'. *Psychotherapy*, Volume 25, 1988, pp. 171–180.

Parloff, M.B.: 'Shopping for the Right Therapy'. *Saturday Review*, 21 February 1976, pp. 135–142.

Parloff, M.B.: 'Can Psychotherapy Research Guide the Policymaker?: a Little Knowledge May Be a Dangerous Thing'. *American Psychologist*, Volume 34, 1979, pp. 296–306.

Paul, G.L.: 'Strategy of Outcome Research in Psychotherapy'. *Journal of Consulting Psychology*, Volume 31, 1987, pp. 109–119.

Perlman, B.: 'A National Survey of APA Affiliated Master-Level Clinicians: Description and Comparison'. *Professional Psychology: Research and Practice*, Volume 16, 1985, pp. 553–564.

Peterson, D.R., Eaton, M.M., Levine, A.R., and Snepp, F.P.: 'Career Experiences of Doctors of Psychology'. *Professional Psychology*, Volume 13, 1982, pp. 268–277.

Pinsof, W.M.: 'Integrative Problem-Centered Therapy: Toward the Synthesis of Family and Individual Psychotherapies'. *Journal of Marital and Family Therapy*, Volume 9, 1983, pp. 19–35.

Prochaska, J.O.: *Systems of Psychotherapy: a Transtheoretical Analysis* (2nd edition). Homewood, Illinois: Dorsey, 1984.

Prochaska, J.O., and DiClemente, C.C.: *The Transtheoretical Approach: Crossing the Traditional Boundaries of Therapy*. Homewood, Illinois: Dow Jones-Irwin, 1984.

Prochaska, J.O., and Norcross, J.C.: 'The Future of Psychotherapy: a Delphi Poll'. *Professional Psychology*, Volume 13, 1982, pp. 620–627.

Prochaska, J.O., and Norcross, J.C.: 'Contemporary Psychotherapists: a National Survey of Characteristics, Practices, Orientations, and Attitudes'. *Psychotherapy: Theory, Research, and Practice*, Volume 20, 1983, pp. 161–173.

Robertson, M.: 'Some Observations from an Eclectic Therapist'. *Psychotherapy: Theory, Research, and Practice*, Volume 16, 1979, p. 18–21.

Robertson, M.: 'Training Eclectic Psychotherapists'. In Norcross, J.C. (ed.): *Handbook of Eclectic Psychotherapy*. New York: Brunner/Mazel, 1986.

Rotter, J.B.: *Social Learning and Clinical Psychology*. Englewood Cliffs, NJ: Prentice-Hall, 1954.

Ryle, A.: 'Cognitive Psychology as a Common Language for Psychotherapy'. *Journal of Integrative and Eclectic Psychotherapy*, Volume 6, 1987, pp. 168–172.

Smith, D.S.: 'Trends in Counseling and Psychotherapy. *American Psychologist*, Volume 37, 1982, pp. 802–809.

Smith, M.L., Glass, G.V., and Miller, T.J.: *The Benefits of Psychotherapy*. Baltimore: John Hopkins University Press, 1980.

Stiles, W.B., Shapiro, S.A., and Elliot, R.: 'Are All Psychotherapies Equivalent?' *American Psychologist*, Volume 41, 1986, pp. 165–180.

Stricker, G.: 'Some Viable Suggestions for Integrating Psychotherapies'. Paper presented at the second annual conference of the Society for the Exploration of Psychotherapy Integration, Toronto, May 1986.

Strong, S.R.: 'Interpersonal Theory as a Common Language for Psychotherapy'. *Journal of Integrative and Eclectic Psychotherapy*, Volume 6, 1987, p. 173–183.

Strupp, H.H.: 'On the Basic Ingredients of Psychotherapy'. *Journal of Clinical and Consulting Psychology*, Volume 41, 1973, pp. 1–8.

Strupp, H.H.: 'The Outcome Problem in Psychotherapy: Contemporary Perspectives'. In Harvey, J.H., and Parks, M.M. (eds.): *Psychotherapy Research and Behavior Change: 1981 Master Lecture Series*. Washington, DC: American Psychological Association, 1982.

Wachtel, P.L.: *Psychoanalysis and Behavior Therapy: Toward an Integration*. New York: Basic Books, 1977.

Wachtel, P.L.: 'Integration Misunderstood'. *British Journal of Clinical Psychology*, Volume 22, 1983, p. 129–130.

Wachtel, P.L.: *Action and Insight*. New York: Guilford, 1987.

Watkins, C.E., Lopez, F.G., Campbell, V.L., and Himmell, C.D.: 'Contemporary Counseling Psychology: Results of a National Survey'. *Journal of Counseling Psychology*, Volume 33, 1986, pp. 301–309.

Weiner, I.B.: *Principles of Psychotherapy*. New York: Wiley, 1975.

Wilson, G.T.: 'Psychotherapy Process and Procedure: the Behavioral Mandate'. *Behavior Therapy*, Volume 12, 1982, pp. 291–312.

Wolfe, B.E., and Goldfried, M.R.: 'Research on Psychotherapy Integration: Recommendations and Conclusions from an NIMH Workshop'. *Journal of Consulting and Clinical Psychology*, Volume 56, 1988, pp. 448–451.

Yates, A.J.: 'Behaviour Therapy and Psychodynamic Therapy: Basic Conflict or Reconciliation and Integration?' *British Journal of Clinical Psychology*, Volume 22, 1983, pp. 107–125.

## ECLECTICISM AND INTEGRATION IN COUNSELLING AND PSYCHOTHERAPY: MAJOR THEMES AND OBSTACLES

### JOHN C. NORCROSS AND LISA M. GRENCAVAGE

### POSTSCRIPT

We would modestly assert that the selection of our paper for this collection is more a testament to the special section in which it was embedded and to the vital interest in psychotherapy integration than to our literary talents. The supporting context of that section (Volume 17 No. 3) was provided by Arnold Lazarus's erudite 'Why I am an Eclectic (Not an Integrationist)', Bernard Beitman's rejoining 'Why I am an Integrationist (Not an Eclectic)', and Stanley Messer's sage 'Cautionary Notes' regarding uncritical acceptance of both eclecticism and integration in counselling.

In the short period of time since we co-authored the article, the integration movement has evolved and grown rapidly. The tripartite characterisation we advanced – theoretical integration, technical eclecticism, and common factors – still accurately defines the basic parameters of the movement. However, the boundaries among these three thrusts have become less rigid and more permeable in the ensuing years. Technical eclectics cannot disregard theory any more than theoretical integrationists can ignore technique. Without some commonalities among disparate schools of therapy, moreover, theoretical integration would be impossible.

The empiricism of eclecticism and the theory of integration may, in fact, be complementary rather than antagonistic approaches to the same goal. The research and clinical data of empiricism can form the basis for theories of psychotherapy integration, just as the theories of integration can guide the search for data of the eclectics (Arkowitz, 1992). All the spokes co-exist more peacefully and operate more harmoniously under the superordinate umbrella of psychotherapy integration.

At the same time, emerging directions are evident in each of these three thrusts. In *theoretical integration*, the narrow preoccupation with a psychoanalytic-behavioural hybrid has given way to broader examination of other conceptual syntheses. Cognitive and interpersonal therapies seem to be the most popular elements to incorporate into a meta-theory, with systems theory following closely behind (Norcross and Prochaska, 1988). In *technical eclecticism*, the meaning of the term is being broadened to denote the combination not only of specific clinical procedures but also of therapist relationship stances (Lazarus *et al.*, 1992). One way to conceptualise this enlargement, paralleling the notion of 'treatment of choice' in terms of technique, is how clinicians determine the 'relationship of choice' in terms of their interpersonal presentation. While continued progress is being made toward the development of specific treatments for different diagnostic groupings of clients, psychological therapies are increasingly matched to client variables beyond diagnosis, e.g. patient goals, defensive patterns, situational demands. And in *common factors*, there is a nascent consensus that the most productive path will combine unique factors *and* common factors, integrating useful differences and fundamental similarities among the schools. Some progress has also been achieved in delineating and operationalising genuine commonalities (e.g. Goldfried, 1991; Grencavage and Norcross, 1990; Saltzman and Norcross, 1990), a necessary step if the common factors approach is to meaningfully influence psychotherapy training and practice (Mahrer, 1989).

Another emerging direction is the integration of psychotherapy itself with broader areas of psychology, such as cognitive, social, health, and psychobiology (e.g. Horowitz, 1991; Schwartz, 1991). The discipline of psychotherapy has become inbred and hence cut off from potentially useful developments in the behavioural sciences (Arkowitz, 1991). While it is still early to tell, advances in these affiliated fields may contribute greatly to our understanding and development of a comprehensive psychology of behaviour change.

Integration in various guises will represent the psychotherapeutic *zeitgeist* of the 1990s. Eclecticism is the modal theoretical orientation of American (Norcross *et al.*, 1989) and British (Norcross *et al.*, 1992) psychotherapists and its prevalence may be rising (Jensen *et al.*, 1990). The movement has matured to the point where compendia on integration are appearing on both sides of the Atlantic (Dryden, 1992; Norcross and Goldfried, 1992). The integrative fervour will apparently persist well into the 1990s: a panel of psychotherapy experts portend its increasing popularity through the second millennium (Norcross *et al.*, 1992).

The obstacles to mature integration identified in the 1989 article continue unabated – intrinsic investment in private theories, inadequate commitment to integrative training, divergent epistemologies and ontologies, insufficient empirical research, and the absence of a common language for psychotherapists. However, the growing emphasis and proliferating number of integrative therapies raise a potential contradiction: the integration of today may become the single-school approach of tomorrow. Integrative therapies may, ironically, become the rigid and institutionalised monoliths which the movement set out to combat in the first place. Such a scenario hints at visions of Institutes for Integrative Psychotherapy and certification of integrative clinicians (Arkowitz, 1992).

Should this occur, the nettle will not have been grasped. We envisage an evolving framework for integration rather than a fixed, static school. Required is an open system that can generate new theories, new therapies, and new research. Whether or not integration can successfully navigate between the perils of haphazard syncretism on the one side, and the dangers of ideological institutionalisation on the other, will largely determine its continuing contribution to psychotherapy in the forthcoming millennium (Lazarus *et al.*, 1992).

## REFERENCES

Arkowitz, H.: 'Psychotherapy Integration Comes of Age'. *Journal of Psychotherapy Integration*, Volume 1, 1991.

Arkowitz, H.: 'Integrative Theories of Therapy'. In Freedheim, D.K. (ed.): *History of Psychotherapy: a Century of Change.* Washington, DC: American Psychological Association, 1992.

Dryden, W. (ed.): *Integrative and Eclectic Therapy: a Handbook.* London: Open University Press, 1992.

Goldfried, M.R.: 'Research Issues in Psychotherapy Integration'. *Journal of Psychotherapy Integration*, Volume 1, 1991.

Grencavage, L.M., and Norcross, J.C.: 'Where are the Commonalities Among the Therapeutic Common Factors?' *Professional Psychology: Research and Practice*, Volume 21, 1990.

Horowitz, M.J.: 'States, Schemas, and Control: General Theories for Psychotherapy Integration'. *Journal of Psychotherapy Integration*, Volume 1, 1991.

Jensen, J.P., Bergin, A.E., and Greaves, D.W.: 'The Meaning of Eclecticism: New Survey and Analysis of Components'. *Professional Psychology: Research and Practice*, Volume 21, 1990.

Lazarus, A.A., Beutler, L.E., and Norcross, J.C.: 'The Future of Technical Eclecticism'. *Psychotherapy*, Volume 29, 1992.

Mahrer, A.R.: *The Integration of Psychotherapies.* New York: Human Sciences Press, 1989.

Norcross, J.C., and Goldfried, M.R. (eds.): *Handbook of Psychotherapy Integration.* New York: Basic Books, 1992.

Norcross, J.C., and Prochaska, J.O.: 'A Study of Eclectic (and Integrative) Views Revisited'. *Professional Psychology: Research and Practice*, Volume 19, 1988.

Norcross, J.C., Alford, B.A., and DeMichele, J.T.: 'The Future of Psychotherapy: Delphi Data and Concluding Observations'. *Psychotherapy*, Volume 29, 1992.

Norcross, J.C., Dryden, W., and Brust, A.M.: 'British Clinical Psychologists: I. A National Survey of the BPS Clinical Division'. *Clinical Psychology Forum*, Volume 40, 1992.

Norcross, J.C., Prochaska, J.O., and Gallagher, K.M.: 'Clinical Psychologists in the 1980's: II. Theory, Research, and Practice'. *The Clinical Psychologist*, Volume 42 No. 3, 1989.

Saltzman, N., and Norcross, J.C. (eds.): *Therapy Wars: Contention and Convergence in Differing Clinical Approaches.* San Francisco: Jossey-Bass, 1990.

Schwartz, G.: 'The Data are Always Friendly: a Systems Approach to Psychotherapy Integration'. *Journal of Psychotherapy Integration*, Volume 1, 1991.

## 2: THE CONTEXT OF GUIDANCE AND COUNSELLING

# THE PERSONAL AND THE POLITICAL

## PAUL HALMOS

*The term 'counselling' is used liberally to convey paedagogical, casework and clinical meanings. The indiscriminate use of the term by institutions of health, welfare, and education often conceals the intention to appear more solicitous to clients than the institution can in fact afford to be. The central fact of counselling is the use of the counsellor's total and global personality in effecting changes in the personality of the client. This factor is shown to be potently present even in behaviour therapy where it would be disclaimed. Counselling, therefore, is a* personalistic *process. Today energetic political attacks are levelled against individualistic, piecemeal, and privatist solutions of man's problems. The political accusers charge counsellors, social caseworkers, psychotherapists and others with a desertion of their moral duty to change evil systems and with distracting attention from the really important public miseries inflicted on man by these systems. Politicisation of the personalists and a kind of hybridisation of the two kinds of social concerns is suggested by these critics. In this paper, the incompatibilities of the personal and political roles are stressed, and a continued protection of the integrity of these meliorist roles is advocated.*

The hazard of asking a sociologist to address himself to the matter of counselling is that he will address himself to the sociology of counselling. Now we all know that sociology today is ubiquitous and oversold, and that some people are not much inspired by it. Such people as these think that the indecent exposure of sociology has about as much to do with the propagation of ideas as the other thing has with the propagation of the species. These sceptics, I feel, are ungenerous, for sociological understanding can be a source of solace to us when distressed by the bewildering predicaments of social life (if we manage to forget that, but for sociology, those predicaments may well have been less severe). Nowadays, where there is political recalcitrance, sociology is often not far away. People have become aware of this and tell us. And so, while we sociologists are in the process of finding out about society, society is in the process of finding out about us. Just the same, I will not try to run away from the consequences of this and attempt to pass as a counsellor. Instead of fleeing from my sociological role I shall play it by attending to three aspects of counselling which are of interest to sociology. *First*, I will attempt a definition of the concept of 'the counsellor'. *Second*, I will try to outline the pervasive central value-affirmations in

First published in the *British Journal of Guidance and Counselling*, Volume 2 No.2, Juley 1974.

the practice of counselling. In both of these first two I will underline the *personalistic* nature of counselling. Then *third*, I will comment on the contemporary political take-over bid of personalistic counselling.

## THE CONCEPT OF 'THE COUNSELLOR'

I interpret the concept 'the counsellor' much more widely than people have generally done. I have understood this term to mean that *anyone who uses his own personality professionally to bring about changes in the personality of another by modifying the other's self-image is a counsellor*. This definition makes no distinction between 'counselling' and 'psychotherapy', and places all forms of personalist consultations within the 'counselling' rubric.

Indeed, I have been in the habit of speaking of 'the counselling professions', and of the ideology shared by these professions as 'the counselling ideology'. I chose 'counselling' as the label for this group of miscellaneous professionals because they are essentially advice-givers. No matter how strenuously non-directive they describe their work in their protestations, their purpose is clearly to effect change through some sort of guidance. The other labels, such as 'psychotherapist' or 'social caseworker', conceal this central fact in the counsellor's role. Of course, there is often a sincere aspiration to be 'non-directive', but this *is* an aspiration, not an achievement. It is only an achievement in an unexpected way: the aspiration to respect the client's integrity – in spite of its imperfections – prevails upon the client as a model more influentially than the aspiration to prevail upon the client could possibly achieve. This is the old story of people who do not as you say but as you do. The more painstakingly non-directive and client-centred we are, the more we are likely to gain recruits to our ethics of respect and to our philosophy of tolerance. The critics of counselling, of course, won't accept even this: Marcuse's freak-notion of 'repressive tolerance' (Marcuse, 1969) is thrown at the counsellors' sinful liberal souls.

Trying to define the class of roles to which I attach the label 'counsellor', I have come across some marginal and anomalous instances of usage which I must briefly consider if only to discourage these usages. Take, for example, the practice of our Open University of referring to some of their staff as 'counsellors'. When we consider the roles of these counsellors we learn with surprise that what they are specifically prohibited from doing is counselling. Senior officers of the Open University recently explained how the role of the counsellor was defined by that university. They write:

*'Counsellors are advised that they should not attempt to re-organise the student's life or to intrude themselves on his personal or family circumstances.* If a counsellor comes upon problems which lie outside his province, e.g. of a social welfare or of a psychiatric nature, and if he believes that these are seriously affecting a student's capacity to study, he should on no account attempt to deal with them himself, but should report the matter immediately to his Senior Counsellor' (Beevers and Cronhelm, 1973, italics mine).

They do not tell us whether the Senior Counsellor is allowed to counsel, and whether in the Open University a counsellor is a counsellor only when he is senior. One may also mention in passing that in the Open University the counsellor is explicitly given 'a defined tutorial role' yet he is expressly told not to teach! No doubt the unique nature of the Open University dictated the employment of personal course-advisers for students so that students can be compensated for the absence of the usual supportive staff–student relationship available to students in other universities. But regrettably – and this is all that I take issue with – by calling these advisers 'counsellors' they suggest the provision of personal services which they do not in fact make available or wish to make available. Of course, we are all aware of the fact that a 'tutorial role' and a 'counselling role' may imperceptibly merge. But by explicitly ruling out the genuine counselling functions the only so-called Open University counsellors who will counsel are those who disobey the rule of 'not intruding on the student's personal life'.

There are other educational institutions in which the opacity of the counsellor's role is deliberately perpetuated, so that, by now, the professional identity of this role is more uncertain than it need be. To make things worse – at any rate for the non-professional public – confusion is brought to full term by the practice of recognising such specialisms as 'investment counsellors', 'central heating counsellors', 'funeral counsellors', 'beauty counsellors', and so on.

There have been various reasons why the term 'counsellor' has been so confusingly and arbitrarily adopted. Sometimes it is brought into the picture because it is a testimonial to the compassionate character of an institution. Such institutions welcome the solicitous, concerned, and personally intimate connotations of the label, though they make sure that these connotations are not taken literally. Others adopt the label defensively so as to show that they are not psychoanalysts or psychotherapists but *only* counsellors. They are not deeply probing and interminably searching investigators who – while school governors and senates are not looking – surreptitiously try to convert perfectly respectable educational institutions into psychiatric clinics or even casework agencies (Newsome *et al.*, 1973). Much of the initial American usage of the term in the contexts of school-counselling, vocational counselling, student counselling, and the like, came about with the assumption that there was in fact a buffer state between the clinics and the schools in which the counsellor could claim some sort of a precarious sovereignty. And so disclaimers of clinical affiliation were *de rigueur*.

Then there has also been a curious inconsistency in the use of the term elsewhere: why, for example, should we speak of 'marriage guidance counsellors' but hardly, if ever, of 'child guidance counsellors'? I do not know.

Clearly counselling appears to be practised in many settings if one takes the use of the label as definitive. My definition aims at limiting the number of settings to a group in which the counselling regimen shares certain fundamental characteristics. This definition may help to put an end to subterfuges, euphemisms, and tactical exploitations of the professional label. It will, at least, identify the large and comprehensive *genus* of counselling of which the many variations of theory and practice are mere *species*. Yet to qualify for membership in this *genus* the minimum qualifications of my definition would have to be met.

### THE FAITH OF THE COUNSELLORS REVISITED

In *The Faith of the Counsellors* (Halmos, 1965a) I advanced the proposition that the *counsellors – on their own showing –* relied on transcendental categories of faith in the conduct of their counselling work. Their dependence on metatheoretical beliefs and metapsychological postulates is followed up not only by stark proclamations of faith but also by prescriptions of a practice of interpersonal communion. The humanistic faith of the counsellors is announced in a scientific-clinical idiom, yet it enshrines the principle that the technician's personality is more important than his technique and that the total personal orientation of the counsellor is a vital ingredient of counselling effectiveness. This is what Nelson (1968) meant when he said that 'points of view which are in any sense instrumental in character, scientific in intent, or specific in purpose are subordinated to vital interpersonal engagement.' To know or to understand are not sufficient qualifications for a counsellor. According to Wrenn (1966) '. . . it is all-important that the counsellor really cares for his client . . . ', and even if counsellors are unable to agree with the behaviourist on the anatomy of this global caring, their dedicatedness and warm-heartedness continue to be essential characteristics of their work. Clearly their commitment has no so-called scientific rationale: it is a credo.

As a sociologist studying the ideological orientations of key social change-agents in our culture, I have focused on the counsellors since they seemed to be somewhat neglected by my sociological colleagues in their study of social change-agents in twentieth-century industrial societies (Halmos, 1970). I – as so many others – have concluded that industrial civilisation has evolved these change-agent roles as successors to the roles played by the pastoral and priestly counsellors of the pre-scientific age. The sociological hypothesis I should like to entertain goes somewhat beyond this trite observation. I would venture here to suggest a set of hypotheses about the social system itself, hypotheses of a functionalist character. According to these, societies have always institutionalised and are likely to continue to institutionalise the role of the counselling person as a functional requisite for the maintenance of any society. This functional requisite is an amenity or resource for those (1) who fail to secure their share of supportive communion with others, or (2) who miss out on rehabilitative dependency situations in which they can realign their developmental career by reviewing it or reliving it, or (3) who can understand themselves only through confiding their thoughts and sentiments in another. Of course, these needs are ordinarily met through the informal and intimate relationships of families, friendships, and acquaintanceships, but those whose needs are the most insistent are usually and especially the ones who cannot establish or maintain these nourishing informal relationships and have to take recourse to their institutionalised surrogates. These three interlinked 'counselling needs' are universal, and no social system can be even imagined which could do away with the institutionalised surrogate-resources for those with unmet counselling needs.

Sociological theories which fail to assign a prominent function to counselling needs are usually the ones which identify the concept of 'social change-agent' with the political-technological-economic in-itiators of macro-social change. I, on the other hand, consider the counselling role as a role of change-initiating even if the micro-social change it can initiate registers on the social system only slowly and cumulatively. So that the sociological neglect of this may be rectified, we must now try to regard institutionalising of counselling as no less a functional requisite of the social system than, say, division of labour, leadership, the prolongation of marital pair-bonding, or the care for the aged.

My analysis was not always a popular one. That the counselling activity is primarily a formalised core-activity and is to be found in all on-going intimate social relationships was not a particularly attractive idea to those professional workers who were still looking for a rationale for their professional status as experts and as possessors of credentialled skill. That the core-experience of counselling was a Buberian I-and-Thou feeling of rapport and that the various reports and case-studies trailing after these experiences contained all kinds of hardly-concealed confessions of faith was not popular with practitioners who thought that they had to compete with unpious surgeons, engineers, architects, and so on, for the status of 'professional' workers.

Since *The Faith of the Counsellors*, however, developments in counselling theory have continued to supply evidence for my conclusions with a most remarkable consistency and with an ever-growing specificity. First there was Fiedler's work to show that the therapist's affiliation to a psychotherapeutic school was of lesser significance than his ability to empathise with the patient (Fiedler, 1950a; 1950b). Then the later Whitehorn and Betz study (1954) added much substance to the kind of thinking started by Fiedler. Soon after these there was Carl Rogers more influentially intervening and listing as necessary and sufficient (*sic*) conditions of therapeutic change (**a**) the counsellor's empathy with the client, (**b**) the counsellor's positive affective attitude towards the client, (**c**) a degree of the counsellor's genuineness, and (**d**) a degree to which the counsellor's affectivity and intensity match those of the client (Rogers, 1957; 1961). Closely following these specifications Truax (1963) and Bergin (1963) concluded that those therapists who scored high on 'empathy, unconditional positive regard, and mature, genuine, and integrated behaviour' were the ones who produced positive results. A somewhat shorter list comprising 'warmth, empathy, and genuineness' was awkwardly – though accurately – described later (Carkhuff, 1966) as 'the core facilitating interpersonal conditions' of counselling.

These factors in their togetherness as well as severally have been the centre-piece of counselling theory during the last six or seven years. The central doctrine is stated by Rogers without any ambiguity: 'The facts seem to suggest' writes Rogers, 'that personality change is initiated by *attitudes* which exist in the therapist, rather than primarily by his knowledge, his theories, or his techniques' (Rogers, 1961). During recent years there have been a large number of studies to test the therapeutic effectiveness of what by now has been sanctified into the trinity of 'accurate empathy, non-possessive warmth, and genuineness'. The conclusions of these studies have been most ably summarised by Truax and Mitchell (1971), who skirt around the faith of the counsellors in non-clerical attire yet not without signs of piety. They do not say that being a counsellor is the same as being a friend, but they do seem to say that not having the vital attributes of a friend precludes one from acting as a counsellor.

What Truax and Mitchell call the 'commonality' of the counselling stance with stances of lay and civic life and with stances of the non-professional world, is the basic core-content – or what I myself call the *personalist* content – of counselling work. This content is clearly to be distinguished from what is 'technical', for they regard this commonality as more important than technique or knowledge. According to them, and according to the whole tenor of scores of current papers, a failure in the global and unanalysable commonality or core-content is a failure in technique and, therefore, in counselling. I say 'unanalysable' because the operational and behavioural components of these basic attitudes do not, and in principle cannot, replace the *Gestalt* of their total *facade*. Notwithstanding these perceptions of total personal relationships, these writers still wistfully retain an analytic and positivistic posture. As an act of another kind of faith they declare, 'no science or applied science has ever progressed without simplifying', and add, 'once we understand the complex by virtue of simplifying, we may be able to put the parts back together again in order to match the complexity we are interested in, but then we will have *control* over it' (Bergin, 1971, my italics). A credo of 1984 if there ever was one! Take the *Gestalt* of the core-experience to pieces and after you have done so Bergin thinks that you can put the core-experience together again. You might as well say that if you take Beethoven's Ninth Symphony to pieces and consider the physical and tonal qualities of each note separately you will be able 'to put together' and 'explain' the total *Gestalt* of the symphony.

But such reaffirmations of analytic and reductive faith remain unconvincing, especially as they are interspersed with equally frequent denials of faith. The sociologist of culture is obliged to observe that what began as a clinical-analytic and clinical-behaviouristic movement relapses into totalistic and phenomenological confessions. 'We want to emphasise', write Truax and Mitchell, 'the therapist-as-person before the therapist-as-expert or therapist-as-technician.' Naturally and very properly they fight a rearguard action: 'Knowledge of patient pathology and strength, a clear conceptualisation of the knowledge we have gathered from psychoanalytic, client-centered, existential, and eclectic sources, should not be cast aside. We see our findings as adding to, not undoing, efforts of the past' (Truax and Mitchell, 1971). If knowledge from 'existential' sources is to be eclectically added to knowledge from 'psychoanalytic' sources, the 'addition' would require some superordinate arithmetic: one can no more 'add' these two than one can add two apples and three bananas. Over and above the reductive and deterministic paradigm the paradigm of the personalist vision so strongly attracts these two evidently tough-minded researchers that they do not notice their position as one of *credo quia absurdum*. The faith of the counsellors remains unexorcised from the ideology of the counsellors. Faith continues to haunt.

Those counsellors who are not only flirtatious with behaviour therapy but actually carry on an affair with it may now look on with a superior smile, with a smile of complacency: 'we', they may now be saying, 'are certainly not guilty of harbouring personalist skeletons in our laboratory cupboards!' But is this really so?

In a correspondence which I had with Joseph Wolpe on the pages of the journal *Discovery* (Halmos, 1965b) I commented on Wolpe's article on behaviour therapy which had appeared in the previous issue of that journal (Wolpe, 1965). I explained there that Wolpe and other behaviour therapists had openly confessed to relying on what they were pleased to call the 'reinforcement function' of the behaviour therapist's personality. The sympathy (*sic*) of the behaviour therapist for the patient, Wolpe had written, is supposed to arouse in the patient certain 'non-specific emotions' which are incompatible with the patient's anxiety and will, therefore, inhibit that anxiety. And so, the 'non-specific' sympathy of the therapist arousing the non-specific positive emotions of the patient is retailed to us as a mechanistic-behaviouristic regimen. It seems to me that what is being asserted here is a Buberian I-and-Thou relationship reissued in the camouflage of a behaviouristic terminology. No analytic reductions of the non-specific *Gestalt* of the sympathy or of the equally non-specific positive emotions of the patient are being offered. When challenged, the behaviourist will invite us to consider the molar concept of sympathy as consisting of the molecular elements of such things as an attentive facial expression, perhaps a warm interest, such comments as 'is that so?' or 'really?' and the like, and other encouragements expressed or shown to make the client continue to communicate. But the counsellor becoming aware of his sympathy for the client does not say to himself, 'I am being attentive and encouraging therefore I must feel sympathy'. He does not infer his molar state by perceiving its alleged molecular components. He is directly and immediately aware of his sympathy, and this awareness will if anything be weakened by separate awareness of the various molecular components, such as 'I say, I am being attentive' or 'Fancy, I am being encouraging!'.

Of course, behaviourists such as Skinner (1953) might call 'sympathy' a mere 'explanatory fiction', presumably asserting that the *Gestalt* does not have an existence apart from its constituent parts and that 'sympathy', 'fear', 'anger' and so on are fictive totalities. Only their behavioural-physiological components exist; the pattern of their existence adds nothing. And yet the behaviourists themselves continue to rely on 'explanatory fictions'. Wolpe talks about sympathy and about friendliness, expecting us to pay due respect to these molar notions and respond to the verbal stimuli with consent. Evidently the molar notions to which the words relate are still useful as stimuli or evocations not only to the behaviourist's audience but also to the behaviourist himself: he too needs the consolations of explanatory fictions and of global images! Chefs who too have to eat – and judging from their girth like to eat – will nevertheless enjoy a plateful of *tournedos Rossini* and it will not be spoilt by their knowledge of what a carcass of beef looks or smells like. In fact we could not survive without explanatory fictions, and this puts a strain on the idea that these global outcomes are 'fictional'. The behaviourists themselves are unconvincingly irregular in their practice: they are furtively molar and ostentatiously molecular.

But the nature and function of sympathy was not the only source of confusion in Wolpe's account. He uses discourse in which the concepts continue to be non-specific: for example, 'the therapist stimulated assertive responses . . . ' What does this 'stimulated' mean? Does it mean anything less than a global personal encouragement, assurance, persuasion, and suggestion? An approving acceptance? Or even the expression of liking for the patient? Wolpe recounted how he prevailed upon the anxious patient: 'I impressed on her that she had been an adult for a long time; that her relatives had no business to try to run her life; and that she should not conceal the resentment that she so appropriately felt.' But how does the behaviour therapist 'impress' such a thing on the patient? Surely by making it clear to the patient that her resentful behaviour will not make her unacceptable or unlovable in the eyes of the therapist.

It is hardly unimportant to note that on this occasion Wolpe's mean number of interviews with patients was 30 and that the sheer perseverance and reasserted interest of the therapist's attentions to the patient could not but amount to a demonstrative and manifest acceptance of the patient's person as worthy of being diligently helped by the therapist. One is reminded of Bernard Shaw's wisdom: never mind that it is only flattery, what matters is the thought that you are believed to be worth flattering.

Wolpe, in reply to my criticism, admitted that 'a friendly general atmosphere between patient and therapist is, of course, desirable for prosecuting behaviour therapy (like any other therapy)' (Wolpe, 1965). But how dare he assume that such a non-specific stimulus will be in any sense potent enough when behavioural indicators of sympathy are certainly not agreed upon and when these indicators inevitably fall short of adding up to sympathy? The model and *raison d'être* of behaviourism is the machine that can be taken to pieces and can be reassembled again into full working order. Behaviourism is indefensible unless the response is totally accounted for as a reaction to behaviourally identifiable stimuli. 'A friendly general atmosphere' is not and cannot be arrived at by adding up so many behaviourally identifiable stimuli. Indeed, I should go as far as to say that at any time when a claim is made that this has been accomplished one of two things must have happened: either an existing friendly general atmosphere has been destroyed, or its essential totality has not been reassembled from known atomic elements. If the global notion or what it stands for can be exhaustively and without remainder translated into a collection of mechanical stimuli, and if this fact can be made known to the participants of the situation of a 'friendly general atmosphere', the outcome of this awareness will be self-stultifying. The behaviour therapist continues to use the global and mystical notion of sympathy because he himself is dependent on the evocative power of this mentalistic image. The behaviour therapist must really stop slipping aces into the game which he has secreted in his sleeves and which do not really come from the behaviouristic pack at all.

In fact, we are back at square one: the sympathy, and the general friendly atmosphere is 'the empathy, warmth, and genuineness', the personalistic trinity that we have already encountered. But Wolpe is adamant. He tells me that 'the feelings of the therapist are not therapeutic' (Wolpe, 1965). Having admitted to the therapeutic potency of sympathy and friendliness one wonders what he can possibly mean by this denial? That the therapist does not or need not feel the sympathy and the friendliness, and that it is enough if he pretends to these? If he believes this, he is more credulous than the average schizophrenic patient who senses insincerity and bad faith a mile off.

Behaviour therapists concur with the counsellors about the core-conditions of effective therapy, however unwittingly. We have here a consensus which is the more impressive as it is so persevering. But if these core-conditions are to be so inflexibly basic to the counselling function, whether behaviouristic or personalistic, how are we to train counsellors so that they are equipped with a skill of providing these core-conditions? Can we train people in empathy, warmth, and genuineness? The answer is already being offered by our counselling theoreticians who are telling us that one of the 'central elements' in the training of counsellors is 'a therapeutic context in which the supervisor communicates high levels of accurate empathy, non-possessive warmth, and genuineness to the trainees themselves' (Truax, 1970). Those who train counsellors must have the personalist core-conditions themselves so that their trainees can also acquire these. 'Interns at a college counselling centre', write Pierce and Schauble (1971), 'made significant gains in this facilitative core only if they had an individual supervisor who was himself functioning at a high level of empathy, positive regard, genuineness, and concreteness' (we need not be distracted by the fourth category 'concreteness', by the Trinity's growth into a Quarternity: the God-head remains one, the personalistic orientation remains global!).

Of course, way back psychoanalysts began to insist on a training analysis, and the current 'discovery' that the trainers must dispense the same regimen to their candidates as that which their candidates are to master and apply is in a direct line of succession: the logic is the same. But whereas in the past 'insight-giving' techniques were discussed almost autonomously, nowadays counsellors think less about their skill to elicit insight in their clients than about their own feelings and about the clients' feelings in response to theirs. The counsellor is required to furnish only the so-called core-conditions of 'accurate empathy, non-possessive warmth, and genuineness' (Carkhuff, 1966), and so long as these core-conditions are provided, insight eliciting is to a large extent a function of the core-conditions.

According to current writing on counselling, indeed, the core-conditions are not only necessary but *sufficient* conditions of counselling. This is by no means universally held: unlike Rogers, Krumboltz (1965, pp. 7–8) explicitly states that the core-conditions are necessary but not sufficient. But for the majority '*Fühlung ist alles*', as Goethe said, and self-knowledge is supposed to be the by-product of the correct feelings. Just the same, 'analysis', or exploration to achieve insight,[1] is not entirely excluded from the new counsellors' goals. The core-conditions, 'the therapeutic context' as Truax (1970) puts it, usually determines 'the level of self-disclosure', and presumably the level of accretion in insight as well. Things used to turn on the counter-transference in the past; now the pivot is represented by the core-conditions. Academic and theoretical knowledge or technical acumen are secondary. Bergin (1971), discussing the concept of 'spontaneous recovery' of untreated patients, not only attributes this result to the empathy, warmth, and genuineness of untrained lay persons, but goes so far as to say that the qualified professionals who have been selected on academic or political (*sic*) grounds are disqualified by their intellectual and technical committedness! We have now reached the stage when a well-selected lay person is regarded as therapeutically superior to a qualified professional, especially a professional who has been trained by personalistically low-level trainers.

One feature stands out in high relief in these accounts of the training of counsellors: without a personalistic dedication of the trainer, no personalistic dedication of the trainee is likely to be elicited. Unless there is charisma – 'gift of grace' – in the trainer, the acolyte will not be advanced *by him* in counselling proficiency. The behaviourist is committed by his theory of human conduct to break up the charismatic I-and-Thou relationship between trainer and trainee on the one hand, and between counsellors and clients on the other, into atomic stimuli and atomic responses. These atomic particles must – in his view – add up to the global stimuli and responses of the interpersonal relationships. I suggest *first*, that this addition will never represent the total personal orientation of the counsellor, and *second*, that a mechanistic-behaviouristic fragmentation of the global-personal acts is itself an arbitrary stultifying influence on those acts. Eye-movements, postures, gestures, specific verbal stimuli and responses will not add up to, or exhaust, the *Gestalt* of sympathy, but an insistence on this arithmetic may have the unintended consequence of gratuitously destroying the vision of a global humanistic sentiment.

What is affirmed here in the ideology of counselling is a central experience of some moment and of ancient standing. One could possibly get nearer to its meaning by starting with something that Logan Pearsall Smith said, which is that 'the test of vocation is the love of the drudgery it involves'. One could adapt this here and say that 'the test of the counselling vocation is the love of empathy, non-possessive warmth, and genuineness, which the counselling drudgery involves.' This love transfers the focus of the action in an area which is mystical-existentialist and not behaviouristic-deterministic. Go and study the literature of counselling and you will find a legion of admissions to this effect, hedged round with creditable efforts not to let these admissions halt tough-minded enquiry, diligent technical exploration, and disciplined behaviouristic-deterministic logic. At the end of the day, the paradox not only survives but does and must rule our minds and our practice. I believe that the teaching and reiteration of this is a heuristic, down-to-earth, and intensely practical matter for counsellors and their trainers and not a wistful theological irrelevancy.

## THE POLITICISATION OF THE COUNSELLORS

Today the counsellors, those highly individualised change-agents, have become the targets of moral and political criticism and condemnation. They are being accused of taking refuge from a malignant social world and of crawling back into the womb of accurate empathy, of non-possessive warmth, and of genuineness. They are alleged to exclaim, 'Let the social world go hang so long as our dyadic intimacies are kept cosy and reassuring', and they are made responsible for humanism having gone clinical in a world which has gone critical. They are being charged with desertion of their professed moral principles of concern, for it is said that their counselling preoccupations distract from the situational miseries of their clients. Counselling is a subterfuge, a 'con' to persuade others to seek non-political solutions to their politically inflicted miseries. The welfare state itself is a sham for it employs legions of counsellors and other personal service professionals to make people submit to existing institutions and accept existing values. The political polis is shown to depoliticise the citizen almost analogously to the way in which the theocratic state depoliticised him with the aid of religious bribery and terror.

The political critic is much angered by theories about 'insight' and of the necessity of 'self-exploration'; these he regards as anti-political smoke-screens. Biographical exploration of clients is pointless, for everything that parents do in a nursery or teachers do in the school is totally determined by society's wars, unemployment, poverty, alien-ation, humiliation of minorities, and other attributes. On the other hand, if the counsellor does not probe, and if he focuses entirely on the present, dispensing his paternalistic core-conditions, he is only lubricating his own sense of worthwhileness and is impertinently condescending into the bargain. The political radical critic brands the counsellors and their ilk as counter-revolutionaries.

The political accusations which are unstintingly made are supported by some such rhetoric as this: 'exploring the infantile libidinal life of a negro adolescent charged with grievous bodily harm, and ignoring the caste-system in which the nursery of that infantile-libidinal beginning was set is about as much to the point as trying to quench the thirst of a man lost in the Sahara by redrawing his faulty maps.' Or it goes like this: 'empathy, warmth, and genuineness role-played for the benefit of some inadequate client will no more make up for the inadequacies of the social and educational system which produced him than a shot of morphine will compensate for an amputated limb.' Or like this: 'to counsel a woman for an anxiety condition when she is on an 18-months waiting list for the gynaecological repair of a condition causing her discomfort and anxiety helps her somewhat less than a health service without waiting lists.'

The critics state their case bluntly and uncompromisingly. The British pamphlet *Case Con*, published by revolutionary social workers, attacks the social work establishment in every one of its issues. For the uninitiated let me explain that *Case Con* is a take-off name to ridicule a respectable former social work journal called *Case Conference*. You will no doubt observe the allusion to the alleged crass hypocrisy of the whole idea of social casework. *Case Con* sums up its position by declaring its opposition to the use of social workers as tranquillisers and agents of social control, who thereby help to buttress the present system. In the US there is a multitude of groups (Perucci, 1974) and of publications from *Insurgent Sociologist* to *Radical Therapist*, which strike similar and even more strident notes. The *Radical Therapist*, for example, demands a radical reappraisal of the individualistic and therapeutic orientation to social ills:

'Therapy today has become a commodity, a means of social control. We reject such an approach to people in distress. We reject pleasant careers with which the system rewards its adherents. The social system must change. But to be true instruments of change therapy and therapists must be liberated from their own forms of oppression. Nor is it enough to pursue a medical model and try to develop popular programs to "treat the masses". Therapists must understand their place in the changing social and political reality; thus therapy must become more politically aware. No therapist, no person, can claim detachment from social contact. Each human act is a social and moral statement: a political fact . . . ' (Anon., 1970).

Writers on counselling are much aware of these interpretations of their function. Arbuckle (1970) observes that 'counsellors and counsellor educators appear to be agreeing more and more that the function of counsellors can no longer be limited to individual and small group counselling . . .' Moore and Margolis (1970) writing in the same journal as Arbuckle report on the attitudes of the high-powered panels set up by the United States Federal Government to study the Pupil Personal Services and tell us that the members of the panel saw 'the psychologist as one more establishmentarian'. Moore and Margolis go on to say that 'the social worker is often viewed now as the establishment's enforcer, the snooper, and the keeper of the bureaucratic gates'. The panel members describe the counsellor 'as a "sorter" who insures that the poor, the black, and the Chicano will not be exposed to roles and futures above the level of competence, as perceived by the counsellors.'

Almost an identical point is made by the New York journal, *Social Work*, where we read:

'The detoxified addict, phenothiazine-controlled mental patient, and rehabilitated convict have much in common, e.g. lack of job opportunities, imminent dependency, and a high probability of returning to the deviant sub-culture. Without massive changes in opportunity structures, treatment and rehabilitation perpetuate myths. Motivating clients to train for a job that does not exist is dishonest' (Segal, 1972).

The resoluteness and the righteous certainty of this statement are impressive: you, counsellors, are not really change-agents but agents of the *status quo*. You must take a long look at the personalist roles you have been playing and snap out of them. The notion of being a personalist change-agent is a sham, but you can redeem yourselves by changing your role-conception and by becoming political change-agents. It is reiterated by the critics that there must be a liaison and a marriage between the personalist and political roles, though it is clear to all concerned which of the partners is going to be the male chauvinist pig. But assuming that the liaison is an equitable one, is a hybrid – a judiciously balanced personal-political role – a possibility? My view is that these two roles are incompatible. A fusion between the two roles, such as 'radical counsellor' or 'radical psychotherapist', is a chimera, rather like a 'fire-fighting stoker' or 'abstemious addict'. One stands in wonderment in front of this composite figure, this double agent, this sphinx with a compassionate feminine face and with a lion's claws. Admittedly, one is somewhat reassured by the thought that hybrids do not reproduce themselves. No doubt, my psychological hypothesis that the two roles cannot be fused is capable of being tested. But until such time as it is falsified, I should like to offer the following reasons why I regard the movement to politicise the counselling profession as mistaken:

**1.** The personalist orientation of counselling demands a strong preference for relating oneself to another by a single-minded cultivation of openness, of receptivity, and of *listening*. Political initiative and action demands a display of certitude and determination and a habit of emphatically *telling*. Counselling is always tentative; political action is tentative much less frequently and only when tactics dictate it – otherwise it is peremptory.

**2.** The personalist cultivates a style and a philosophy of non-directiveness, and even if this expresses a mere aspiration and not an accomplished fact, it is an influential and infectious aspiration. The political actor's style is the style of the advocate, the protagonist, and the persuader.

**3.** The political role is Machiavellian: people are treated as means to abstract or at least impersonal ends, such as 'the welfare of the community' or 'the prosperity of the state'. The personal role addresses itself to clients who are ends in themselves. 'To be a leader of men', said Havelock Ellis, 'one must turn one's back on them.'

**4.** A good deal of the political role-playing is acted out on the stage, in front of multitudes, audiences, and committees: the platform performances are totally impersonal and the caucus performances tactical-manipulative. In other words, the political performance is either a histrionic or a courtroom kind of performance in response to a larger or smaller aggregation of unspecific people, whilst the personal performance is always in response to the unique and concrete presence of a single person.

**5.** The political role aims at conclusive and statutory results. Changing the system is changing the rules, the relationships, and the structure of relationships. In the personalist orientation the aim is invested in the ongoing personalist action, in the process of pursuing a goal.

**6.** The political actor questions the moral legitimacy of the counselling function altogether and indeed has no place for individualistic orientations in his scheme of things. The personalist agent, on the other hand, does not reciprocate with the same deprecatory allusions of irrelevance or counterproductivity. The counsellor does not as a rule cast doubt on the *raison d'être* of the political agent.

**7.** The political radical must begin by attacking what there is, criticising and denouncing. To change the system he has to marshal all his available ire and venom against it. The very inertia of his radical critique carries him into sceptical and even cynical diagnoses – such as, for example, that counsellors are entrepreneurs or mercenary agents rather like stockbrokers or scrap iron dealers, or that counsellors practise for the good of their souls and require clients as mere intrumentalities to achieve their own personal salvation. The personalist counsellors, on the other hand, must work on the benign assumption that their own empathic, warm, and positive approach is genuine, for without this genuineness they know that they would be ineffectual. Of course, they may self-consciously set out to be genuine, and this willed genuineness would be self-defeating, but for the well-known voluntaristic truth that a deliberate and willed application can be and is self-fulfilling and self-validating.

This last item in the list of distinguishing features has an important corollary: whilst the radical critique tends to debunk the very virtues of personal service without which it could not make his own utopia plausible (Halmos, 1974), the intensely humanistic sensitivity of the counsellor is entirely capable of making him into a recruit for the radical cause. This is so even at the level of reflection: for the political radical and the critical sociologist, scepticism about human motives is prophylactic; for the counsellor, it is toxic.

### CONCLUSION

The central paradigm of the counselling ideology is that an accurate empathy, a non-possessive warmth, and genuineness welded together in a global personalistic orientation are the essence of practice and the pivot of theory. This is so, even when the counselling purports to be behaviouristic. The affirmation of this central paradigm is an act of faith, and the faith of the counsellors is thus a dominant and decisive characteristic of their function.

But this faith is intensely personalistic and is certainly at variance with the commitment of those who equally fervently believe in the supremacy of political intervention. According to these, man's kindness to man is a by-product of the system's kindness to man. I have argued that there is room in this world for both points of view to co-exist and for their respective professional roles also to co-exist. I pleaded that any attempt at a hybridisation of the roles was a mistake. By all means intensify your efforts to politicise those whose talents and predilections lie in the direction of impersonal political action. But no social system, least of all the favoured utopias, can come about and subsist without a generously staffed personal service to individuals. Above all, the whole *raison d'être* of the visionaries of social betterment is that they help in the creation of societies in which human relations are empathic, warm, and genuine. Therefore baiting those who make it their profession to practise these virtues, however haltingly and gropingly, is hardly a sensible position to take up.

## NOTES

[1] Naturally, the concept of insight too cries out for a definition, and to avoid a lengthy digression I should like to cite my definition of it which I offered some seventeen years ago: 'insight is the individual's ability to relate the effect of a present experience to that of a past one provided that the latter determines the basic quality of the former' (Halmos, 1957). Whether 'insight-eliciting' is achieved through a scrutiny merely of a presenting situation (secondary insight) or through some persistent probing into the earlier history of the individual (primary insight) will not break up the unitary concept of 'counselling' in my definition. Whether the counsellor seeks only secondary insight for his client or primary insight, he is a counsellor (Halmos, 1957).

## REFERENCES

Anon.: 'A Manifesto'. *The Radical Therapist*, Volume 1 No. 1, April-May 1970.

Arbuckle, D.S.: 'Educating Who for What?' *Counselor Education and Supervision*, Volume 1 No. 1, 1971, pp. 41–48.

Beevers, R.H., and Cronhelm, E.: 'The Role of the Counsellor in the Open University'. In *Student Counselling: Preparation, Roles, Functions and Status*. Proceedings of the Fourth Conference on Student Counselling, University of London Institute of Education, 27 February 1973 (mimeo).

Bergin, A.E.: 'The Effects of Psychotherapy: Negative Results Revisited'. *Journal of Counseling Psychology*, Volume 10 No. 3, 1963, pp. 244–250.

Bergin, A.E.: 'The Evaluation of Therapeutic Outcomes'. In A.E. Bergin and S.L. Garfield (eds.): *Handbook of Psychotherapy and Behaviour Change*, pp. 217–270. New York: Wiley, 1971.

Carkhuff, R.R.: 'Training in Counseling and Psychotherapy: Requiem or Reveille?'. *Journal of Counseling Psychology*, Volume 13, 1966, pp. 360–367.

Fiedler, F.E.: 'A Comparison of Therapeutic Relationships in Psychoanalytic, Non-Directive, and Adlerian Therapy'. *Journal of Consulting Psychology*, Volume 14, 1950, pp. 436–445(a).

Fiedler, F.E.: 'Concept of the Ideal Therapeutic Relationship'. *Journal of Consulting Psychology*, Volume 14, 1950, pp. 239–245(b).

Halmos, P.: *Towards a Measure of Man*. London: Routledge, 1957.

Halmos, P.: *The Faith of the Counsellors*. London: Constable, 1965(a).

Halmos, P.: 'Behaviour Therapy'. *Discovery*, November 1965, p. 62(b).

Halmos, P.: *The Personal Service Society*. London: Constable, 1970.

Halmos, P.: 'The Moral Ambiguity of Critical Sociology'. In R. Fletcher (ed.): *The Science of Society and the Unity of Mankind*. London: Heinemann, 1974.

Krumboltz, J.D.: 'Promoting Adaptive Behavior: New Answers to Familiar Questions'. In J.D. Krumboltz (ed.): *Revolution in Counseling*. Boston: Houghton Mifflin, 1965.

Marcuse, H.: 'Repressive Tolerance'. In R.P. Wolff (ed.): *A Critique of Pure Tolerance*. London: Cape, 1969.

Moore, D., and Margolis, G.: 'A Review of the Leadership Training Institutes for Pupil

Personal Services'. *Counselor Education and Supervision*, Volume 10 No. 3, 1970, pp. 219–223.

Nelson, B.: 'The Psychoanalyst as Mediator and Double Agent: an Overview'. In M.C. Nelson (ed.): *Roles and Paradigms in Psychotherapy*, p. 3. New York: Grune and Stratton, 1968.

Newsome, A., *et al.: Student Counselling in Practice*. London: University of London Press, 1973.

Perucci, R.: 'In the Service of Man: Radical Movements in the Professions'. In Paul Halmos (ed.): 'Professionalisation and Social Change'. *Sociological Review Monograph*. No. 20, 1974, pp. 179–194.

Pierce, R.M., and Schauble, P.G.: 'Toward the Development of Facilitative Counsellors: the Effects of Practicum Instruction and Individual Supervision'. *Counselor Education and Supervision*, Volume 11 No. 2, 1971.

Rogers, C.R.: 'The Necessary and Sufficient Conditions of Therapeutic Personality Change'. *Journal of Consulting Psychology*, Volume 21, 1957, pp. 95–103.

Rogers, C.R.: 'The Process Equation of Psychotherapy'. *American Journal of Psychotherapy*, Volume 15 No. 1, 1961, pp. 27–45.

Segal, B.: 'The Politicisation of Deviance'. *Social Work* (New York), Volume 17 No. 4, 1972, pp. 40–46.

Skinner, B.F.: *Science and Human Behavior*. New York: Macmillan, 1953.

Truax, C.B.: 'Effective Ingredients in Psychotherapy: an Approach to Unravelling the Patient-Therapist Interaction'. *Journal of Counseling Psychology*. Volume 10 No. 3, 1963, pp. 256–263.

Truax, C.B.: 'An Approach to Counselor Education'. *Counselor Education and Supervision*, Volume 10 No. 1, 1970, pp. 4–15.

Truax, C.B., and Mitchell, K.M.: 'Research on Certain Therapist Interpersonal Skills in Relation to Process and Outcome'. In A.E. Bergin and S.L. Garfield (eds.): *Handbook of Psychotherapy and Behavior Change*. New York: Wiley, 1971.

Whitehorn, J.C., and Betz, B.: 'A Study of Psychotherapeutic Relationships between Physicians and Schizophrenic Patients'. *American Journal of Psychiatry*, Volume 3, 1954, pp. 321–331.

Wolpe, J.: 'Behaviour Therapy'. *Discovery*, November 1965, pp. 62–63.

Wrenn, C.G.: 'Foreword'. In J.D. Krumboltz (ed.): *Revolution in Counseling*. Boston: Houghton Mifflin, 1966.

# THE PERSONAL AND THE POLITICAL
## LÉONIE SUGARMAN

### POSTSCRIPT

Paul Halmos died several years ago and so I feel especially fortunate to have heard him in 1974 deliver a version of his paper 'The Personal and the Political' at the Sixth International Round Table for the Advancement of Counselling in Cambridge. It was a stimulating and provocative presentation, and none of its fire is lost in the transformation from the spoken to the written word. Its inclusion in this volume is a tribute to Halmos's memory. This postscript differs from the others in that it is not written by the author of the paper to which it refers, and so, obviously, it cannot represent a personal statement of how the author's ideas have changed and developed. Rather, it is a brief assessment of the current status and relevance of some of the key issues Halmos addressed.

Halmos's assertion that counsellors use their personality 'to bring about changes in the personality of another by modifying the other's self-image' is not seriously contentious. It is inherent in the preference for the term 'person-centred' rather than 'non-directive' counselling. It is also indicated in the continuing emphasis in counsellor training and professional development on self-reflection along the lines of: Which clients do I find difficult to work with, and why? What is it in me that helps and hinders my work with a particular client? How are my feelings for a particular client influencing the therapeutic benefit of the counselling for the client? By the same token, the power of the personality of the counsellor to influence is indicated in traditional psychoanalysis where analysts deliberately avoid giving of themselves so as to facilitate patients' projection. Acceptance of Halmos's assertion also implies asking which approach is appropriate for which counsellors, as well as for which clients and/or which issues.

A second strand of Halmos's thesis (the pivotal role played by the trinity of empathy, warmth and genuineness in all forms of counselling) was a precursor of the search for commonalities across different models of counselling that has since occupied considerable research energies. Whilst the question of whether these person-centred qualities are sufficient to produce therapeutic change in clients is still debated, there is general agreement that they are, at the very least, instrumental in building an effective working relationship based on trust and respect. It is not surprising, therefore, that they are found in the practice of effective practitioners, irrespective of the attention they are given in any theoretical orientation which the counsellor imbibes. Halmos criticises such eclecticism, arguing that one cannot add apples and pears. Maybe so, but it is possible to have a fruit salad where the flavour of each fruit gives something to the whole whilst still retaining its distinctiveness.

A controversial element in Halmos's comments on the personalistic 'core conditions' is his assertion that they are articles of faith – believed, but unproven and unprovable. Debate continues as to whether and how the core conditions of counselling can be measured and analysed, but developments in qualitative and process research methodology have challenged the imperialist position of the experimental paradigm. Different types of knowledge, in addition to that derived from scientific experiments, are somewhat more readily acknowledged than in the early 1970s. Even if no resolution is achieved, debating the measurability of the core conditions challenges us to examine the bases of our convictions and attempt to tease out the role of personal values and value judgments. That what we do is not value-free is, again, an idea which has grown in acceptability. The values (or personality) of the counsellor are reflected in the theoretical approaches and techniques to which a counsellor is attracted.

A third strand in Halmos's paper concerns the condemnation of the personalistic orientation by political activists and the pressure on counsellors to become more political. These issues impinge, if anything, more acutely on members of the helping professions in the 1990s than in the 1970s. At the personal level, counsellors doubtless still grapple with moments of self-doubt: Am I really helping? Does what I do really make any difference? In view of the enormity of the task of overcoming the restricted opportunity-structures of many client groups, such doubts reflect a realistic assessment of the limited amount that any one individual or, indeed, profession can achieve.

During the last two decades there have been many calls for the expansion of the counsellor's role beyond work with individual clients, and it is now virtually impossible for most practitioners to restrict themselves in this way. The squeeze on resources and the calls for accountability have meant that increasingly counsellors have had to learn how to fight for their own patch. Whilst counsellors may not like this element of their role – they went into the profession to help individuals, not to fight political battles – this is not to say they cannot learn how to fulfil it. There can be eclecticism if not integration. The personalistic and political roles can co-exist, although the partnership may be stressful. In fighting for the right to operate on the basis of the values central to the counselling enterprise, counsellors can employ the strategies of the political activist. Time and energy spent in fighting the system is, of course, time and energy taken away from work with clients. Counsellors may not like this, but they have been forced to learn how to do it.

I have regularly returned to Halmos's paper ever since its publication, and it is one which I recommended to many generations of Masters degree students. By no means everyone agreed with what Halmos had to say. Some, indeed, became quite angry with his assertions. But the passion of his exposition is energising and the issues it raises are important. 'The Personal and the Political' jolts readers into considering or re-considering the values, assumptions, aspirations and limitations of counselling and counsellors. In the same way as counsellors cannot do their clients' work for them, so all counsellors must travel the road of becoming and being a counsellor for themselves. 'The Personal and the Political' can help to propel them along this path. It is, perhaps, this above all else that keeps the 1974 paper by Paul Halmos as relevant today as it was nearly twenty years ago.

## MENTAL HEALTH AND EDUCATION:
## COUNSELLING AS PROPHYLAXIS

### PETER P. DAWS

*Though school counselling is concerned primarily with prevention rather than cure, in practice the urgent needs of the wayward and the sick leave little time for genuinely preventive work. Furthermore, effective prophylaxis in the strong sense of laying foundations of robust mental health, competence and well-being in* all *children must involve the whole school to some degree, and particularly a team of willing and able teachers working along with the school counsellor on curriculum development in personal and social education. Though the needs of the few can be met by one-to-one counselling, the needs of the many will be answered only through group work. Trained counsellors must take the initiative in such work. They will retard the mental health movement if they permit their colleagues to feel complacently that the appointment of a school counsellor is an ample school contribution to the objectives of preventive psychiatry. Mental health is every teacher's business.*

It has been repeatedly emphasised since the beginning of the school counselling movement in the mid-sixties that its purpose is prevention of breakdown rather than the rescue of those who are already casualties, and that it is intended to serve the normally occurring needs of all children and not the psychotherapeutic needs of a disturbed, unhappy few. A number of factors have been responsible for this prophylactic conception. One important factor was the initiative of the National Association for Mental Health, which was then preoccupied with finding an appropriate form of expression for its concern with the preventive rather than therapeutic aspects of its work. Seminars were held in Bristol (1963) and in York (1966) under the chairmanship of Lord James of Rusholme, attended by a small but varied group of professional workers in the fields of medicine, education, psychology and social work, to consider the school's responsibility for protecting and promoting the mental health and well-being of children. They recommended that school counselling be considered as one potentially valuable contribution to the protection of the mental health of children (NAMH, 1970).

In addition to the NAMH's concerns, there were other reasons for the emphasis on the problems of *normal* children. It was for instance necessary to allay the anxieties of some psychiatrists and psychologists who feared that counsellors in their enthusiasm might undertake psychotherapeutic tasks with very disturbed children and perhaps also delay the referral of

First published in the *British Journal of Guidance and Counselling*, Volume 1 No.2, July 1973.

such children to specialist psycho-medical services. It is also clear that those who began the training programmes at the Universities of Keele and Reading in 1965 had an essentially educational rather than clinical view of the purposes to which trained counsellors would address themselves, all rather neatly and simply summed up in those days as *educational, vocational* and *personal.* Today, there are approximately ten courses claiming to be school or college counsellor training programmes to some extent. They are very varied in their content. Some claim to prepare counsellors 'to do something' for disturbed pupils; none of course prepares counsellors to 'treat' such pupils. All would claim to be concerned with preventive work in the field of mental health.

## DEVELOPMENTAL COUNSELLING AS PROPHYLAXIS

Of the theoretical models available at the time when the first British courses in school counselling were set up, that of developmental counselling seemed to fit best the preventive and protective spirit. The writings of Wrenn (1962) and Tyler (1961) have particularly familiarised us with this model. In the course of their development all children are confronted with a series of challenges and transition points which they must adjust to, master, or come to terms with in some way. In Tyler's descriptive phrase, these are opportunities to progress or regress. All children experience the rapid physical changes of puberty and must come to terms with their dawning sexuality. All must work through a changing relationship with adults and authority, including parents, as they move through adolescence, and all must find an identity, if only to face and accept what the world has imposed upon them. All must feel their own way into the adult, post-school world that will be much less considerate and forgiving than school. Furthermore, each child confronts these common challenges and stresses from his own unique standpoint and must therefore find the answers that best suit him. Instruction in universal remedies and solutions is not enough; there is need also for individual counselling if young people are to extract the maximum profit in personal growth from these challenges and not be at times overwhelmed by them. Where there is readily available to young people a counsellor who has considerable understanding of the developmental hurdles that lie before them, including the less certain or predictable ones like bereavement, it is assumed that such young people are enabled to grow into strong, mature personalities better able to withstand life's pressures. They have been protected from the crippling consequences of suffering overwhelming stress unaided.

Such briefly is the theoretical viewpoint of developmental counselling. It has the appearance of idealised and professionalised *parenting* in its purposes, though the counselling relationship through which these objectives are achieved is much more like *befriending*. Basically, the intention is to encourage and protect the child's development not by excluding the pressures of life but by helping him to cope with them and the potential impediments to his development. One would hardly quarrel with the theory. But in practice, one is unlikely ever to achieve the numbers of counsellors that such an ambitious conception implies. They are not likely to in the United States either. In Britain, the transition from school to work or to higher education is the only common developmental hurdle that we have recognised as requiring the guiding help of professional expertise, and even here there are not yet many schools where educational and vocational guidance aspires to – let alone achieves – a very lofty ambition.

## COMMON COUNSELLOR ROLES AND THE PREVENTIVE PRINCIPLE

The reality of the counsellor's current position is that he commonly finds he is the only trained person to serve 800 or more pupils, and is given only a part-time counselling brief anyway. In such circumstances, what expression can be reasonably given to the notion of counselling as preventive work? More often than not, crisis-counselling occupies most of his time. He may be asked to 'deal with' the most disturbed children in the school on the grounds that this is where the greatest need lies and that his training fits him better than anyone else in the school to understand them and help them. Most counsellors see the fatuity of attitudes that proscribe them from attempting to do anything for disturbed pupils – on the grounds that their training is inadequate – but which exhort them as teachers to do what they can for such pupils in the classroom. The counsellor may therefore undertake supportive work with such children, working in close collaboration with the specialist psychomedical services and perhaps also with parents. Certainly a strong case could be made for such a therapeutic counsellor (*vide* Maguire, 1971), but such work can only be termed preventive on the grounds that terrible situations should at least be prevented from becoming unendurable.

Another kind of role that the counsellor may find himself pushed into, though he will resist it strenuously, is dealing with all the school's misfits: that is, those whose behaviour is institutionally and perhaps even socially unacceptable – the truants, the persistently violent, the anti-authority nonconformists, the underachievers and poorly motivated, and so on. Most counsellors will resist such a brief partly because they see themselves as identifying and responding primarily to children's needs and problems and only secondarily to those of the school, and partly also because the counsellor's task is made difficult if not impossible if he is perceived by pupils as another arm of the school's disciplinary process. Again, it is straining the notion of prevention to apply it to remedial work with the deviant, the delinquent and the maladjusted, even though it is evident that disapproved behaviour is often a symptom of excessive strain and disturbance.

Perhaps the commonest role that is given the counsellor – and which he fashions for himself – does qualify as prophylaxis, but only in the weakest sense of that term. The counsellor attempts to identify, with the help of colleagues, all cases of distress and disturbance. The more serious cases are referred to the specialist agencies; the walking wounded are helped in school, either by himself or by a colleague to whom the pupil has preferred to take his problem. The preventive element here lies in the assumption that most psychiatric disturbance begins in small remediable ways and can be prevented by vigilant early detection and helpful intervention. It is a role that only weakly expresses the preventive principle, because an attempt is made to identify the needs not of all children, but only of those who are already flying distress signals. It is always crisis-counselling. Its image is clinical rather than educational.

Of course, prophylactic mental health services in education need not focus upon pupils. They can choose instead to focus upon environmental inadequacies and stresses, intending to remedy the former and alleviate the latter. Much pupil disturbance for example originates in the home, in the inadequacies and hostilities of parents. Some school counsellors prefer to become school-based home-visiting social workers, feeling that in doing so they are getting at the roots of a pupil's disturbance. Others, with a taste for diplomacy and with a sense of compassion for a faltering and ailing colleague, attempt to do what they can for those teachers who are producing more than their fair share of unhappy and hostile pupils. Such milieu therapy, such environmental manipulation and rectifica-tion, is again prophylactic only in the weakest sense. It derives from responding to those children who are already in the process of breaking down.

Another common counsellor role is centred upon careers work (educational and vocational guidance) and provides a very partial and fragmentary expression of the purposes of developmental counselling. To have helped pupils to make wise educational and occupational choices is to have prevented some potentially serious cases of maladjustment and personal misery. Because of the narrowness of its focus of concern, however, it too cannot be said to be a very strong expression of the preventive principle, however generally useful it undoubtedly is.

Thus despite the emphasis that has been consistently put upon the preventive as distinct from the remedial character of school counselling by originators, theoreticians, trainers and practitioners, one finds only secondary attentiveness to the processes and objectives of prevention in the common counselling roles that have emerged. This is partly the result of counsellors being a scarce resource. To identify and respond to *all* the personal developmental needs of children would require thousands of counsellors. We have, perhaps, 300. Furthermore, it is predictable and perhaps justifiable that in the competition for benefit from a scarce resource the needs of the disturbed and unhappy should have priority over the less pressing ones of the competent and the confident. But perhaps we should question the view that individual counselling is the main or the most appropriate vehicle for the achievement of mental health objectives in schools. In the end counselling must restrict itself to attempting only what it most appropriately can, and we must desist from claiming for counselling more than this. What is left undone should at least be very evidently so, and counsellors should be prepared in co-operation with other staff to seek more appropriate ways of achieving those prophylactic purposes for which one-to-one counselling proves to be less suited or too costly.

### LEVELS OF PREVENTIVE WORK

The counselling movement with its emphasis on preventive work in the mental health field has followed by little more than half a century the inauguration of the School Health Service, whose concern has been to protect the physical health of children. The pioneering example of that service provides a useful guide for the development of sound prophylactic measures by those concerned with protecting and enhancing the mental health of children. The provision of school meals, milk and health education has added significantly to the benefits obtained from routine medical inspection of all pupils. By the same token, mental health provision must do more than merely screen the total school population regularly for signs of distress and maladjustment (a modest level of provision that we are still far from achieving). It must make positive steps to provide healthy children with insight and skills so that their vulnerability to breakdown is reduced. To change the medical analogy: a mental health equivalent of inoculation is needed, providing whatever will increase the child's protection against the adverse effects of stress. Of late, there have been visionary moves to bring mental health more explicitly within the prophylactic purposes of the School Health Service (Francis, 1966). The coincidence of such progressive thinking and the development of school counselling services makes it doubly ironic that the School Health Service is to be disbanded in 1974 and its medical and social work components relocated within hospitals and social service departments. If preventive mental health work is to be taken seriously by schools, the starting-point is to recognise especially *vulnerable* children – those who are particularly *at risk* in some sense or other. There are three main classes of vulnerable child: (**a**) those who will be subject to some special form of stress or risk, such as immigrant and coloured children, the handicapped, the sexually active, children in care, the immature school leaver, the bereaved, etc.; (**b**) those whose capacity for coping with normal stresses is atypically low – that is, delicate children and dull children; and (**c**) those whose deviant and delinquent behaviour will bring down upon them the wrath and the censure of the rest of us. If children within these categories can be identified before they are showing evidence of adaptive stress (though of course deviance and delinquence are often themselves distress signals) some genuinely preventive work can be undertaken. They can be helped to understand in advance the kinds of challenge and stress that lie ahead for them, and can be given the insights and competences they specifically need to deal with them effectively. Such work will require a teaching or group guidance approach rather than individual counselling, though counselling will be an invaluable support service.

But the strongest expression of the preventive principle in secondary school work is that devoted to the personal and social education of *all* pupils, for such work genuinely attempts to anticipate the developmental needs of all children, or at least those needs that are universal. It is an economically sensible alternative way of meeting the objectives of developmental counselling outlined at the beginning of this paper. It lacks only the sensitivity that counselling would have of responding to the unique individual needs of children. It implies such areas as health and sex eduction, moral education and personal relationships, social educa-tion, careers education (including self-awareness work, decision-making, and uses of leisure), and so on. It implies that time will be found on the timetable, that competent and willing staff will be available for the innovative curriculum planning that is required as well as for doing the work. It also implies a considerable opportunity and responsibility for the counsellor, who can help his colleagues appreciate the mental health objectives of such work and the ways in which they are most effectively achieved in group work. This requires of the trained counsellor a co-ordinative function and an educative one as far as his colleagues are concerned.

Finally, it must not be overlooked that environment-focused (as distinct from pupil-focused) preventive work is possible and desirable. If all children were wanted children, welcomed by emotionally secure and loving parents, mental health casualties in our society would be more than halved. This implies a very ambitious conception of parental education far beyond the counsellor's or even the social worker's insinuation into a disturbed home on behalf of a reactively disturbed child. Similarly, great benefits would accrue to the mental health of children if schools were purged of unnecessarily stressful values, customs and practices, and staffed by caring and vigilant teachers. This, too, implies a degree of institutional change and of attitude change in many teachers that goes far beyond the friendly quiet word with the harassed and fractious teacher. Though one cannot ask counsellors to involve themselves in the emotional education of parents-to-be, except as part of the upper school's personal and social education programme, it is legitimate to ask them to find acceptable ways of introducing their insights and their values to colleagues for their consideration. After all, counsellors are in the best position to evaluate the impact of the school and of individual teachers on pupils. They can say where the shoe is pinching. It is long-term work and should only be undertaken with modesty and humility, but the counsellor's potential value as an agent of change on the educational scene may prove to be his most important long-term contribution to preventive psychiatry.

### CONCLUSIONS

Let us summarise the observations, the arguments and the recommendations:

**1.** Pupil-focused preventive work has three levels which in increasing order of strength are (**a**) the deviant and the distressed, (**b**) vulnerable children, and (**c**) *all* children. Few counsellors go beyond the first stage except to be involved in educational and vocational guidance.
**2.** Contextual or environment-focused preventive work has two main

areas: the school and the home. Here, too, what is done by counsellors is frequently remedial rather than preventive: help for an irascible teacher or intervention in a disturbed family. Counsellors should find opportunities to acquaint their colleagues with their philosophy, their values and their insights so that mental health objectives may become more explicitly evident in the ethos of the school.

**3.** The pressure of coping with the immediate and the urgent is likely to keep counsellors crisis-oriented and therefore only weakly involved in prophylactic work, the major contribution to which is more likely to be personal and social education programmes and not individual counselling. It follows that if the counsellor is to put his training to serve prophylactic purposes in a stronger way he must take the initiative in guiding teams of colleagues and in co-ordinating their endeavours. The counsellor should also try to make time to be personally involved in the personal and social education programme. It will serve to introduce him to his possible clients and it will refresh him for the more emotionally draining work of counselling the distressed.

There is a real danger that the prophylactic role of the counsellor has been so widely emphasised and disseminated that the minimal sense in which most counsellors serve preventive ends (a situation unlikely to change very much) will go unrecognised. Heads of school may then feel that the mental health needs of their school are being adequately met by the trained counsellor. In fact, a strong prophylactic programme is not so cheaply achieved. It requires a team of suitable teachers, curriculum planning and a share of the timetable for all children. It would be a pity if the gap between the counsellor's prophylactic image and the realities of his work was allowed to retard rather than enhance the rate of progress in developing a positive educational programme to give all children sound foundations to their mental health.

Finally, a postscript. A paper on counselling and the implications for education of preventive psychiatry must at least question the assumption that the secondary school is the most appropriate place to start making special provision for the protection and enhancement of the mental health of children. Quite evidently, many cases of serious adolescent disturbance could have been identified during the primary school years and more effective help given. If suitable primary school teachers were offered something analogous to the counselling training now available to secondary school teachers, the mental health movement in education could be helped to spread effectively down to the youngest pupils. Three purposes could be considered: (**a**) the prompt identification of disturbed children, (**b**) the early involvement of parents in any work that is undertaken, and (**c**) the development of suitable personal and social education programmes. This way it may be possible to bring help to those parents who cannot readily admit their own inadequacies or their children's disturbance and who resist their children's referral to a child guidance clinic. The coming dismemberment of the School Health Service gives an added urgency to the development of a primary-school-based mental health movement.

### REFERENCES

Francis, H.W.S.: 'The Medical Examination of Children in Relation to the Prevention of Mental Ill-Health'. *The Medical Officer*, Volume 116, 14 October 1966, pp. 209–214.

Maguire, U.: *The Effectiveness of Short-Term Counselling on Secondary School Pupils*. PhD thesis, University of Keele, 1971.

National Association for Mental Health: *School Counselling*. London: NAMH, 1970.

Tyler, L.: *The Work of the Counselor*. New York: Appleton-Century-Crofts, 1961.

Wrenn, C.G.: *The Counselor in a Changing World*. Washington: American Personnel and Guidance Association, 1962.

# MENTAL HEALTH AND EDUCATION: COUNSELLING AS PROPHYLAXIS

### PETER P. DAWS

## POSTSCRIPT

Half our population will have only hazy memories at best of the values that informed educational developments in the 1960s, a halcyon decade of individualism, tolerance and optimistic belief in the perfectability of man. The prophylaxis paper was written in a professional climate that took for granted that teachers were firstly teachers of children and only secondarily teachers of subjects. Children's personal, social and moral development were considered no less the responsibility of schools than their scholastic development. There was a deeper understanding of the world of children, more empathy with the stresses they faced and the suffering they experienced, and a consequently greater sense of the *in loco parentis* (supplementary parenting) role that schools had to bear. Schools were becoming persuaded of the need to provide courses on such topics as health, sex, careers, practical communicative competence, oral as well as written (not merely 'compositions'), and decision-making. The term 'personal and social education' was becoming familiar. 'Life skills' was still some years away; 'gender education', 'multicultural education', 'economic awareness', 'assertiveness training' and 'empowerment' even further distant.

The school counselling movement, one expression of the child-centred initiative of the 1960s, was still in its infancy, still unfamiliar other than as a strategy for addressing the needs of the 'walking wounded': the unruly, the depressed, the under-motivated, the bereaved and others who did not conform or who were in obvious difficulties. To ensure sensible school practices and appropriate strategies of staffing and in-service preparation, a common conceptual framework was needed to relate the quasi-therapeutic provision for the faltering few, through interviews (pastoral care, guidance and counselling), to the classroom provision that addressed the personal and social developmental needs of all children. The Schools Council supported this child-centred trend with a number of curriculum development projects, including the widely influential Humanities Project (Stenhouse *et al.*, 1970). Its recommended blueprint for careers education also appeared at that time (Schools Council, 1972). The emergence of child-centred purposes and practices seemed set to gather momentum in our schools without neglect of traditional scholastic purposes.

But the momentum faltered. 'Black Papers' (see e.g. Cox and Dyson,

1969a; 1969b) protested the loss of traditional single-minded scholarly pursuit and the devotion of valuable school time to 'mickey mouse' subjects, but they were not at the time particularly persuasive, for the achievement of school-leavers in public examinations at O- and A-levels had been consistently rising throughout the 1960s and would continue to do so through the 1970s. Where was the evidence of a decline in standards? More significantly, the oil crisis occurred in the early 1970s to accelerate our economic decline. Government was bereft of effective policies to reverse or arrest it. At such times, scapegoats are sought. In 1976, James Callaghan, fuelled by Shirley Williams, opened the Great Debate and secured broad assent across Parliament to his charge of educational decline and neglect of the requirements of the labour market, and also to his diagnosis of their causes. When he left office with the change of government in 1979 after the Winter of Discontent, the task of denigration and reform passed to another able woman with scores to settle with Elizabeth House.

The emphasis in educational reform since 1979 has been on curriculum updating, particularly in science and technology, the reaffirmation of traditional values, learning objectives and methods of instruction ('back to basics'), and the establishment of a marketing approach to parental selection of schools, based on published assessment of how well pupils have been enabled to achieve the scholastic goals set for them by the nation. Whatever one's views of such priorities and criteria of school assessment, the pressures upon teachers that have resulted have offered precious little classroom or teacher time to spare to help children come to terms with the challenges of their own biology, personal relationships and complex social requirements. Only in the cross-curricular themes are such matters prescribed: health (including sex) education, careers education, and economic and industrial education. Unfortunately, the suggestion that health and sex can be addressed within the science syllabus reinstates a 1940s view that these topics are largely a matter of physiology and plumbing, a view found wanting and discarded in the 1950s. Furthermore, it has yet to be demonstrated in the face of considerable professional scepticism that adequate learning can be achieved in the cross-curricular themes. The pressures that teachers currently feel in covering the requirements of the subject syllabuses in the time available to them suggests that they will find little time to refer to these themes even when they are competent to address them, which itself implies a daunting programme of in-service training to cultivate competence and enthusiasm.

Teachers, who recognise that children preoccupied with personal difficulties and anxieties are in no frame of mind to address core subjects with any effective enthusiasm, deplore the neglect of vigilance to ensure the well-being of all children, and deplore also their enforced abdication of surrogate parental responsibility where children show evidence of the need for help. In addition, the requirement to relate to parents as consumers whose custom must be persuaded by 'performance indicators' has made more difficult the development of the co-partnership role, which had been seen as a promising route for the delivery of care – though in truth, state schools still had a long way to go to gain acceptance among parents of the co-partnership model (Schools Council, 1968). Sadly, teachers also recognise that the world of children and the developmental guidance and support available to them today are not noticeably improved since the 1960s. We do not know whether the extent of child abuse, including sexual abuse, has increased in recent times, though public awareness of it certainly has. The sexual mores of the young were not in those pre-pill days as precocious as they now are: at risk of contracting genital herpes as well as cervical cancer, not to mention AIDS, in addition to the more long-standing STDs. Single-parent families were fewer before the divorce rate soared; so was the extent of maternal employment. The current clamour for pre-school provision is fuelled not by a Plowden-inspired concern for children's development but by women's demand for a safe and cheap place to dump their infants so that they may be freed to work. The latch-key kids of yesterday are now more numerous but no longer excite concern.

The country that does not care for its young destroys its future. Since mediaeval times, Europe has been affronted by England's indifference to, neglect of and brutality towards its children (Pinchbeck and Hewitt, 1969; 1973; de Mause, 1976). Briefly, the conscience of the nation asserted itself through the two public services of education and social work. Neither was allowed to exercise such unwontedly child-centred values for long, and both have been publicly chastised for their temerity. When the inadequacies of our parenting become too obviously a focus for public examination, the nation rallies to divert attention and condemnation towards other targets, however implausible. One may confidently assume that our schools are safe from the intrusive clamour of child-centred theorists and practitioners for the foreseeable future.

## REFERENCES

Cox, C.B., and Dyson, A.E.: *Fight for Education*. London: Critical Quarterly Society, 1969(a).

Cox, C.B., and Dyson, A.E.: *The Crisis in Education*. London: Critical Quarterly Society, 1969(b).

de Mause, L. (ed.): *The History of Childhood*. London: Souvenir Press, 1976.

Pinchbeck, I., and Hewitt, M.: *Children in English Society* (2 volumes). London: Routledge & Kegan Paul, 1969; 1973.

Schools Council: *Young School-Leavers: Enquiry 1*. London: HMSO, 1968.

Schools Council: *Careers Education in the 1970s*. Working Paper 40. London: Evans/Methuen, 1972.

Stenhouse, L., *et al.*: *The Humanities Project: an Introduction*. London: Heinemann, 1970.

# COUNSELLOR INTERVENTIONS IN ORGANISATIONS

KENNETH GRAY

*A counsellor occupies a potentially facilitative role in an organisation. Ways in which the counsellor can facilitate the development both of individuals and of the organisation of which they are members are discussed and are related to organisational transitional change and fantasy life. Possible interventions with individuals, groups and the organisation are outlined with the accent on development.*

For many counsellors, counselling is about working with clients in the one-to-one session; in some settings, the work focuses on the concerns and development of a small group of clients. Most workers see counselling, other than the purely supportive kind, as a more or less intensive activity which is designed to assist *individuals* to change their way of life, to look at aspects of their behaviour and attitudes which are ill-founded, and to put them in closer touch with reality. In this sense, counselling is a creative attempt to help the client to recognise maladaptive behaviours and to change them.

Nelson-Jones (1982) recognises that the target of counselling interventions may be (**i**) the individual, (**ii**) the individual's primary groups, (**iii**) the individual's associational groups, or (**iv**) the institution or community. This present paper addresses (iv) by considering counselling which is targeted on the organisation as a whole though is mainly implemented via work with individuals and groups.

In so far as the organisation has a life of its own, beyond the individual lives of its members, it can relate to people and thereby can be a recipient of transference. Members of an organisation project qualities on to their organisation as if it possessed those qualities. This transference relationship to the organisation means that people unconsciously enact attitudes, desires and expectations from the past towards the organisation, and that the latter becomes invested with psychological meanings. Such concepts have been utilised in the management of medical centres and psychiatric hospitals (Levinson, 1969; Simnel, 1929; Reider, 1953).

In this sense, the focus of the counsellor's activity can be on psychodynamics which are multipersonal. The development of this theme requires a consideration of the developmental nature of organisations, the psychological factors which block change, and the kinds of counselling interventions which may be helpful in assisting change.

First published in the *British Journal of Guidance and Counselling*, Volume 12 No.1, Jan. 1984.

## THE DEVELOPMENTAL NATURE OF ORGANISATIONS

Organisations are tools to help man continue and develop certain kinds of behaviour which are, thereby, encouraged and directed. To this end they have characteristics such as an internal structure and sub-systems which carry out particular functions. A college, a hospital, or a voluntary agency, for example, may have a staff hierarchy with given roles and a designated or evolved formal system of internal government. Its action parts may be departments which carry out the professional work. There will also be other parts which are no less significant, such as management sub-systems. Most organisations have a chart which shows the roles of staff and gives an indication of their levels of responsibility and of the particular tasks they are designated to perform. Because the roles are filled by people, however, such a chart gives only a superficial view of the actual organisation.

Organisations cannot change and develop without people changing. Sometimes it is possible to enhance the organisation by reassigning roles to match people, and sometimes people leave and are replaced by others more suited to the immediate requirements of the system as a whole and the roles they are to fill. Frequently, though, there is a limit to the reassignment of roles and to recruitment. Yet organisations need to change in order to meet the changing needs or demands of their environment. Organisational responses which have been successful in the past may be inappropriate to the present.

An organisation is a complicated interplay of reality and fantasy for its members. Anyone seeking to facilitate the development of the organisation has to take account of this. It does not mean that reality and unconscious fantasy must necessarily both be considered when applying one's model of change. But if the counsellor works with the consciously perceived and consensually validated reality, then he or she should not be surprised by factors which arise from fantasy. Conversely, anyone working with fantasy only, or indeed treating both reality and fantasy as fantasy (as some techniques appear to require), will also need to take account of mutually agreed reality.

**Organisational development: a reality view.** The attention paid by Jung (Jacobi, 1967) to the single transition of the mid-life, which he called the crisis of 'individuation', has been recently extended by Levinson *et al.* (1978). It is claimed that individuals pass through a series of life transitions and that their ability successfully to negotiate these is determined, in part, by their previous transition experiences. A counsellor who is aware of this will be able to assist a client to recall previous transitions and to identify the skills acquired then in order to make use of them in the new transition. Furthermore, acquiring knowledge of the internal nature of transitions will alert the counsellor to possible feelings present in the client. With a view to making use of the same approach with the organisation, it is appropriate to ask whether they too pass through transitions, and how. This subject has been investigated by Greiner (1972), who considers that growing organisations move through at least five distinct phases of development, each being a relatively stable growth period which ends in a transition crisis. Similarly, Chandler (1962) has concluded that organisations may undergo phases of development because of the strategies they evolve to meet new external demands or threats. Other studies (Starbuck, 1971; Fouraker and Stopford, 1968) show that organisations develop, broadly speaking, through at least four identifiable phases with further phases related to ever-increasing complexity.

*Figure 1:* **Phases of organisational development**

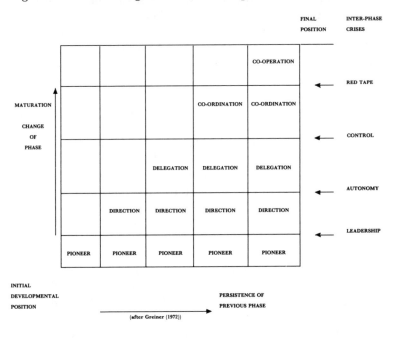

The phased development of an organisation is shown in figure 1. Note that each phase of stable growth is succeeded by a crisis for the organisation. At the outset, the individual pioneer is seeking growth through creativity, and communication within the organisation is frequent and informal. As growth occurs, however, the pioneer finds that increasing complexity burdens him or her with responsibilities of management. This *crisis of leadership* can be resolved by appointing a general manager who has the requisite skills. This person will introduce a structure which is more suited to the needs of the organisation and will direct the work of junior staff, who lose autonomy in decision-making and become specialists. This period ends with the *autonomy crisis*, in which the latter (having more direct knowledge of the work than the senior staff) seek substantial rights in decision-making.

If this crisis is not surmounted, juniors will have feelings of futility and leave. The organisation itself may fail. If the general management are able to delegate, so that control is given to more junior managers, then a new period of growth can occur; the decentralised scheme means that people on the ground can respond more quickly and senior staff concentrate on the exceptional cases. After some time, the general management will become anxious over losing control in a highly delegated system in which some individuals and groups will have begun 'to do their own thing', moving away from the principal concerns of the organisation as a whole. This *crisis of control* is sometimes tackled by increased centralisation, but the more successful organisations effect greater co-ordination between their sub-units. There will be investment in organisation-wide planning and review schemes, and some units might be merged. This proliferation of schemes eventually causes a *red-tape crisis* in which bureaucratic procedures take precedence over innovation. It seems that the only successful way forward is to stress interpersonal co-operation; Greiner (1972) suggests that this phase 'emphasises greater spontaneity in management, action through teams, and the skilful confrontation of interpersonal differences'. A matrix structure is often implemented: in other words, teams with relevant membership focus on appropriate tasks.

There are several consequences to be noted by counsellors concerned with the healthy development of the organisation in which they participate. First, it is important to identify *where* one's organisation is in the process of development. The needs of individuals may depend on this siting. During the pioneer phase, individuals will need opportunities for direct and informal communication with others, and some staff will need counselling about their suitability to take on the main leadership roles. In the autonomy crisis, members of the organisation will need to understand what delegation means to them: for example, taking more or fewer decisions, accepting or giving up responsibility. An obvious time when counsellors can intervene is at the red-tape crisis, when co-operation between people can be strengthened. Of course, it is not always clear which phase of development an organisation is in. The crisis boundaries are often diffuse, rather than sharply defined.

Second, the counsellor must recognise that there will be *persistence* of ways of working from previous developmental phases. For example, delegated powers may be overruled, anxiety over confronting differences in a co-operative venture may encourage regression to bureaucratic procedures and centralisation, and there may be insufficient surrender of autonomy in a co-ordinated phase. If the organisation is embedded in a larger structure, as a college is in a local education authority, then its opportunities to move from one phase to another may be limited. In the co-ordination phase in a college, bureaucratic procedures may be partly imposed by the local authority, and it may then be more difficult to overcome the red-tape crisis. This particular issue is connected with that of *boundary management*, considered below. It falls to the general management to operate at the interface between the local and the larger organisation.

Third, when an organisation resolves one crisis, the solution it finds will inevitably lead to another one. In other words, the solution becomes the problem. Solutions which were good in one phase of development may not work in the next. However, an awareness that there will be a crisis to be overcome will be helpful. In addition, the experience of having gone through a prior transition may be valuable in itself. A great opportunity exists for the counsellor actively to teach colleagues about the development of their organisation and to intervene at times of crisis to encourage people to take stock and, by seeking positive changes, to avert a deterioration of the organisation.

**Organisational development: a fantasy view.** At and between the transitions in development, individuals will also have unconscious perceptions of the organisation and their own unconscious fantasies. Many of these are constructed in order to reduce personal anxiety – neurotic, existential, or psychotic. From a client-centred viewpoint, neurotic anxiety arises when the person has a subconscious perception of a threat to the consistency of his or her self-concept. Various defences, such as denial or distortion, may then be invoked (Stefflre and Grant, 1972). In psychoanalytic terms, ego defences such as simple projection, regression, introjection and displacement will be summoned (Freud, 1966). In the case of simple projection, the individual will attribute to another person or persons a characteristic that is in fact his or her own: incompetence or feelings of hate may be so projected. The organisation, because of its size and diversity of membership, provides a wide range of suitable recipients for such projections. Through this mechanism, the person making the unconscious projection diffuses his or her own boundaries, confusing both others and him or herself about what is within and without.

In this situation, action may be based on unreality and it may happen that events are then the 'neurotic problems of individuals writ large in organisational terms' (Soper, 1972, p. 703). The neurotic defence is a disability of the individual in the organisation. It leads to a lack of effectiveness because it obscures reality. The counsellor's role here is clearly to help people be aware of the projections they use and of the ones they take on board. Ways of doing this include, for example, encouraging people to test out how real are their projections on to specific individuals and groups, by offering alternative views of how the other person is, and using the empty-chair technique of Gestalt therapy.

The fear of non-being is the context for the individual's existential anxiety (Shaffer and Galinsky, 1974). In the organisation a person may vigorously assert his or her independent existence to combat this fear, but the energy may be poured solely into the assertion itself and not be available for the tasks of the organisation. Some people, however, seem to be able to make a considerable identification with the organisation: their existence is assured, providing the organisation itself survives. In such cases, energy may be directed into organisational survival; whether there is any external need for its continuation will be ignored. Here, too, there is an opportunity for counsellors to question or confront people.

Jacques (1955; 1976) advances the view that all social systems are used as defences against psychotic anxieties – in particular, persecutory and depressive anxieties. He considers that individuals in organisations externalise the unconscious impulses which would otherwise produce psychotic behaviour and that these are then shared in a fantasy organisation through the mechanisms of projective and introjective identification by its members. Projective identification is more than simple projection in that an active interpersonal effort is involved to place into another person aspects of one's inner state (Langs, 1977). A suitable choice of recipient may be induced to take on such aspects (Laing, 1971) and to act them out. In defending against paranoid anxieties, the individual puts his or her bad impulses into particular persons in the organisation. Alternatively, people may introject these bad impulses from the pool of fantasies. In defending themselves against unconscious depressive anxiety, which occurs when there is an unconscious realisation that other people contain both good and bad impulses, members of an organisation will tend to split its personnel into a good majority and a bad minority. An actual majority group may then emerge through a process of introjective identification with each other and by a joint attack on some scapegoat group. In transactional-analysis terms, the symptomatic outcome is known as the 'Aren't they awful' game (Berne, 1963) and is frequently heard in organisations.

There are specific consequences of anxiety-reduction fantasies and perceptions in educational establishments. Some teaching staff frequently split 'ordinary teachers' as a majority group from the 'bad' administrators and managers, and some students split all staff into a minority group. In cases where divisions are not based on here-and-now issues, confrontation between the majority and minority groups is not likely to be productive. Instead the counsellor's role here is (**a**) to maximise real communication between members of majority and minority groups so that fantasy has less opportunity to take over, and (**b**) to help individuals and groups to confront each other over their real differences and to assist them to resolve these through negotiation (and power if relevant) rather than allow differences to be denied or defused.

A special case of depressive anxiety defence occurs when a person leaves the organisation permanently, in that the bad impulses may be projected into him or her and thus taken away completely. A gift to the leaver is often seen as a recompense for carrying away the bad material. Similarly, a new member of the organisation may be in receipt of good impulses from others. New counsellors may enter in this way and trade on these impulses for a time, but it is likely that as they become real people to the other staff, the projections will be taken back.

The flow between an organisation and its environs, and between the sub-units of the organisation, is regulated by boundaries. These boundaries are equivalent to the boundaries which distinguish the individual self from the world of other selves and things. For an organisation, the flow of ideas, feelings or materials across a boundary is mediated by relationships between people. A highly permeable boundary which is mediated by considerable traffic will lead to an organisation or sub-unit which is not clearly distinguishable from its surroundings. For integrated student services units in polytechnics, for example, an optimum boundary permeability exists between ineffectively low levels of activity associated with a 'hard' boundary and very high levels of traffic associated with a 'soft' boundary, leading to a loss of group identity for the unit staff. This may be seen as the conflict of external pressure and group cohesion (Berne, 1963).

Traffic across such boundaries enhances the effectiveness of the organisation if no disagreements, feelings of anger, etc. are selectively withheld. If there is withholding, then the lack of negative feedback may render an organisation or sub-group complacent and vulnerable to catastrophe. As far as internal boundaries are concerned, one of the counsellor's interventions will be to help junior members express their disagreement with senior members, and to assist senior members to accept such disagreements. This will mean *seeking* to counsel organisation staff where disagreements exist *in potentia*, or are being denied or diffused. A further task is clearly to make people aware of the importance of the management both of their own boundaries, and of the organisation and sub-unit boundaries.

### FACTORS BLOCKING CHANGE

Apart from the defences particular to individuals, many other factors inhibit positive change in organisations. These may be expressed in various ways at the conscious level, for example by focusing on conspicuously heavy costs, by requiring the effects of change to be predictable, by asserting that certain matters are beyond question of change, and by seeking the perfect solution while not implementing any solution. These irrational responses, however, are merely symptoms of concealed or underlying conscious or unconscious wishes.

At the conscious level, individuals may have goals which conflict or appear to conflict with those of the organisation. In cases where the individual is unable to make this overt, he or she may block change by various means. The counsellor's role is to help the person look at whether this conflict can be brought into the open, and if so, how. The counsellor's role may then be extended to facilitate discussions in which these matters may be resolved. In some cases it may not be possible to compromise or otherwise meet the individual's needs, but he or she is then in a clearer position to make choices about the future. Apart from real and perceived conscious needs, the work of the unconscious may produce obstructive symptoms in organisational life. The use of the organisation to reduce neurotic and psychotic anxieties has been discussed. In addition, mental material which belongs to the *collective unconscious* of people in the organisation may be taboo. This may include considerations of social class, race, or religious belief.

### ESTABLISHING INTERVENTIONS FOR THE COUNSELLOR

It goes without saying that nothing written here is intended to direct counsellors away from their work with individuals; such work, in addition to its personal worth to the client, will have valuable spin-off for the organisation. Nor is it being advocated that the counsellor should take on the role of an organisation-development specialist, who is usually invited in to solve some particular organisational problem, and so begins with a role accepted to some degree by the organisation, or at least its general management. The counsellor's entry to the organisation may not be regarded in the same light. Some organisations would prefer to see their counsellors as dealing with the unfortunate, but inadequate, casualties of a system which works to the benefit of most of the people most of the time. The counsellor will then have to develop an acceptance of these further aspects of his role and to establish a brief to work with organisational issues, as well as with individuals and groups of people.

A number of role factors are to be considered when making interventions from inside an organisation as a member: these are role definition, role stress, role overlap, and other people's roles. In attempting to work with the organisation, the counsellor is extending or re-defining his or her role. This may provoke conflict with the senior person who traditionally defines the counsellor's role. Conflict may also arise with persons who perceive themselves as occupying overlap or contiguous roles such as staff development officers, organisation development consultants, and specialised trainers. Role stress is the experiencing of mismatch between the counsellor's definition of his or her role and the definitions given by others. Consequently, it is important to negotiate with others in order to reduce such conflict and stress. This may include negotiating about the proportion of the counsellor's work time to be spent on this new function, and requires an internal study of competing needs.

The possible strategies for the counsellor fall into four areas: working with individuals, with groups within the organisation, and with the whole organisation; and, just as important, seeking support for him/ herself. Each of these will now be considered in turn.

In *working with individuals*, the counsellor may be able to intervene with the person in the most senior role and/or with other persons. Organisation-development specialists often refer to the importance of 'top down' operation. By this they usually mean gaining the confidence of the people at the top of an organisation and making sure they *do* desire change, that they *own* their request to the specialist. It is highly desirable however that the top managers do not spell out what the changes should be in detail, as this reduces the number of degrees of freedom for change in the organisation, and limits the opportunities for subsequent work by the specialist. As a counsellor working with the person in the senior role, some of the goals will be to:

❖ *feed back* data from counselling and elsewhere indicating *how* the organisation functions;
❖ *clarify* with him or her whether this is how it should perform;
❖ *establish* the discrepancies between actual and desired performance;
❖ *contextualise* the organisation's position in terms of possible schemes of development;
❖ *seek* a commitment to set up a change process;
❖ *assist* the client to understand and deal with his or her anxieties about change and its consequences, and to contain that anxiety so that detailed but possibly precipitate detailed changes are not implemented or attempted;
❖ *review* possible ways of engaging in organisational change (Sherwood, 1972).

The author believes that if the person in the senior role in the organisation is unwilling to see that change is desirable, then beneficial changes of substantial dimensions cannot be brought about through negotiation. Willingness to institute change is not, however, enough; he or she must be able benevolently to encourage change without specifying the details. A basic trust and optimism in the change process has to exist or be engendered, while at the same time containing the competing anxieties.

In intervening with other persons, it is important to note that a few individuals will be so rigid and inflexible as to be almost unsusceptible to pressure for change. It may be that these individuals really do need their defences for psychological stability, and that manipulating them or forcing them to adjust will severely disrupt their lives. Such people should be respected and permitted to exclude themselves. Of course, difficulties arise in very small organisations when this is so, and then the needs of the organisation will inevitably be balanced against their personal needs, particularly where they occupy key roles.

Most people, however, are prepared to review themselves, their role, and what changes are desirable. One way of undertaking this is for the counsellor to work with small groups of staff, or individuals. This kind of work with individuals and groups requires not different skills and understanding from the counsellor – it is still counselling but it involves the counsellor in a more active organisational role. Besides being available to those members of the organisation who are in distress or have personal concerns, he or she has to identify individuals and categories who hold importance for the development of all. Naturally, some people will present themselves for developmental work when a norm begins to be established, but in the early stages, the counsellor must take an active position. Some readily identifiable categories include those who are newly arrived, those who are about to leave, those who have taken on new functions or changed roles, those who fill more than one role, those who are actively seeking to change what is happening, those who have outstanding qualities, those who are managers, representatives, delegates etc., and those who seem to be in stasis. In these categories will be people who are aware, unaware and marginally or pre-aware of the significance of *personal development* for their personal effectiveness at work. Marketing of what the counsellor has to offer should take account of this.

In the case of the *aware person*, what he or she needs is usually a clear message about what is on offer and how it is relevant. At the margin of such awareness the *pre-aware person* is almost conscious of personal developmental needs, and if the right situation can be created by the counsellor, then sufficient insight can be achieved to go about meeting them. The right situation means opportunities for what Cox (1978) calls 'third level disclosures', which are not available readily to introspection.

Frequently this means helping people to make conceptual links between feelings and ideas of which they are aware and events in their work or elsewhere, be they past or present, and to provide opportunities to work through related cognitions and affects. This can be highly significant for the organisation. In one example, a staff member prosecuted vigorously a particular issue against his manager. In a discussion with the counsellor it became clear that, although some of this was grounded in current reality, a separable element was based on a difficult relationship with a previous superior *of the same name*. This connection had not, of course, been made, but was readily available. In another case, an individual was aware of his difficulties in confrontive and stressful situations involving people in authority. He had made some connection with difficulties with his parents in childhood and was able to recall traumatic experiences and express his feelings about them, freeing his intelligence for use in his current responsibilities. For these and other events to occur, the counsellor actively has to work at creating the opportunities. This means building trust, and offering conceptual input where this may help people make links.

The *unaware person* is not in the fortunate position of being able consciously to seek the services of the counsellor, although he or she may be referred or arrive as a result of unconscious promptings. The effective counsellor to the organisation will *recognise* and *offer assistance* in some way, and perhaps counsel such individuals. Unfortunately, recognition of a person's mental conflicts is often obscured because the unaware person's work provides opportunities for the release of energies which derive from internal conflicts. Manic overactivity, excessively competitive struggles, and the setting of achievement goals beyond realistic possibility, may all be obscured by the way the organisation functions. The counsellor's *recognition* of these events will be enhanced by noticing the normative values of his or her organisation relating to conformity/individualism, competition/co-operation, authoritarianism/democracy, and so on, which may serve to screen such conflictual symptoms in individuals. By way of example, the need to be maternal may be enacted by an indivdiual representing employees because the organisation behaves in a paternal mode; on the other hand, excessive maternal nurturing may be reinforced by an organisational norm that there can never be enough nurturance, as in *some* child-care establishments or social-work facilities.

In *working with groups*, it may be noted that there are two kinds – those which have an existence already, and those called into being by the counsellor. The former are likely to have some defined purpose in the organisation – for example, staff groups with a common task which involves them in working together – although there may also be informal groups, such as a religious study group meeting in the lunch hour. The difference between pre-existing and specially created groups is that the former *may* call upon the counsellor to help them in some way (perhaps to enhance their communication skills or to facilitate a higher level of trust between members), *or* the counsellor may identify them as groups whose receipt of counselling help would be potent for the organisation – for instance, all departmental managers. A group called into existence by the counsellor is a training laboratory but may develop into a group with an organisational purpose.

The kind of group work will depend on the counsellor's range of skills and interests, and what he or she feels comfortable with in the organisation. The author has offered T groups, encounter groups, seminars and talks, skills workshops, induction meetings, discussion groups, and video workshops. In the first example, the author offered a T group with the task of 'studying interpersonal relations here and now in this group'; enough staff responded to permit two groups to run in parallel for a full year, once a week. Although staff found the groups puzzling at first and were somewhat dismayed and anxious that the author offered no leadership in the expected sense, sufficient trust was developed that the group members could work on intimate aspects of their personal lives. Sometimes this was very painful for them and uncomfortable for other group members. One young staff member said, near the very end of the group, 'I feel that I've grown up in this group'; he is now taking a much more active part in the development of a part of the organisation in which he is interested.

*Working with the whole organisation* as a large group is as yet a relatively unexplored area. The dynamics of such groups have been mainly investigated by psychoanalytic workers (Kreeger, 1975) although some more recent work has been reported by Rogers (1980). The only occasions on which most organisations come together as a large group is when the members are to be *talked at* by someone, or for entirely *social* reasons, or when things have got so bad that *mass meetings* are called. In this section, we are not considering the above possibilities but the alternative of working with the large group without being in the midst of crisis.

The large group is an opportunity to allow some of the fantasies of individuals to be expressed and to be countered by reality. If the group can become safe enough, individuals may work on their own feelings in some depth. The author has jointly staffed four large groups of some 40 persons responsible for the peer management of a course, in which deeply held feelings were explored. It is most important for the large group to proceed at its own pace, and not be pushed by the facilitator into anxiety-provoking disclosures. Large groups contain massive potential for creative planning and have been shown to be able to manage their own work in highly creative and satisfying ways (Houston, 1980).

Working with the large group is also highly pertinent to the fantasy view of the organisation expressed above. The paranoid and depressive defence mechanisms are strongly aroused in most people in a large group. Because they are the earliest defences to be constructed in human development, they are strong and can easily give rise to unconsidered movements in the group dynamic.

*Professional consultative support* in individual counselling, whether it takes the form of supervision with a more experienced person or consultations with peers, is essential. The elements of the counsellor's work with the organisation are also enhanced by consultative support. Support will have at least the following components:

(**a**) opportunity to express feelings and ideas about the organisation and to explore them adequately;
(**b**) a common language with the consultant, since counsellors may find that they do not have the same vocabulary as organisational development specialists;
(**c**) exploration of the stresses arising for the counsellor from his or her own organisational role and role stress;
(**d**) recognition of the myths and rituals of the organisation;
(**e**) comparative input about other organisations or sabbatical visits to them.

## CONCLUSION

In this paper some information on the developmental nature of organisations has been given, and potential counsellor interventions with individuals and groups have been considered in the light of this information. The author hopes that the focus on organisational patterns may prompt other counsellors to review how they work with and within their organisational host, and by encouraging such review activity, enable counsellors to gain a greater acceptance of the organisational aspects of their role.

## REFERENCES

Berne, E.: *The Structure and Dynamics of Organisations and Groups*. New York: Ballantine, 1963.
Chandler, A.D.: *Strategy and Structure*. Cambridge, Massachusetts: MIT Press, 1962.
Cox, M.: *Structuring the Therapeutic Process*. Oxford: Pergamon, 1978.
Fouraker, L.E., and Stoppard, J.M.: 'Organisation Structure and the Multinational Strategy'. *Administrative Science Quarterly*, Volume 13 No. 1, 1968, pp. 47–64.
Freud, A.: *The Ego and the Mechanisms of Defence*. London: Hogarth, 1966.
Greiner, L.E.: 'Evolution and Revolution as Organisations Grow'. *Harvard Business Review*, Volume 70 No. 4, July/August 1972, pp. 37–46.
Houston, G.: *On Becoming a Self Directed Course*. London: South West London College, 1980 (mimeo).
Jacobi, J.: *The Way of Individuation*. London: Hodder & Stoughton, 1967.
Jaques, E.: 'Social Systems as a Defence Against Persecutory and Depressive Anxiety'. In Klein, M., Heiman, P., and Money-Kyrle, R.E. (eds.): *New Directions in Psychoanalysis*. London: Tavistock, 1955.
Jacques, E.: *A General Theory of Bureaucracy*. London: Heinemann, 1976.
Kreeger, L. (ed.): *The Large Group*. London: Tavistock, 1971.
Laing, R.D.: *The Politics of the Family*. London: Tavistock, 1971.
Langs, R.: *The Therapeutic Interaction*. New York: Aronson, 1977.
Levinson, D.J., Darrow, C.N., Klein, E.B., Levinson, M.H., and McKee, B.: *The Seasons of a Man's Life*. New York: Knopf, 1978.

Levinson, H.: *Reciprocation in Industrial Organisations and Health*, Volume 1. London: Tavistock, 1969.

Nelson-Jones, R.: 'The Counsellor as Decision-Maker: Role, Treatment and Responding Decisions'. *British Journal of Guidance and Counselling*, Volume 10 No. 2, 1982. pp. 113–123.

Reider, N.: 'Transference to Institutions'. *Bulletin of the Menninger Clinic*, Volume 17, 1953, pp. 58–63.

Rogers, C.R.: *A Way of Being*. Boston: Houghton-Mifflin, 1980.

Shaffer, J.B.P., and Galinsky, M.D.: *Models of Group Therapy and Sensitivity Training*. New Jersey: Prentice Hall, 1974.

Sherwood, J.J.: 'An Introduction to Organisational Development'. In Pfeiffer, J.W., and Jones, J.E. (eds.): *The 1972 Annual Handbook for Group Facilitators*. La Jolla, California: University Associates, 1972.

Simnel, E.: 'Psychoanalytic Treatment in a Sanatorium'. *International Journal of Psychoanalysis*, Volume 10, 1929, pp. 70–89.

Soper, E.: *Organisations in Theory and Practice*. London: Heinemann, 1972.

Starbuck, W.H.: *Organisation Growth and Development*. Harmondsworth: Penguin, 1971.

Stefflre, B., and Grant, W.H.: *Theories of Counseling*. New York: McGraw-Hill, 1972.

# COUNSELLOR INTERVENTIONS IN ORGANISATIONS
## KENNETH GRAY

### POSTSCRIPT

I was prompted to write the paper reprinted above in two ways. The first was through a conviction that I developed fairly quickly as a student counsellor that working with individual clients, while worthwhile for them and in itself, was not always the most cost-effective way of helping them and others potentially like them in the college. Spending all one's time with individual clients can lead to a lack of awareness of the processes of the organisation which provide the opportunities for the clients' particular neurotic, existential or psychotic imperatives to emerge. I am reminded of the anecdote of the person saving a whole series of people from drowning in a river who, recognising that these individual acts of heroism were proving repetitive, set off upstream to find out who was pushing them in or why they were falling in. It is my experience that sometimes the organisational river itself has been diverted by well-meaning folk who are unaware of the impact on individuals in its new path.

Second, I was helped to see the organisation as an entity by my work for six years on the staff of the South West London College counselling course (now transferred to Southwark College). The course provided one of the few (at the time possibly the only) Rogerian large-group experiences in counselling training in the UK. Students had the option of pursuing a very wide range of counselling approaches (psychoanalytic, transactional, existential, person-centred, etc.) but the course was peer-managed through staff and student participation in the large group, comprising 40 or more people. There was no initial timetable of workshops or other activities; the staff did not specify how or what work was to be done, but provided flexible structures through which decisions could be taken, and both individual and community contracts were made for learning and peer assessment. The work was resource-intensive but large numbers of people took the course and the waiting list was always long.

It was the experience of seeing quite primitive defences emerge in the large group (which was in essence an organisation at work in one room) that alerted me to the same processes in organisations such as colleges, particularly when they are going through unsettling periods of change. This experience was not confined to the staff role in a mainly student large group. The staff group itself was almost a large group when gathered together for residential staff meetings two or three times a year. In my view, it was often necessary for the staff group to work at – if not through – some fairly basic object-relations problems (for example, envy and jealousy) before these issues could be progressed in the course group with students.

I still hold to the view which I formed then that counselling training should always include some exposure to large-group process in a learning set-up because (**a**) most trainees will go on to use their skills in an organisational context of some kind and (**b**) the large group can allow trainees to experience and identify their more primitive responses which they can then take to supervision and/or therapy.

Another aspect of organisations which is worth reflecting on is that their complexity is not possible to resolve to a single point. When working with individuals, I often found that they talked about events which were not fully clear to me; but after a while, I realised it was not essential for me to understand them – merely enough that they were enabled fully to understand for themselves. As in the case of the individual, it is necessary to tolerate uncertainty and ambiguity when working with organisational content and processes.

Organisational change is almost always a change from one complex position to another. The new situation can appear simpler because of a revised perspective (rather like looking along ranks of soldiers on parade rather than through the rows, recognising the planets to be in the elliptical orbits of a solar system rather than Keplerian epicycles, or seeing Paris from an airliner instead of at street level) and at that moment of insight it is often possible to act effectively to steer the organisation (or large group). But the intervention made will result in change, and then insight becomes occluded, so one has to generate a new perspective.

As I became more experienced, I became more interested in managing organisations. At the same time, however, I saw that there were all kinds of pressures on leaders – on the Senior Tutor on the course and on College Principals – which I in my turn would need to experience and work with. Most of our understanding of leadership in organisations relates to hierarchy: most organisations are line-managed. But the course was not of this kind (though it has to interface with a line-managed college then and now), and the trend more generally was towards other structures – the matrix, team teaching, and colleges in which management responsibility was devolved to a larger number of staff and traditional departments did not exist. I wanted to understand how the pressures might exist in these various structures for the people who exercised leadership.

Some of these pressures arise from the nature of the tasks, whether the right functions have been assigned to the leader, and to what extent the organisation has been distorted from the ideal task-determined structure by personal interests. But the most interesting factor (from a counselling perspective) is the leader's personality and how that, in turn, may create organisational pathology which then impacts on potential clients.

I suspect that many managers have a strong obsessional streak. In moderation, this is helpful in its desire for clarity and order. But carried too far, it may hinder creativity in others through too much bureaucracy, and lead to an over-reliance on authority (which tends to reduce corrective feedback from staff). Under stress, this streak produces perfectionism: energy is bound up in seeking better solutions than the situation requires. It has been suggested (Kernberg, 1980) that the major regression force or stress is frustration of the leader's dependency needs. If the leader seeks to meet his or her dependency needs inside the organisation, then the special relationship(s) created may tilt the organisation away from the task structure. Hence, in my view, the importance of all leaders of organisations having external consultative arrangements.

Finally, I said in the paper that this interest in the organisation was not in competition with the organisational development (OD) specialist. I have revised that view. Organisational health is too important to be left to the specialist: it should concern us all.

### REFERENCES

Kernberg, O.: *Internal World and External Reality.* New York: Aronson, 1980.

# 3: EDUCATIONAL AND CAREERS GUIDANCE

# THE SOCIAL CONDITIONS, CONSEQUENCES AND LIMITATIONS OF CAREERS GUIDANCE

## KENNETH ROBERTS

*The recent influence of developmental theories of occupational choice upon guidance practice in Britain is criticised. It is suggested that people do not typically 'choose' occupations in any meaningful sense: they simply take what is available. Moreover, the career of the typical industrial worker cannot be meaningfully understood in terms of self-actualisation and implementing a self-concept: guidance work based upon these concepts is accordingly unrealistic. An adequate theory for understanding school-leavers' transition to employment in Britain needs to be based around the concept not of 'occupational choice', but of 'opportunity structure'. Guidance should concentrate not on raising unrealistic expectations, but on helping people to adjust successfully within the opportunity structures open to them.*

### DEVELOPMENTAL THEORY AND PRACTICE

At the grassroots the practice of careers work is never a simple application of academic theories. Organisational convenience, professional considerations and sheer practicalities inevitably intrude. Nevertheless, ideas can influence practice, and during the last twenty years the most influential ideas in the careers work field have undoubtedly been the developmental theories of occupational choice initially formulated by Ginzberg *et al.* (1951) and Super (1957). The appearance of these theories promised a much-needed shaft of light. Research was assembling a miscellany of data on topics such as how school-leavers learn about their first jobs, the satisfactions they hope to derive, and the sources of advice they feel to have been the most helpful. The developmental theories offered to place this otherwise embarrassing wealth of information into a meaningful order and, in addition to this, carried implications for guidance services that, in Britain, were fast becoming renowned for their ineffectiveness. The practice of vocational guidance had previously drawn its main theoretical inspiration from the 'square-pegs-in-square-holes' thinking derived from differential psychology. The developmental theories seemed to possess greater scientific validity in the sense of explaining ordinary vocational behaviour, and to suggest a wider range of guidance strategies.

The principal implications of the developmental theories for guidance

---

First published in the *British Journal of Guidance and Counselling*, Volume 5 No.1, January 1977.

strategies are two-fold. Firstly, they focus attention on attributes of the individual client – his self-understanding, knowledge of the world and aspirations – and suggest that vocational welfare will be enhanced by facilitating their development. Secondly, by insisting that vocational development be treated as a cumulative process analogous to other dimensions of psychological growth, in which the successful completion of early developmental stages is necessary before subsequent tasks can be effectively addressed, the theories draw attention to the early stages of vocational development as the time when the foundations can be laid for effective later maturation. Hence, in the context of other favourable forces, the popularity of the developmental theories has encouraged an intensification of careers work within education. The schools have begun to take careers guidance seriously. Today careers teachers are not only designated, but increasingly are specifically trained and organised in their own professional association. Concurrently, in the 1960s, the Youth Employment Service (now the Careers Service) became increasingly an educational service aiming to stimulate the development of careers programmes in secondary schools, rather than an employment service concerned with job-finding and following-up the vocational progress of young school-leavers.

In the course of a research project amongst careers officers around 1969 (Roberts, 1971), I discovered that the idiom of the developmental theories had become a conventional wisdom amongst the professionals. The careers officers were mostly emphatic about the need for a developmental approach, and virtually unanimous in their conviction that guidance should be a progressive rather than a once-and-for-all exercise. They were critical of their own Service's earlier crisis-counselling *modus operandi*, which they agreed did 'too little, too late', and saw themselves as shaping a new, genuinely educational form of guidance. They understood the need to play non-directive and essentially supportive roles in deepening their clients' self-awareness and knowledge of the world. The development of careers work in secondary schools, therefore, found widespread favour among them, though at the time the careers officers were rarely experiencing all-round success in their attempts to introduce such ventures.

The argument which will be presented in this paper is critical of these trends in careers work and of the theories that have lent encouragement to them. I shall argue that, as descriptions or explanations of how young people embark upon their working lives, the theories are false and inconsistent with the known facts, and that their prescriptions for careers work are therefore unlikely to have their intended benign consequences. Indeed, I shall argue that in some ways the prescriptions are likely to prove positively harmful, and – equally important – that they are deflecting scarce resources from where these resources would make a more useful impact.

## OPPORTUNITY STRUCTURES AND THE IRRELEVANCE OF 'CHOICE'

I used the developmental theories as a source of hypotheses in my own initial enquiries into the transition between school and work, only to conclude with strong reservations about the theories themselves (Roberts, 1968). I have found no cause since to change my initial conclusion: that a different type of theory employing *opportunity structure* rather than *occupational choice* as the key concept is required in order to understand school-leavers' transition to employment in Britain.

There are two major blocks of evidence which interpretations of work entry need to take into prominent account, and which are crucial in order to understand the conditions and limitations surrounding the practice of careers guidance. The first block revolves around the proposition that neither school-leavers nor adults typically choose their jobs in any meaningful sense: they simply take what is available. In western countries considerable lip-service is paid to the ideal of a free labour market. The direction of labour finds little favour; instead, we possess the concept of occupational choice. It may seem only common-sense to assume that this concept corresponds to real processes. But how much choosing actually occurs?

In practice, studies conducted in various parts of Britain have rarely found the majority of school-leavers entering jobs reflecting their stated preferences. In his Sheffield study, Carter (1962) found that only a third of the boys and a half of the girls entered the types of jobs they were aiming for when interviewed prior to leaving school. Similarly in London, Maizels (1970) found that only a third of her school-leavers obtained jobs reflecting their aspirations. To predict the type of job that a school-leaver will obtain, the most relevant information concerns not what he would ideally like to do, but his educational qualifications and to a lesser extent the occupational status of his parents, together with the local job opportunity structure (Central Advisory Council for Education, 1959).

Furthermore, the choices that are available to individuals are rarely difficult to make. Job preferences are not mere matters of individual taste but are determined by a system of stratification. From much of the material disseminated for careers guidance purposes, one would hardly imagine that we live in a society in which occupations are arranged in a hierarchy, the main structure of which is well-known and agreed among the public-at-large, including adolescents. Guidance materials written for secondary-school pupils stress how different occupations demand and allow for the expression of different interests, abilities and aptitudes. There is considerably less emphasis upon the inequalities in income, power and prestige around which other differences in values and life-styles crystallise to shape what is commonly known as the class structure. The relative desirability of different occupations is socially structured, and treating the individual's occupational choice as a problem requiring careful investigation and systematic guidance only mystifies the blunt facts of the situation.

Social-class differences combine with the role of the family as the normal agent of primary socialisation to generate considerable inequalities of educational and hence socio-economic opportunity with the result that few individuals move far away from the level of the social hierarchy into which they are born (Boudon, 1974). Despite the talk about deepening young people's awareness of the world in which they live, there are few signs that these aspects of social reality are accorded prominence in careers education: nor perhaps could they be, in any constructive way. Yet no-one operating in this area can realistically ignore the manner in which social-class differences pervade occupations, education and patterns of family life so as both to inhibit individuals' scope for genuine occupational choice and to limit the influence that careers guidance is able to exert.

Of course, the social structure allows some scope for individuals' aspirations to make a difference. The 16-year-old school-leaver with two O-levels may not qualify to become a surgeon or architect, but he enjoys a fair degree of lateral scope for choice amongst different industries and trades. Nonetheless, the room for manoeuvre available to any individual can become very circumscribed when he finishes his schooling. Young people are not equipped with a fully comprehensive knowledge of jobs even after following careers education courses. Furthermore, as the time to leave school approaches and passes, possibly after a number of unsuccessful applications and interviews, pressures to take any job that is offered soon become dominant. Although occupational choice is not just a myth, if entry into employment is to be properly comprehended at least equivalent emphasis needs to be placed upon the opportunity structures

created by the manner in which educational and occupational stratification entwine with the role of the family. These opportunity structures
constrain both individual school-leavers and careers advisers, and
operate whatever the inclinations or aspirations of the individuals
involved might be.

Once in the labour market, the most useful information for predicting
career movements concerns not people's aspirations but the types of jobs
they currently hold, and the connections between past and future jobs
become increasingly tight as individuals progress into their working lives
(Blau and Duncan, 1967). In general, patterns of job mobility amongst
young workers do not represent a gradual unfolding of ambitions. Job
changes are as likely to be away from as towards original aims (Carter,
1962; Maizels, 1970). The career patterns of beginning workers are best
explained as responses to the rewards of stability and mobility in different
occupations (Swift, 1973). Individuals climb ladders when they are
sufficiently lucky to enter occupations in which progressive careers are
available. For many young workers, however, there are no career ladders
to climb. During adolescence as during adulthood, many individuals are
destined to move laterally through a succession of jobs in order to
maximise earnings, cope with redundancy, alleviate boredom, reduce
travelling costs and realise other marginal benefits.

Given the phrase's everyday as distinct from its social science
connotations, the Careers Service has been sardonically mistitled for
many of its clients. Opportunity structures limit the genuine careers that
are available, restrict the scope for individual occupational choice, and
likewise circumscribe the role available for vocational guidance.

### ANTICIPATORY AND OCCUPATIONAL SOCIALISATION

The second block of evidence with which we have to contend shows that
for the typical industrial worker, his career cannot be meaningfully
understood in terms of self-actualisation and implementing a self-concept
and, therefore, that careers work based upon these notions is unrealistic.
It is more usual for individuals to have to tolerate a lack of fit between
their self-concepts and the occupations they practise. As Maizels (1970)
has observed: 'Since few occupations allow for the full use of talents, while
a large proportion of jobs for adolescents, as adults, require little
technical or other skill, any match achieved is minimal. In many cases it
depends upon the capacity of the individual to modify his inclinations,
and to function with many of his known and unknown talents dormant.'

Job dissatisfaction may not be widespread, but this is no testament to the inherently satisfying nature of the occupations that many individuals practise. It owes as much to human adaptability and the capacity of individuals to accommodate to work that offers few intrinsic satisfactions. Different jobs offer different types of rewards, and processes which reduce cognitive dissonance help individuals to concentrate upon whatever satisfactions happen to be available. The concept of occupational choice highlights one aspect of this process, portraying individuals as selecting jobs that promise the satisfactions they particularly value. The concept of occupational socialisation, however, draws attention to complementary and at least equally important processes. Socialisation is a life-long rather than merely a childhood process. It occurs at work just as significantly as in school and home. In their various workplaces, individuals are informally taught to look for, value and derive the particular satisfactions that the careers upon which they have embarked can offer. The instrumental orientations characteristic of most workers in routine assembly-line jobs may help to explain why they entered such employment (Goldthorpe, 1968), but they are also the consequence of adjustment to the reality of the situation (Beynon and Blackburn, 1972).

In occupations that are intrinsically satisfying and rewarding, such as medicine and social work, the job can become an individual's central life interest and pervade much of his leisure time (Parker, 1971). In such occupations, novices may learn to take a pride in their skills and eventually acquire professional identities (Merton, 1957). Elsewhere, however, occupational socialisation is more a matter of learning how to disengage from the task in hand and enjoy secondary gratifications, such as the company of one's mates or 'beating the system', that can make a tedious job tolerable (Beynon, 1973).

Socialisation is always a conservative process. Although it can occasionally transcend and reshape, the 'self' is initially and necessarily a product of social structures: hence the responsiveness of students' aspirations to their educational experiences. However little students in Britain gain from explicit vocational guidance, a hidden curriculum based around the processes of educational selection that operate throughout their school lives enables them to learn their places in the social pecking order. Distinct climates of expectation become associated with particular educational careers and are internalised by pupils, with the result that levels of aspiration are closely related to the types of secondary school and the streams within them through which individuals pass (Hargreaves, 1967; Ashton, 1973). Accordingly, students' aspirations can best be understood not as preliminaries to decisive occupational choices, but as products of anticipatory socialisation. Once in employment, under the influence of comparable processes, even school-leavers who do not fulfil their declared ambitions tend to modify their aspirations in line with their attainments and the values inherent in their occupational experience.

The implications of the above for careers guidance are considerable. Sociologists and psychologists inevitably stress different aspects of the process of work entry. The former's professional concerns lead to a stress upon collective tendencies: the ways in which certain types of people enter particular types of jobs. In psychology, in contrast, the focus is upon the individual, with interest concentrated upon how and why, given similar opportunities, different people enter different occupations. Both perspectives undoubtedly have something to contribute, but my concern is that an under-estimation of the importance of sociological processes biases the theory and practice of careers work.

In seeking to understand the entry into employment it is misleading to set a developmental process of occupational choice at the centre of the scene. A more realistic course is to conceptualise careers as unfolding into patterns dictated by the opportunity structures to which individuals are exposed, and to treat ambitions as reflecting the influence of the structures through which they pass, with job satisfaction depending upon individuals learning to appreciate whatever intrinsic or extrinsic rewards their careers can offer. This theory will not fit all situations, for all theories must necessarily condense a more complicted everyday reality, identify key processes, and accord prominence to those considered crucial. But the fit with reality is helpfully close, particularly in respect of individuals who enter employment immediately upon leaving school in contemporary Britain. Since these individuals comprise the majority of the population, this opportunity structure theory realistically sketches the context in which guidance must operate.

## THE ROLE OF CAREERS GUIDANCE

Possibly the most important truth to digest is that guidance itself – providing clients with information and advice and encouraging conse-quent reflection – functions within closely circumscribed parameters. In providing advice and job information, guidance merely lubricates more basic processes of occupational selection. Careers officers frequently remark that although they offer all the facilities of an employment exchange, they never actually 'place' anyone in employment: placement is done by employers. To careers officers this realisation is irritating since the constraints upon their own influence are so manifest and immediate. Counselling in an educational setting is less immediately inhibited, and appears therefore to offer greater professional satisfaction. No form of counselling however can create access to jobs that do not exist or from which individuals are structurally disqualified.

In the final analysis, therefore, guidance must be a matter of assisting individuals within the opportunity structures to which they have access. Vocational guidance cannot make jobs more rewarding, nor create employment opportunities for personal growth and development. No amount of guidance can change the realities of work in an industrial society. Extolling careers work in schools as if it could extend to all adolescents the opportunities for personal enrichment at work currently available to only a few, or to widen the horizons of individuals whose scope for occupational choice is presently limited, merely obscures the reality of the situation.

There is evidence that circumstances usher guidance into a lubricating role irrespective of practitioners' private inclinations and stated intentions. American sociologists have described the 'cooling-out function' that college counsellors find themselves performing (Clark, 1960), and have drawn attention to the 'educational decision-makers' whose actual as distinct from manifest role is to direct students along educational routes leading to later opportunity structures that they are judged capable of entering (Kitsuse and Cicourel, 1963). Casework is unavoidably socially conservative. It deals with individuals, and although it may influence them, it does not change social structures.

If the role of careers guidance is closely circumscribed, the corollary is that its impact must be marginal. This inference is supported by research findings (Rothney, 1958; Campbell, 1965). There is no study of school-leavers in Britain in which the Careers Service, careers teachers, or any other body offering vocational guidance has emerged as a major influence. This used to be treated as a ground for criticism. Commentators asked how the Youth Employment Service could be strengthened so as to increase its impact. A calmer interpretation, however, suggests that these criticisms are misplaced. The role of careers guidance is so structured by other influences upon the entry into employment that its own contribution must inevitably be incidental. Careers teachers and careers officers are not going to change fundamentally the forces which govern the movement of young people into work.

Rather than detracting from the potential importance of career work, however, acceptance of these realities makes it all the more vital that the strategies adopted should be those that will maximise the available gains. To do this we need valid theories correctly interpreted. My fear is that mistaken emphases in careers work could entail consequences that will admittedly be marginal but may nonetheless be unwelcome. Feeding students with the widest possible range of job information so as to broaden their horizons irrespective of their actual prospects may leave them less able to adjust to the opportunities they eventually find. Assisting all young people to acquire self-knowledge and crystallise related occupational self-concepts before they enter work may similarly leave them less adaptable when faced with the constraints of job availability. No harmony is guaranteed between individuals' aptitudes and occupational requirements, and guidance may have the effect not of closing but of widening the gap. Refusal to recognise the limited role that careers guidance can play will not change other social institutions for the better. The net result may be that young people will become less able to adjust to the world as it is.

### THE NEED FOR AN EMPLOYMENT SERVICE

Careers work should concentrate upon practical employment problems. This may sound obvious, but experience suggests that 'careers' is too readily transformed into an educational concern. Given the limited role that guidance can play, it is important that it be directed to the areas of most relevant need. There is indeed cause for concern that whilst careers work in schools has been intensified, the guidance of young workers – which could make a greater impact – has been neglected.

In many ways, the increasing development of school-based guidance services is discriminatory. Those who have the most to gain from such services are the students who prolong their education beyond the statutory leaving age. Apart from being the most in need of information to help them make competent educational decisions, it is they who have the greatest scope for occupational choice. Designing vocational services to meet the needs of these particular young people, however, adds yet further disadvantages to those already suffered by the educationally and occupationally less privileged.

Vocational embellishments in the school curriculum are not intrinsi-cally undesirable, but a greater need for the majority of young people, who leave school at the earliest opportunity, is to be offered an employment service that treats their employment problems seriously. As a result of being involved for over a decade in studying the vocational problems of young workers, I have become conscious of the lack of support available to them at the end of their school life and when they later seek to change their jobs – especially during periods of unemployment. Casualties of these crises are still often left unattended on the fringes of the labour market, and in danger of growing adrift from other social institutions. Such problems are growing rather than diminishing, as the recent NYEC working party's report demonstrates (National Youth Employment Council, 1974). The work of the Careers Service in this area has made little progress, and on balance has probably deteriorated over the last twenty years. Yet it is here that their services are most needed, and most likely to be effective.

Rather than offering general job information and encouraging the crystallisation of self-concepts, therefore, guidance should concentrate upon helping them to face the practical problems of working life. School-leavers need precise information about the jobs actually open to them and where they can be found. Dissatisfied young workers need similar information about alternative jobs, and realistic advice about the probably limited satisfactions they can expect to find in the other forms of employment available to them. Many also need help to adjust to the demands made upon them in working life.

All too frequently, however, such assistance is not available. Careers officers dislike crisis counselling. Their objections are understandable, but school-leavers face crises whether or not the Careers Service cares to respond. While we have a labour *market*, finding a job will always involve uncertainty, strain and tension. For over a decade the Careers Service has been disengaging itself from 'routine' placement and follow-up work. For school-leavers, however, finding a job has never been a routine matter; nor has job-changing for those already in employment. Yet when young people seeking jobs visit their careers office, their needs are often dealt with briefly by a clerk or employment assistant. Unfavourable impressions of the Service inevitably follow.

A good employment service means basically a good employment exchange service, closely linked to industry and able to provide its clients with the qualified attention they need. To some this may sound like turning back the clock and dismantling the progress of recent decades, for careers work has been fighting hard to lose its labour exchange image and to gain recognition as a basically educational service. It is indeed cutting across recent trends to suggest that there is nothing fundamentally wrong with labour exchanges provided their services are delivered effectively. But, as I have argued, there are grounds for disputing whether recent trends have been wholly in the right direction.

In short, guidance has a limited role to play. If it is to play that part effectively within the limitations set by opportunity structures, it is vital that it gets its aims and priorities right. In this context, the danger of the developmental theories is that they over-estimate the importance and scope of the individual's range of occupational choices. They consequently encourage the adoption of unrealistic aims, and fail to target resources to the areas of greatest need.

## REFERENCES

Ashton, D.N.: 'The Transition from School to Work'. *Sociological Review*, Volume 21, 1973.

Beynon, H.: *Working for Ford*. Harmondsworth: Penguin, 1973.

Beynon, H., and Blackburn, R.: *Perceptions of Work*. London: Cambridge University Press, 1972.

Blau, P.M., and Duncan, G.D.: *The American Occupational Structure*. New York: Wiley, 1967.

Boudon, R.: *Education, Opportunity and Social Inequality*. New York: Wiley, 1974.

Campbell, D.P.: *The Results of Counseling*. Philadelphia: Saunders, 1965.

Carter, M.P.: *Home, School and Work*. Oxford: Pergamon, 1962.

Central Advisory Council for Education: *15–18* (Crowther Report). London: HMSO, 1959.

Clark. B.R.: 'The "Cooling-Out" Function in Higher Education'. *American Journal of Sociology*, Volume 65, 1960.

Ginzberg, E., *et al.*: *Occupational Choice*. New York: Columbia University Press, 1951.

Goldthorpe, J.H., *et al.*: *The Affluent Worker: Industrial Attitudes and Behaviour*. London: Cambridge University Press, 1968.

Hargreaves, D.: *Social Relations in a Secondary School*. London: Routledge & Kegan Paul, 1967.

Kitsuse, J., and Cicourel, A.V.: *The Educational Decision-Makers*. Indianapolis: Bobbs-Merrill, 1963.

Maizels, J.: *Adolescent Needs and the Transition from School to Work*. London: Athlone Press, 1970.

Merton, R.K., *et al.*: *The Student Physician*. Harvard: Harvard University Press, 1957.

National Youth Employment Council: *Unqualified, Untrained and Unemployed*. London: HMSO, 1974.

Parker, S.: *The Future of Work and Leisure*. London: MacGibbon & Kee, 1971.

Roberts, K.: 'The Entry into Employment: an Approach towards a General Theory'. *Sociological Review*, Volume 16, 1968.

Roberts, K.: *From School to Work*. Newton Abbot: David & Charles, 1971.

Rothney, J.W.M.: *Guidance Practice and Results*. New York: Harper, 1958.

Super, D.E., *et al.*: *Vocational Development: a Framework for Research*. New York: Teachers College, Columbia University, 1957.

Swift, B.: 'Job Orientations and the Transition from School to Work: a Longitudinal Study'. *British Journal of Guidance and Counselling*, Volume 1 No. 1, January 1973.

# THE SOCIAL CONDITIONS, CONSEQUENCES
# AND LIMITATIONS OF CAREERS GUIDANCE
## KENNETH ROBERTS

## POSTSCRIPT

The 1977 paper was my ultimate contribution to a debate that began in the 1960s about the extent to which young people's occupational preferences played a causal role in their career development and, therefore, the extent to which individual guidance could affect outcomes. My contentions were: firstly, that career progression was determined primarily by the structural relationships between family backgrounds, educational attainments and processes of recruitment into the jobs available in local labour markets; secondly, that such consistency as existed between school-leavers' expressed aims and the jobs they entered was mostly due to aspirations being shaped by the same influences as actual opportunities, not to individuals genuinely choosing their occupations; and thirdly, that mismatches between aspirations and occupations entered were usually resolved by individuals modifying their aims.

To recollect that these arguments were not embraced warmly in careers guidance circles is an understatement. The implication was that guidance could have only a limited impact, and that pretensions such as bringing vocational self-actualisation within everyone's reach were simply unrealistic. My arguments were not accepted instantly by all the interested parties, but history seemed to resolve the debate in my favour at the end of the 1970s, though possibly only for the time being. The disappearance of school-leavers' jobs and their replacement by a succession of schemes and unemployment made it difficult to continue to argue that young people's choices were directing their career development.

It is rarely possible to attribute specific policy effects to particular research projects and publications. My arguments could hardly have lessened careers guidance's difficulties in gaining increased public funding. They could also have contributed to the political pressure for guidance to pay less attention to individuals' own interests and inclinations in preference to presenting the realities of labour markets. Devolving careers guidance budgets to employer-dominated Training and Enterprise Councils is likely to amplify these pressures.

I can speak more confidently about the opportunity structure theory's influence on research. The emphasis in studies during the 1980s was not on young people's choices but on how their opportunities varied by sex, race, educational attainments and, in particular, where they lived. It is perhaps noteworthy that the Economic and Social Research Council's 16–19 Initiative (see Banks *et al.*, 1992), which was centrally concerned with young people's routes into the labour market in the late-1980s, did not even measure its core samples' job aspirations, and yet there were as many psychologists as sociologists involved in this research.

I have always felt some guilt that the opportunity structure theory necessarily stresses the limitations rather than the scope for guidance to make a difference. Guidance can smooth most young people's (and adults') transitions into and within the labour market. With particular individuals, guidance undoubtedly can make a difference to career outcomes. The potential benefits of guidance are maximised when advice is related to placement, as has traditionally been the case in Britain's Careers Service, which explains its generally superior record against comparable services in other European and more distant countries. However, the main comfort from the opportunity structure theory for guidance practitioners is probably that failings during the transition into employment are not typically due to poor guidance but to lack of opportunity, and the crux of such problems in modern economies lies in socially defined success being available to only a few.

I have not changed my mind; I remain an advocate of the opportunity structure theory. A recent article in the *Sociological Review* (Roberts and Parsell, 1992) restates the theory, taking account of the changes in young people's opportunities in training, education and employment since the 1970s. On my reading of the evidence, the transition into employment has been restructured not destructured, and new courses and schemes have mostly been assimilated into longer-established relationships between social origins, educational success and employment outcomes. However, there has been one significant change: nowadays school-leavers' aspirations are often too distant from their immediately awaiting opportunities to be modified into alignment. So there are more young people than in the past who hope that their current occupations will be temporary. Needless to say, whether their hopes are realised will be more dependent on future trends in the structure of opportunities than on the strength of the individuals' desires – assuming, of course, that the theory really is valid.

## REFERENCES

Banks, M., *et al.*: *Careers and Identities*. Milton Keynes: Open University Press, 1991.
Roberts, K., and Parsell, G.: 'Entering the Labour Market in Britain: the Survival of Traditional Opportunity Structures'. *Sociological Review*, Volume 30, 1992.

# ARE CAREERS EDUCATION PROGRAMMES IN SECONDARY SCHOOLS A WASTE OF TIME? ~ A REPLY TO ROBERTS

### PETER P. DAWS

*Vocational guidance and the careers education programmes which vocational theorists currently argue should span the secondary school years imply that entry into employment is the outcome of choice processes exercised on significant differences among available jobs in respect of the talents they require and the kind and extent of opportunity for self-fulfilment that they offer. Because Roberts (1977) has questioned these assumptions, the case is here argued that careers education programmes (CEPs), if begun early enough, can exert an influence upon all young people's educational and occupational choices, and that such an influence is educationally and socially defensible.*

Roberts denies a number of commonly implied assumptions of vocational guidance. He asserts that for the majority of school leavers entry into employment is the outcome not of a process of reflective thinking and choosing but of strong socialisation forces operating within a limited structure of occupational opportunity; and that there is in any case little meaningful choice because the jobs available offer no opportunity for the application of talent, nor significant promise of self-fulfilment. Careers education programmes (CEPs) cannot therefore achieve the purposes conceived for them, and indeed may prove disturbing to many young people by raising expectations that are inevitably to be frustrated. The most that schools can hope to achieve, argues Roberts, is the provision of help with occupational adjustment (another socialisation responsibility) – by no means a negligible purpose.

### WHO HAS NO CHOICE?

An ambiguity in Roberts' argument requires initial comment: it is not clear to which young people he intends to refer by the phrase 'the majority of school leavers', for whom he claims there is no choice and therefore no choosing. It seems likely that he refers to those who leave school without any formal educational qualifications with which to approach an employer. But this is no longer a majority of school leavers, and of them a significant number find opportunities in industrial training programmes.

In any case, it will be argued below that CEPs can be a significant and beneficial influence upon the occupational thinking of the prompt school

First published in the *British Journal of Guidance and Counselling*, Volume 5 No.1, January 1977.

leaver as well as upon the more educationally committed and able pupil. It is also worth noting that those who elect to leave school as soon as they are permitted to, without the benefit of a CEP, are not necessarily the same as those who might choose to leave school promptly *after* experiencing one.

### WHAT ARE THE OBJECTIVES OF CEPS?

In his general premise, Roberts is correct: CEPs do assume that meaningful vocational choices and preferences are possible for all pupils, and that the CEP will help each pupil to make the most suitable choice in the light of his own needs and wants. CEPs also have an adjustive or socialisation purpose – namely, to acquaint pupils with the nature of working life, its opportunities, expectations, demands and rewards, so that they may be optimally equipped to seek, obtain and keep a job. All pupils should be aware of the total range of jobs potentially accessible to them, and of the requirements, irritations and stresses as well as the rewards that are commonly associated with those jobs. Specifically, they should know of the satisfactions inherent in the job tasks, those that are offered by the social environment within which the job is done, and those that are offered by the life-style available outside working hours to those who do the job. CEPs are primarily concerned to help young people determine the kind of life that they want, and in that context to consider which among the jobs realistically available to them offers the most likely and approximate fit to what they seek as a style of life and as a satisfying way of 'making a living'. To achieve this, CEPs must first help pupils to achieve a degree of accurate and full self-awareness, including a realistic sense of personal strengths and limitations, a capacity for accurate calculation of the probabilities of their achieving what they find attractive, and a shrewd knowledge of what they might do – well in advance of meeting selection processes – to prepare themselves for those processes (another anticipatory socialisation function).

It is worth emphasising, then, that there *is* a socialisation element in CEPs. There is also however – as we shall see later – a concern to combat dysfunctional aspects of the anticipatory socialisation processes to which children have been subjected in their neighbourhoods and their homes.

### WHAT ARE THE VOCATIONAL OBJECTIVES OF THE SCHOOLS WITHIN WHICH CEPS APPEAR?

Before this century, all schools, even state schools, were class-confirming institutions in no manner concerned to promote social mobility. But when, following the 1902 Education Act, elementary schools ceased to be an educational cul-de-sac for the children of the labouring poor and were placed end-on to the secondary schools, giving access to a fortunate few via free-place scholarships, then state schools began, however tentatively, to be an agent of social mobility through the process of identifying and promoting talent. Arguably, there were humanitarian feelings behind this trend. Certainly there were economic ones: changes in the structure of work had brought an increase in the number of jobs requiring numeracy and literacy, and other forms of skill that could not be acquired without a sound foundation in the basic scholastic skills. The demand for 'middle-class' labour was accelerating faster than the capacity of the middle class to produce it.

There have been many educational changes and proposals during this century intended to extend the possibility of educational achievement and therefore social mobility to working-class children, and perhaps also intended to reduce social inequalities of access to educational (as well as other) resources. Examples are the Hadow Report (Board of Education, 1927), the 1944 Education Act that resulted from it, the introduction of less class-biased procedures for allocating children to grammar schools, the Labour Party's commitment to introducing comprehensive second-ary education in 1964, and the trend towards the abolition of within-school streaming. The spirit of these changes was well expressed by Edward Boyle in his introduction to the Newsom Report, when he said that '. . . all children should have an equal opportunity of acquiring intelligence, and of developing their talents and abilities to the full' (Ministry of Education, 1963).

One implication of the intention behind these educational changes is that if they are effective there will be a rising proportion of scholastically able children emerging from state education to fill a rising rate of labour-market demand for them. Such children in the majority of cases would be unable to rely on guidance from family socialisation processes to help them move sensibly and appropriately into the world of work. Vocational guidance of the square-peg-in-the-square-hole (talent-match-ing) kind is clearly required, therefore, to ensure an efficient relationship between the output of schools and the economic uses to which it is put.

A further implication of those educational changes is a steady rate of increase in social mobility as measured by inter-generational shifts in level of educational achievement: again this implies that traditional socialisation processes will be an inadequate and possibly misleading guide for those children who are translated by the meritocratic selection process to levels of occupational skill that lie beyond family understanding or expectation. Moreover, children are now retained in school to an age where they are sufficiently mature to play an active part in deciding the directions in which they wish their lives to move; and post-school educational opportunities in further and higher education are now accessible to 'the majority of school leavers'. For all these reasons, CEPs – although only adequately provided yet in a small minority of schools (DES, 1973) – are an essential part of secondary schooling if its purposes are to be achieved efficiently. Whether educational changes have brought about increases in social mobility and a reduction of social inequalities of access to educational resources is an empirical matter, the evidence for which will be considered in the next section. But since these are intentions that underlie state educational provision, it is important that their realisation is not impeded by a failure to provide the CEPs necessary to facilitate such social movements. We should not appear to be only half-hearted in our attempts to achieve our social ends.

## IS EDUCATION INCREASING SOCIAL MOBILITY IN BRITAIN?

In considering whether in practice education is increasing social mobility, there are two issues to be distinguished. One refers to overall increases in educational achievement (disregarding class differentials) which, linked with increased occupational opportunity, have brought steady improvement in inter-generational life chances and experience. The evidence for such steadily rising social improvement has been overwhelming during this century (even though it may not continue) and is the consequence of occupational and educational factors in combination – neither could have achieved it alone. It implies an overall improvement in affluence and a relative increase in middle-class occupational opportunity. It therefore further implies that there has been more upward mobility from the working class than downward mobility from the upper and middle classes. This evidence alone justifies the changes in the structure of education, though it is impossible to know whether the overall improvements would have occurred without such changes. The evidence is also a *prima facie* demonstration of the necessity for professional guidance for children who are carried by the educational process to areas of unfamiliar social and occupational opportunity.

The second question refers to evidence of a more equitable social distribution of valued resources like education. Specifically, is there evidence that social inequalities of access to educational opportunity are declining? The evidence for such decline is undeniable, though its rate is much slower than one might have supposed. Socially structured inequalities are not dramatically altered by changes in any single social institution. The last major investigation into social mobility in Britain was that of Glass (1954). There emerged a picture of a stable social order in which there was very little inter-generational mobility. Certainly, the changes that followed the 1944 Education Act did not have any quick dramatic effects on social-class differences in educational achievement (Ministry of Education, 1954). More recent evidence is more encouraging (see Banks, 1976, chapter 3). For example, Neave (1975) provides evidence that the comprehensive school has resulted in an improvement in the working-class child's chances of educational achievement and also a relative improvement in those chances compared with the effects on middle-class educational achievement.

The most recent evidence on rates of mobility through education has emerged from the first data to appear from a major Nuffield College study. Halsey (1975) has calculated the relative chances of attaining a university education for children from different social levels and born at different periods during this century. He shows that whereas upper-middle-class children born in 1910/29 had a five-times-better-than-average chance of entering university, those born in 1930/49 had only a three-times-better chance. Again, whereas lower-working-class children born in 1910/29 had a less-than-quarter-average chance, those born in 1930/49 had only a less-than-half-average chance. Today, working-class children comprise one-third of all students achieving two or more passes at GCE A-level, and one-quarter of the university undergraduate population (Banks, 1976).

The evidence suggests, therefore, that structural changes in education designed (**1**) to increase absolute levels of educational achievement, and (**2**) to reduce social-class inequalities of access to educational opportunity, have succeeded. In respect of the second ambition the effects have been slow to appear and so far are modest. They are sufficient, nonetheless, to constitute a strong argument for CEPs.

### SOCIALISATION AND OCCUPATIONAL CHOICE

The sociologist's social mobility evidence is not the only kind relevant to establishing that pupils have significant educational and occupational choices to make and that they can be helped by guidance, including CEPs, to undertake them competently. There are also other arguments.

Roberts implies an antithesis between socialisation and choice processes as if the former produced vocational attitudes, perceptions and behaviours that owed nothing to reflective thinking and were impervious to educational influence. In fact, socialisation processes, including those that are experienced in school, provide a framework or context within which reflection and choice take place. Furthermore, some modes of socialisation inhibit reflective thinking and choosing, while others encourage it. CEPs quite explicitly force pupils to think and to reflect upon the effects of all the socialisation pressures to which they have been subjected. They are a way of protecting children from the consequences of a too unreflective and uncritical dependence upon socialisation experiences. In times of rapid social change, home pressures are invariably poorly informed and obsolescent because the occupational experience of the parents is partial and dated. Children need not only to be protected from too vulnerable a dependence upon parental guidance and influence, but to be offered compensatingly a professional, fully-informed and disinterested alternative, if they are to achieve a realistic basis for planning their lives and moving from education to work. The relevant evidence would be that those who experience CEPs achieve a greater sense of personal satisfaction and self-fulfilment than those who do not, but there have been too few schools offering such programmes for any length of time for such evidence to be available yet.

Another questionable implication of Roberts' argument is that socialisation processes are essentially conservative, resulting in children adopting the values, sharing the perceptions and striving to repeat the occupational experiences of their parents, in contrast to the purpose of CEPs which is to help children transcend socially-imposed barriers to a full awareness of choice and opportunity. But some working-class families are ambitious for their children, striving to keep up with the Joneses, in contrast to those who loyally stay down with the Smiths. The precise contribution of socialisation within socially-aspiring families to social mobility in their children is unknown, but it needs to be exposed to inspection and reflection in CEPs just as much as more conservative influences.

The underlying argument here is that there is a personal and psychological aspect to social mobility processes as well as the sociological one: a microcosmic as well as a macrocosmic picture (see Stacey, 1965). It is the individual psychological story that more easily exposes undesirable pressures, whether they be conservative ones that threaten to stifle the fulfilment of a talented child, or mobility pressures that may push someone of modest wits beyond his limits. Professional guidance programmes can counterbalance such forces. Yet even this is a misleading way of stating the situation, for it implies that under certain circumstances parents and schools compete for 'ownership' of children. In fact, CEPs seek to help children own themselves, to become autonomous, self-directing, and less vulnerable to social pressures.

It is not only individual differences of reaction to socialisation processes that a psychological approach reveals. One becomes aware also of certain oversimple uninspected assumptions in the sociological account of occupational behaviour. 'The relative desirability of different occupations is socially structured', says Roberts, who implies also that income, power and prestige are the crucial variables. No differentiation among childhood socialisation processes is implied, though clearly an important distinction is that between *conservative* and *aspiring* ideologies; there are undoubtedly others that lead to quite different sorts of occupational behaviours (an *anti-employment* ideology, for example). Such a sociological oversimplification leads to another, that all people are motivated in the same way in their occupational aspirations to aim as far as possible up the one commonly-perceived occupational hierarchy. In practice, social categories and groups show highly differentiated kinds of perception and evaluation, and individuals within specific categories and groups even more so.

## SOCIAL CHANGE AND WITHIN-CLASS SOCIAL MOBILITY

Two observations about social mobility need to be made if vocational psychologists and sociologists are to understand each other's arguments. First, a successful CEP will not necessarily be reflected in a change in educational or career mobility rates. There is no built-in value assumption within such programmes that social mobility is 'a good thing'. Put another way, a theoretically possible outcome of an effective CEP is that school-leavers choose to adopt values and pursue objectives that are very similar to those of their parents. One must respect a child's right to govern his life in accordance with conservative socialisation processes if he so chooses.

Second, the vocational psychologist's appreciation of what social mobility implies is richer, if less precise, than that of the sociologist, who considers only vertical mobility. To the sociologist, people move up or down or stay where they began. Psychologists are interested also in diverse forms of lateral and geographical mobility, and their preoccupation with choice of *life-style* is their common way of referring to these possibilities. The son of a rural garage mechanic who chooses a job in a car assembly plant in a large city, the doctor's son who chooses to rebel against the family tradition and enter instead the profession of law, the

Fife miner who takes his family to the greater security of the coalfields of South Yorkshire, and whose son then ventures with his guitar into the world of popular entertainment, the squire's son who forsakes the family acres to become a fashion photographer, relying upon his name and his contacts – none of these social movements, which are very real ones in terms of the style of life that characterises them, would have been easy to contemplate let alone achieve earlier in the century, but they are occurring increasingly today. They would not, however, show up as social mobility in a strictly vertical conception of social class.

Nor is inter-disciplinary discussion of social class helped by the sociologist's inclination to consider only occupational criteria. Developmental vocational psychologists are interested in the total life-style of the person and not merely in the way he earns his living. This is partly because job satisfaction and self-fulfilment are often found not in the work tasks that define employment but in other experiences within and outside the working environment which the job makes possible. CEPs are concerned with total life choices and not merely with occupational and educational ones.

This issue draws attention to significant differences between jobs which in the skill sense (e.g. unskilled) are equivalent and which offer real choices therefore to the least educationally qualified school-leaver. A primary objective of CEPs is to help young people find for themselves a mode of employment which, as well as being acceptable *per se*, makes possible a way of life that is satisfying and self-fulfilling for the person who chooses it. The coal mine, the supermarket, the railway yard, the road transport industry, the farm, the factory: unskilled work is to be found in all these and many more working environments, but they are not equivalent environments, nor is the work to be found there. Each has its own climate and flavour, each has different kinds of people within it, and each offers a distinctive way of life both within and outside the job. It is such differences that decide whether the worker finds contentment and a degree of self-fulfilment, not the nature of the job tasks that await him. For children who cannot aspire to more than unskilled labour, it is the purpose of a CEP firstly to enable them to survive wherever they choose to go, and secondly to choose that occupational milieu which promises the most congenial style of life for them.

Roberts is, however, right to point out that CEPs, because they are confined to the years of secondary schooling, can have only a limited socialisation value in securing the satisfactory adjustment of young people to the demands of working life. Indeed, the need for continued help is clearly expressed by developmental theorists, who argue that vocational development is not properly completed by the age of 16. I share Roberts' view that the post-school responsibilities implied should be undertaken by the Careers Service (Daws, 1969/70). I would not of course agree that such work may be regarded as alternative to rather than complementing and extending from developmental guidance programmes in school.

Equally, such developmental responsibilities should be assumed by institutions of further and higher education for their students, though few institutions have developed suitable programmes and guidance practices. The social climate within which educational innovation and guidance processes have developed has yet to question the myth that only the unqualified prompt school-leaver needs guidance. The prevalence of this myth in secondary schools was confirmed by the recent DES survey (DES, 1973), and contradicts Roberts' assertion that CEPs discriminate in favour of those pupils who stay on into the sixth form.

## VOCATIONAL GUIDANCE: LUBRICANT OR CATALYST?

A comprehensively adequate theory of entry into employment must take account of many factors – sociological, economic and psychological (Blau et al., 1956). Explanations derived entirely from one discipline will be inadequate. Furthermore, to demonstrate the importance of anticipatory socialisation does not preclude individual reflection and choice. The former defines the context within which the latter occur. What we do not know with any precision is the *relative weightings* of these processes in deciding the occupational experience of school leavers, particularly their relation to such variables as social class, ethnic group, sex, intelligence, educational qualifications, and age of commitment to an occupational choice.

Moreover, in concentrating on early socialisation and structures of occupational opportunity, Roberts fails to consider many other social processes that imply a need for CEPs to ensure that young people are equipped with a full knowledge of all the opportunities – educational, occupational and social – available to them. Social change brings new opportunity for which traditional socialisation is a misleading guide. Old jobs change and new ones appear. Opportunity broadens. There is legislatively extended opportunity for women and for coloured people. The steady increase in volume of educational achievement, and the trend of diminishing social-class inequalities in access to educational opportunity, each imply growing needs for disinterested, professional guidance through the school years, as does also the more open access to post-school opportunities of increasing flexibility and variety in further and higher education. Roberts further fails to consider the *variety* of socialisation processes in homes, neighbourhoods and schools, all of which imply a need for the kind of counter-balancing and protective socialisation that a CEP should be.

Finally, Roberts in my view has not understood that the relationship between the practice of vocational guidance and the processes of transition from school to work cannot be a simple one because there are two important prescriptive elements in guidance. One is *moral*, and reflects the values to which the practice of guidance is committed – labour market needs, the optimal deployment of talent, individual human fulfilment, and the removal of discriminative practices have all been canvassed as important guiding principles in recent times. The second prescriptive element is *technical*, and refers to the means by which the valued purposes might best be achieved. Because of these prescriptive elements, vocational guidance does not have to confine itself merely to increasing the efficiency with which current processes of occupational placement are concluded. It can strive to challenge and change those processes. In this respect, Roberts' account is useful chiefly in reminding us that there can be other than educational strategies for attempting to influence the process of occupational placement. One might, for example, attempt to modify occupational recruitment and selection processes.

In general, though, the prescriptive implications of Roberts' own proposals are highly conservative. He suggests that guidance services, both within and outside schools, should restrict themselves to the adjustive function of helping young people adapt to the demands of working life. To attempt more, he suggests, is pointless. He is sceptical about the possibility of developing and implementing CEPs capable of influencing the vocational thinking of young people. Developmental theorists, of course, are more optimistic; this paper has been an attempt to justify that optimism. No longer is vocational guidance (or indeed any form of guidance) merely a lubricant of social processes. Today, guidance must also play the role of catalyst in the production of desirable social change. Suitably tackled, it can be an instrument of progressive rather than conservative social policy.

## REFERENCES

Banks, O.: *The Sociology of Education*. London: Batsford, 1976 (3rd edition).

Blau, P.M., Gustad, J.W., Jessor, R., Parnes, H.S., and Wilcock, R.C.: 'Occupational Choice: a Conceptual Framework'. *Industrial Labor Relations Review*, Volume 9 No. 4, July 1956, pp. 531–546.

Board of Education: *The Needs of the Adolescent* (Hadow Report). London: HMSO, 1927.

Daws, P.P.: 'Careers Guidance in the 1970s'. *Careers Quarterly*, Volume 22 No. 1, 1969/70.

Department of Education and Science: *Careers Education in Secondary Schools*. Education Survey 18. London: HMSO, 1973.

Glass, D. (ed.): *Social Mobility in Britain*. London: Routledge & Kegan Paul, 1954.

Halsey, A.H.: 'Sociology and the Equality Debate'. *Oxford Review of Education*, Volume 1 No. 1, 1975, pp. 9–23.

Ministry of Education: *Early Leaving*. London: HMSO, 1954.

Ministry of Education: *Half Our Future* (Newsom Report). London: HMSO, 1963.

Neave, G.: *How They Fared*. London: Routledge & Kegan Paul, 1975.

Roberts, K.: 'The Social Conditions, Consequences and Limitations of Careers Guidance'. *British Journal of Guidance and Counselling*, Volume 5 No. 1, January 1977.

Stacey, B.G.: 'Some Psychological Aspects of Inter-Generation Occupational Mobility'. *British Journal of Social and Clinical Psychology*, Volume 4, 1965, pp. 275–286.

# ARE CAREERS EDUCATION PROGRAMMES IN SECONDARY SCHOOLS A WASTE OF TIME? ~ A REPLY TO ROBERTS

## PETER P. DAWS

### POSTSCRIPT

The aims of collective social action, such as education, are shaped by moral obligation, and its means derive from a broadly held view of how society works. Social scientists of any discipline that examines the work of those employed on carrying out social policy have a dual obligation: (**a**) to set out the present social consequences of practice, negative and positive, intended and unintended; and (**b**) to argue carefully any prescriptions they offer for change in the work of practitioners. Too frequently, our data are partial and over-interpreted, our diagnoses over-generalised, and our proposed remedies based on theories of strictly limited application and insufficient subtlety. In consequence, we fall into two kinds of error: the spread of false diagnoses and prescription; and the discouragement and flawed re-direction of practitioners. Ironically, we are sometimes too persuasive, too influential on practice, and reality changes in line with our message (the self-fulfilling prophecy). The flaws in our analyses and prescriptions become temporarily even more difficult to spot. Marxism is but one, if dramatic, recent example. We would do well to adopt medicine's basic ethical principle: *primum, non nocere* (first, do no harm). I felt that Ken Roberts' thesis would harm valuable developing practice, which was why I challenged it.

The powerful influence of socialisation processes (and not merely conservative ones) to shape children's educational outcomes and occupational destinies was not unappreciated by practitioners. Those who had hoped that educational change following the 1944 Education Act would diminish their influence were made aware how little things had changed in 1954 by two sources of evidence: David Glass' (1954) comprehensive study of social mobility; and the official education report *Early Leaving* (CACE, 1954). The Crowther Report (CACE, 1959) impressively re-affirmed the picture. The received message was not 'give up', but 'there's much more to be done'. Hence the further measures taken in the 1960s: the process of comprehensivisation of the post-primary schools and the decisions to further raise the school-leaving age, to equalise financial access to higher education (Ministry of Education, 1963), and to implement the recommendations of the Plowden Report (CACE, 1967) in the provision of compensatory education in educational priority areas.

It was most inappropriately timed, in 1977, for K. Roberts to present yet again a case for the ubiquitous power of conservative socialisation and for persuading practitioners to desist, therefore, from efforts that assumed 'the facts' to be otherwise. In fact, many school-leavers were moving into educational and occupational spheres beyond those experienced by their parents, even though class differentials were little changed since 1954 (Halsey *et al.*, 1980; Goldthorpe, 1980). After all, that middle-class children no less than working-class children were taking opportunities for upward mobility reinforced rather than weakened the case for CEPs. The macroscopic functionalist picture presented by K. Roberts clearly claimed too much. The discredited Durkheimian compulsiveness he implied for socialisation processes concealed the looseness of causal relationship between them and their outcomes; concealed also, therefore, the extent to which young people found educational and occupational routes contrary to the persuasions of socialisation; and ignored the fact that CEPs were but an additional mode of socialisation interpolated to strengthen children's capacity to make their own choices, informedly and wisely, whether with the grain of traditional socialisation or against it.

Responding to the Roberts and Daws papers, R.J. Roberts (1980) proclaimed, in effect, a plague on both our houses and offered an alternative sociological analysis no less simple-minded, in my view, than K. Roberts', and a prescription so implausible as to invite little risk of diverting teachers from their current practices. His less tendentious ideas, however, stimulated Law (1981) to develop the implications for CEPs of the face-to-face relationship source of children's belief about themselves, their world and their opportunities within it. This has proved a significant contribution to and influence upon, CEP practice, alongside similar but distinctive European Community ideas based on the principle of *alternance*: that CEPs should systematically alternate between in-school instruction and out-of-school experience, in which both teachers and field personnel should have clearly co-ordinated agreement about learning objectives, the means to their achievement and methods of assessment.

In the past decade, the broad sociological picture has changed considerably, at least in respect of where the spotlight and energies are focused. Social class is slightly out of the limelight. More in focus are unqualified school-leavers and the moral imperative to extend the range of 'opportunity structures' to women, ethnic and religious minorities, and the disabled. When the output of school-leavers is diminishing annually, *all* of them are sought by the labour market, provided they have marketable talents. Each of these groups is the subject of laudable initiatives, which are happily unimpeded by fatalistic acceptance of the *status quo*.

### REFERENCES

Central Advisory Council for Education: *Early Leaving*. London: HMSO, 1954.
Central Advisory Council for Education: *15 to 18* (Crowther Report). London: HMSO, 1959.
Central Advisory Council for Education: *Children and their Primary Schools* (Plowden Report). London: HMSO, 1967.
Glass, D. (ed.): *Social Mobility in Britain*. London: Routledge & Kegan Paul, 1954.
Goldthorpe, J.H.: *Social Mobility and Class Structure in Modern Britain*. Oxford: Clarendon Press, 1980.
Halsey, A.H., Heath, A.F., AND Ridge, J.M.: *Origins and Destinations: Family, Class and Education in Modern Britain*. Oxford: Clarendon Press, 1980.
Law, B.: 'Community Interaction: a "Mid-Range" Focus for Theories of Career Development in Young Adults'. *British Journal of Guidance and Counselling*, Volume 9 No. 2, 1981, pp. 141–158.
Ministry of Education: *Higher Education* (Robbins Report). Cmnd. 2154. London: HMSO, 1963.
Roberts, R.J.: 'An Alternative Justification for Careers Education: a Radical Response to Roberts and Daws'. *British Journal of Guidance and Counselling*, Volume 8 No. 2, 1980, pp. 158–174.

# COMMUNITY INTERACTION: A 'MID-RANGE' FOCUS FOR THEORIES OF CAREER DEVELOPMENT IN YOUNG ADULTS

## BILL LAW

*Thinking about career development changes not only in response to the discovery of new empirical evidence but also in response to prevailing social climates. In contemporary Britain both the evidence and the social climate are pointing to yet new formulations of career-development theory in terms which accord overriding importance neither to the explanations offered by the sociologist nor to those offered by the psychologist. Some of this evidence is examined, and a theoretical formulation is attached to it. The implications are that guidance practitioners should see themselves both as applied psychologists and as applied sociologists.*

The struggle for understanding is riven by the capacity of *homo sapiens* to generate more than one explanatory hypothesis for every observation. It is what makes human thought and conversation dynamic, not static. There is always another way of configuring the evidence (cf. Pirsig, 1974).

The opening section of this paper is an attempt to elaborate three propositions: (**1**) thinking about career development is not static but dynamic, continuously reconfiguring available evidence; (**2**) each new attempt seeks in part to resolve problems left by previous attempts; but (**3**) each new generation seeks also to achieve a congruence with the social and cultural ambience in which it is set, so that such ambiences represent a 'readiness' for the acceptance of new ideas about career development (the development and linkages described briefly here are explored in more detail in Law, 1980). This section will then be followed by an attempt to outline an emergent theoretical formulation having some resonance with the preoccupations in contemporary Britain.

## CHANGING SOCIETY: CHANGING THEORY

**Scientific matching theories**. The earliest attempts to crystallise career-development thinking occurred in the wake of movements to formalise careers guidance. Those movements occurred in societies well into a process of change brought about by the application of science and technology to the means of production, distribution and exchange, and by an increasing movement of people both from rural to urban living, and – particularly in the case of the United States – from one national

First published in the *British Journal of Guidance and Counselling*, Volume 9 No.2, July 1981.

culture to another. The demands made by the labour economies of these societies were changing, and so were the informal attachments in neighbourhood and community which had formerly carried people into their places in those economies.

Shertzer and Stone (1971) attribute the first use of the term vocational guidance to Frank Parsons who established his agency in Boston in 1908. The thinking underlying Parsons' work can be summarised in three statements: people are different from each other; so are jobs; it should be possible by study of both to achieve a match between person and job. Similar thinking underlay the establishment in Britain of Juvenile Employment Bureaux in 1911.

As Beck (1963) has argued, a problem posed in part by an increasingly scientific society was likely to be met by a similarly scientific response. Thinking about career development was accordingly dominated increasingly by the assumed need to generate verifiable data about individuals and jobs. The work of the National Institute of Industrial Psychology in Britain between the two world wars rested upon such scientific matching assumptions. The tradition is not dead. Kline (1975) has recently argued for scientific matching theories of career development as a basis for practice, characterising guidance as 'fitting men to jobs' (sic!). And a current project (Kirton, 1979) is addressed to the problem of establishing verifiable differences between jobs, and psychometrically diagnosing the validity of people's perceptions of them.

**Humanistic theories**. By the early 1960s, however, new ideas were being imported from the United States, and were finding fertile soil in Britain in which to take root. Rogers (1951) drew attention to the way in which each individual uniquely and internally configures his or her own experience of self and situation. The dissemination of this thinking in the United States led, for a time, to the virtual abandonment of psychometric techniques. But it has subsequently led to an interest in knowing how best to use psychometric techniques as a stimulus to client participation in helping relationships (Goldman, 1961), and to the development for research and practice of more subtle techniques for identifying the phenomenology of the individual (Gould, 1969; Edmonds, 1979).

Again, Roe (1956) pointed to the way in which individuals seeking work are not merely engaged in the task of economic survival, but are purusing satisfaction for a variety of different sorts of deficit needs or self-actualising motivations. Daws' (1968) argument for a 'comprehensive matching' model for guidance is parallel with Roe's contribution. He argues that more attention should be paid to the way in which people seek satisfactions for needs and values – as well as marketing their talents – in their work. A colleague and I (Law and Ward, 1981) have recently sifted British evidence in support of Daws' contention.

As a further development Super (1957) was among those who applied developmental frameworks to the configuration of evidence about career choice. This articulated an understanding that people do not choose a career in an isolated moment of time, and linked the variety of respects in which today's decision rests upon yesterday's experiences.

Morever, Rogers (1951) refused to accept that career development in particular could be adequately conceived in isolation from general human development. The progressive broadening of frames of reference for thinking about career development has subsequently included Samler's (1961) criticism of the lack of 'psycho-social' material in occupational information, Hayes' (1971) research into the changing appreciation in young workers of the importance of administrative and social working situations, and Super's (1980) massive conception of 'life-space-life-span' as a framework for considering career development.

These ideas invite an understanding of career development in terms of whole persons, each uniquely responding to his or her feelings, needs, and growing experience. They are features which can be subsumed beneath the label 'humanistic'. The Schools Council's Careers Education and Guidance Project defies exact categorisation, but its developmental sequence of stimuli of personal responses to a broad range of career-related issues represents one of the most thoroughgoing implementations of humanistic theory to be developed in Britain.

It is argued here that it is no accident that such ideas emerged more or less contemporaneously in the United States, and were accepted more or less contemporaneously in Britain. They emerged and were accepted to the extent that the societies in which they appeared no longer thought of themselves as supported by a single moral spine transmitting a coherent set of moral messages. Technological changes in communication and transportation had put more voices in each ear and more images in each eye. There was an increasing awareness in these societies of the relativity and vulnerability of their cosmologies. Official, traditional, stereotyped and establishment ways of representing reality to the people became profoundly suspect. Such societies were progressively becoming more of a problem to themselves. In this ambience, thinking about career development which – like scientific matching theory – looked as though it could be used to fit people into unproblematic slots in society, became profoundly suspect. In such a ferment of doubt and re-examination, there was a high degree of readiness for new ideas which invited people to think about career development in terms of how each individual developed in response to a growing, unique, feeling and whole sense of self – a self-concept.

**Functionalist theories**. Up to the late 1960s the story could be told almost wholly in terms of concepts derived from differential, developmental and counselling psychology. But, as Dovey (1980) has pointed out in his discussion of guidance in South Africa, thinking about how people find work eventually touches upon the philosophical and political assumptions that we make concerning the relationship between people and society, and will tend to be accepted or rejected on the basis of those assumptions. The Schools Council Project materials did so, and formed part of a discussion in which sociologists were progressively becoming more involved.

In the Britain of the 1970s it was the sociologists who most sought to reconfigure the evidence. For example, K. Roberts (1968; 1971; 1977) was already arguing that people do not choose jobs: they take what is available. In Roberts' view all the major determinants of occupational status lie outside the individual. They are to be found in the currents of socialisation to which the individual is subjected, and in the vortex of the socially-classified labour economy. The economy controls by what is offered; and an adequate account of the process can be given with little reference to the influence of needs, aspirations, feelings or personal views of individuals.

Readiness for such ideas lay in a growing scepticism concerning the appropriateness of the psychology-bound theories which had preceded them. In particular, the relative contraction of the labour economy – and, in particular, the hard consequences of structural unemployment – were, by the late 1970s, causing many people to rethink the relationship between people and society, placing less emphasis upon the choices of individuals and more upon the requirements of society. The theories of career development which suggested the who-does-what in society is best explained in terms of the functioning of social forces seemed to many like a breath of fresh air into the tedious – some might say 'wet' – obfuscations of introspective psychology.

The ensuing debate has been cast in terms of a discussion concerning the relative importance of accounts offered by sociology and psychology in explaining and predicting career development (Speakman, 1976;

Law, 1976; Daws, 1977; K. Roberts, 1981; Daws, 1981). Some of the interest in the debate may be attributable to the fear that the powerfully functional explanations of the sociologists appear to leave guidance practitioners with little significant to do between the extremes of ovine compliance and bloody revolution.

## EVIDENCE FOR COMMUNITY INTERACTION IN CAREER DEVELOPMENT

But sociologists have not yet finished with thinking about career development. It is now becoming possible to trace the rough shape of newly-emerging conceptions which are drawn on a narrower canvas than that suggested by functionalist theories, yet which still pay careful attention to situational influences in the career development of individuals. These conceptions suggest that the way in which who-does-what in society is decided is the product of a plurality of interpersonal transactions conducted in local settings, and on the basis of interaction within and between groups of which the individual is a member – the 'community'. It is moreover a conception of exchange between the individual and his or her environment which may prove to have significant resonances with emerging preoccupations in our society: notably with pleas for a more human scale and texture to the structuring of our enterprises, and with an increasingly ecological understanding of the relationship between individual and environment.

The term 'community' is notoriously problematic, and it is not used here to connote benign influence in a succouring or protective sense. Instead, it is used for its alternative connotation of plurality of interpersonal exchange. It is, in that sense, a rag-bag concept selected to represent a rag-bag reality. It corresponds in some important aspects with the ecological concept of 'territory' and with the more popular term 'patch'. What characterises the raw data upon which the concept of community interaction draws is not their newness: much has been lying around for some time. It is to be found in their common reference to the importance to our understanding of the exchange which occurs between the individual and the other members of the groups of which he or she is a member.

**Studies in career development.** Such studies include specific enquiries into career development, focusing on approaches and entry to the working world. K. Roberts himself drew upon evidence (Veness, 1962; Maizels, 1970) indicating that a high proportion of school leavers paid a great deal of attention to what they learned in their community contacts (parents, siblings, peers, neighbours, teachers, etc.) in preparing them-selves for career choices and transitions. Carter's (1962) study of the school-leaving experiences of 200 youngsters in five schools in an industrial city in Britain indicates some important distinctions between different types of family values and identifies their influences upon the career aspirations of youngsters. And Gupta (1977) is among those who have provided evidence to support the view that family support can enhance the life-chances of children of working-class immigrant families.

Again, Willis (1977) offers an illuminative account of the interper-sonal influence of the peer group, describing how a small group of working-class lads at school select futures for themselves on the basis of a strong sense of identification with the group. They share the same school with the 'conformists', whom they despise. But tribal affiliation to their own 'non-conforming' group means that for 'the likes of us' the way is going to be different, with better short-term and worse long-term rewards. Membership of the group is the arbiter of choice, leading to distrust of the school's attempts to offer careers guidance, subversion of its attempts to change them, and claims to (and defence of) unsupervised territory in the school in which they can assert and celebrate their own group dominance.

**Studies in the sociology of education.** British explorations into the sociology of education – focusing on the impact of education, family, etc. on the educability of children – provide further elaborations of the concept of community interaction. For example, studies (e.g. Jackson and Marsden, 1962) of the way in which academically-achieving children of working-class families cope with their own prospect of upward social mobility show that the claims of childhood community member-ships are strong. Sometimes such memberships seem to make it imposs-ible for the youngsters to escape, so that the prospect of upward social mobility *via* higher education is rejected; even where the prospect is accepted, they lead to considerable strains between the youngsters and their family and neighbourhood of origin. Some youngsters make the break, and some do not.

More recently, Bernstein (1965) and Lawton (1968) have examined the way in which the differential use of interpersonal communication in working-class and middle-class homes leads to differential systems of identification with groups. The Plowden Committee (1967) made more extensive enquiries indicating the way in which a variety of family influences affect youngsters' use of educational opportunity. Miller (1971) showed that some of these value-laden attitudes could be isolated and shown to be more predictive of educational achievement than could crude sociological criteria, such as membership of a social class.

**Studies in the sociology of the school.** Investigations into the sociology of the school – focusing on the patterns of interaction within schools – extend the emerging attention to ways in which membership of interpersonal groups influences the aspirations of young people. Hargreaves' (1967) participant-observer investigation of social relations in a secondary school outlines the influence on the personal development of youngsters of their membership of subcultures within the school, and of the intended and unintended consequences for the students of the way in which their teachers respond by categorising the students in terms of their perceptions of these subcultures. Furthermore, Ford's (1968) study of social relations in schools indicates that students are much more likely to choose friends from people of like ability and social background, than from the structured social groups which schools form in order to foster social mixing. Membership of a social group tends, then, to override the structural attempts of the school to encourage socially heterogeneous experiences for individuals. The students stick to their own kind. Ford made one other discovery which significantly elaborates that finding: where able children from working-class backgrounds have been selected into working groups for higher ability, those youngsters seem able to disentangle themselves from membership of working-class groups and to view themselves as prospective members of the middle class. The opportunity they have to make friendships with middle-class peers appears to be a significant aspect of this upward aspiration on their part.

The main thrust of such conclusions has received some support from a more recent study by Rutter *et al.* (1979) of the effects upon their students of twelve London secondary schools. The study suggests that 'physical and administrative' features of the organisation of schools (such as the status and sex composition of the schools, their size and available space, the age of their buildings, the teacher-student ratios, the size of their classes, and the type of internal organisational structure they adopt) have little effect on the attendance, behaviour, achievement or delinquency records of their students. But such outcomes seem to be significantly affected by those features of the school which have to do with 'interpersonal contexts' (such as the degree of emphasis placed on doing academic work, the style of interaction in class between teacher and student, the use made of rewards and praise, the extent to which students are able socially to contact and influence their teachers, the extent to which students are given responsibility in the school, continuity of contact with teachers, and stability of student groupings).

**International comparisons**. Weir (1977) has assembled American and Australian evidence closely parallel to the British evidence cited above. Much of her evidence is well-known. It includes, for example, Kahl's (1953) study of 24 'common-man boys' which showed that the sorts of values inculcated at home have considerable predictive power: 'getting-ahead' values suggest that upward mobility is more likely, and 'getting-by' values suggest that it is less likely. Weir also refers to Rosenthal's (1968) study suggesting that teacher expectations sometimes have a powerful effect on student performance in class.

**A mid-range focus.** Such an assembly of evidence re-configures our picture of how who-does-what is decided and, accordingly, it redirects our attention. Its primary focus is neither upon 'big-picture' trends identified by the telescopes of functionalist sociology, nor upon the 'small-picture' refinements afforded by the microscopes of differential, developmental and counselling psychology. Its focus is mid-range: referring to, and demonstrating the importance to our understanding of, the way in which both 'big-picture' and 'small-picture' events occur in the context of 'community interaction' between the individual and the social group of which he or she is a member. The evidence gives foreground significance to the personal exchanges which occur between individuals and the people with whom they are in community contact – notably family, neighbourhood, peer group, ethnic group, and teachers at school. It strongly suggests that, whatever explanatory and predictive significance we may wish to assign to self-concept or to opportunity structure as influences upon career development, that significance will be modified by exchanges occurring between the individual and the groups of which he or she is a member. It moves towards an explanation of career development which is likely to appeal to guidance practitioners working with clients unable to take a perspective on themselves or their situation generated beyond earshot of a shout for a home goal at their local football ground – their 'patch'.

### PROCESSES OF COMMUNITY INTERACTION

The evidence cited above supports a general case for seeking a mid-range focus for theories of career development. But it also leaves us with a further task: to examine the relationship between such a focus and earlier thinking.

**Community as a transmitter of motivation.** A spectrum of influences – ranging between 'small-picture' psychological and 'big-picture' sociological influences – have been identified in a review of evidence undertaken by a colleague and myself (Law and Ward, 1981) concerning motivation for career development. The psychological pole of that spectrum is identified where the roots of motivation are to be found in organismic needs (Roe, 1956). There are then progressively more interactive influences like those between child and early parenting (Bordin *et al.*, 1963), the transmissions of parental values (Kahl, 1953; Carter, 1962), peer-group identifications (Willis, 1977), and member-ship of ethnic groups (Strodtbeck, 1965; Gupta, 1977). More generally sociological influences may be found in social-class membership (Hol-lingshead, 1949; Fogelman, 1979) and in the rewards and incentives offered by the labour economy (Roberts, 1977). The relationship between internally experienced needs and drives, and externally experi-enced incentives and rewards, cannot be described in the simplistic terms of a confrontation between 'self' and 'situation'. The events of motivated career development cannot be described wholly in the psychological terms of needs pursued, nor wholly in the sociological terms of incentives offered. Instead, a great deal of the process of identifying motivation for career development occurs in mid-range transactions involving the participation of parents, family, neighbourhood, peer groups and ethnic group – the rag-bag of community, territory or patch.

The spectrum-configured analysis of data on motivation suggests the possibility of configuring the evidence from the studies mentioned in the previous section in a manner indicated by figure 1. The spectrum is not complete, drawing only upon influences identified by studies cited in this paper. Neither is it possible precisely to order the sequence of influences on such a spectrum. Its purpose is to suggest that crude distinctions between self-concept theory and opportunity-structure theory lack the subtlety of analysis which the evidence now demands. Self-concept theory – although it refers to other sources of influence – is articulated from the left of the diagram; opportunity-structure theory is similarly articulated from the right. A focus upon community interaction – articulated from the middle – unifies the presentation by drawing attention, for example, to the way in which the demands and incentives of the labour economy are learned through a range of community interactions.

*Figure 1:* **Spectrum of self-concept, community-interaction and opportunity-structure influences upon career development**

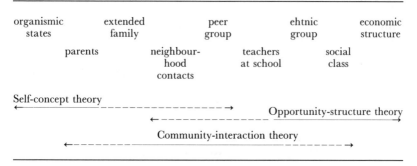

**Community as a modifier of social functioning**. Community-interaction processes, however, do not only *transmit* the effects of 'big-picture' sociological processes: they also *modify* these effects. Social-class attitudes are transmitted to youngsters through their families, but *not* in a way which permits simple prediction from social-class membership (Miller, 1971). Peer-group membership can confirm people in the predictions which functionalist sociology would make for them (Willis, 1977), but it can *also* wean them away from those predictions (Ford, 1968). Although membership of a minority ethnic group is often a crude predictor of low occupational achievement, membership of a highly aspiring (even, to the external observer, 'unrealistically' aspiring), supportive and reinforcing ethnic minority *can* lead to occupational achievement which 'big-picture' sociological categories do not predict (Gupta, 1977).

**Modes of community influence.** The community mediates and modifies structural influences upon individuals. It also transmits its own influence on individuals. And it does so in a variety of identifiable – although overlapping – ways or modes. There is evidence that *expectations* may be transmitted through the values of family or peer group (Carter, 1962; Willis, 1977). The term 'expectation' can be used, therefore, to refer to the cues, pressures, and enticements that are often embedded in membership of groups. There is evidence that *feedback* may be transmitted – in the sense of the messages that people receive concerning their suitability for different sorts of social roles (Bernstein, 1965; Hargreaves, 1967). The term 'feedback' can be used, therefore, to refer to the images that people can receive of themselves by their participation in those groups. There is evidence that *support* may be transmitted – in the sense of the reinforcements to aspiration offered by the parents of some immigrant families (Gupta, 1977). The term 'support' can be used, therefore, to refer to the reinforcements and encouragements that group-membership can entail. There is evidence that *modelling* may be transmitted – in the sense of the opportunity to meet and understand ways of life outside those of the person's origins (Ford, 1968). The term 'modelling' can be used, therefore, to refer to the flesh-and-blood examples which offer specific targets for identification to members of the group. And there is evidence that *information* may be transmitted – in the sense of the direct observations and reports that youngsters are able to have of the work habits and patterns of the people they contact in their day-to-day lives (Veness, 1962). The term 'information-provision' can be used, therefore, to refer to the communication of impressions, images and data which people distil from conversation in the groups of which they are members.

There are undoubtedly other contents to messages transmitted by means of the influence of expectation, feedback, support, modelling and information-provision. Other and future research data will further define and extend our understanding of such modes of influences. But, even within the limits of the data cited here, a near-to-complete account of the way in which community-interaction occurs would require some account to be given of events in each of the 30 cells set out in figure 2.

*Figure 2:* **Sources and influences of community-interaction**

*Sources*

| *Influences* | parents | extended family | neigh-bourhood contacts | peer group | ethnic group | teachers at school |
|---|---|---|---|---|---|---|
| expectations | | | | | | |
| feedback | | | | | | |
| support | | | | | | |
| modelling | | | | | | |
| information | | | | | | |

## THEORETICAL FORMULATION

The closest approach to the formulation of a community-interaction theory has been that of R.J. Roberts (1980), although he claims to have advanced little beyond the threshold of a theory-building undertaking. While paying serious attention to social influence upon career development, he also draws heavily upon the sort of phenomenological perspective proposed by Rogers (and later used in this country by Hargreaves and Willis). R.J. Roberts suggests that an understanding of career development is best achieved by means of a biographical account of the way in which each individual constructs a constantly changing series of representations of self and situation. Those constructions are built from the process of interaction with members of the social group to which the individual belongs. The constructions of reality will, for any individual, show some similarity and some dissimilarity with those of other members of the group. There is, accordingly, no absolutely agreed 'self' or 'society' to arbitrate upon career development. There is only what each individual continuously negotiates from the process of interaction. 'Society' is not a massive and impersonal entity, like that described as 'opportunity structure' in functionalist accounts of career development. It is people: individuals in interaction with members of their various groups, constructing partly-shared representations of where they believe themselves to be. 'Self' is not a static collection of introspective statements, as implied by the humanists' use of the term 'self-concept': it is the changing sense that a person takes in large measure from the feedback that he or she receives from others.

What a person says about self and situation will, accordingly, change according to the particular construction of reality being negotiated with a particular partner on a particular occasion. 'Self', 'society' and 'career' are words which – like 'marriage' (R.J. Roberts' analogy) – mean different things, to different people, at different stages in their lives, and with different audiences. Moreover, the process of interaction does not only involve the accommodation of the individual to shared constructions in the group: it also involves the accommodation of group constructions to those of the individual. Not only are 'big-picture' sociological categories modified by the constructions they receive in particular communities: the constructions of communities are modified by those of the individuals they comprise.

R.J. Roberts' contribution to thinking about career development comes from a sociological tradition which appears to take more pride in the radical pedigree of its propositions (*vide* the title of Roberts' paper) than in the prior assembly of hard empirical data to support those propositions (cf. Karabel and Halsey, 1977). R.J. Roberts' attack on K. Roberts and on Daws is not primarily based on the evaluation of evidence but upon the quasi-political colour of the positions they adopt: K. Roberts for his implications for compliance with the economic and social *status quo*, Daws for the 'liberal-progressive' hypocrisy of trying to serve two masters.

Nonetheless, what R.J. Roberts is in process of developing bears many valuable marks of a theoretical formulation which can respond to the evidence cited earlier. Four marks are particularly worthy of note. First, it assigns foreground predictive and explanatory significance to the person-to-person exchanges which occur in the day-to-day encounters of an individual's life in family, neighbourhood and community. Second, it bridges the apparently irreconcilable claims of self-concept theory and opportunity-structure theory for career development, showing how material highlighted by both types of theory is incorporated in exchanges negotiated at family, neighbourhood and community level: in this sense, community-interaction theory does not supplant but tends to unify existing theory. Third, it descriptively indicates the means by which self-concept and opportunity structure may modify and be modified in that process of exchange, permitting us to understand the senses in which neither self nor situation are fixed and absolute in their influence upon what people do. Finally, in explanatory and predictive terms it contributes significantly to our understanding of why an individual may behave differently to other members of the group in which he or she has membership, and why members of a single social class vary so much in the directions and levels of their aspirations and destinations.

## PARALLEL THEORIES OF GUIDANCE

Theories of career development are attempts to describe, explain and predict what happens. Theories of guidance are attempts to think how we might sensibly intervene in what happens. The former is concerned with what is; the latter with what might and should be.

There are scraps of evidence from studies to suggest not only that it is *possible* to represent what happens in community-interaction terms, but that it is *desirable* for students to be encouraged to foster such community interaction in preparing themselves for their futures. For example, Hill (1969) found that although, in general, youngsters tend to become duller and more apathetic as they approach school-leaving, a minority appear to be able to adopt a more purposive, striving posture. Such youngsters, maintains Hill, are not necessarily more intelligent or academically-achieving than their peers, nor have they necessarily received more help from teachers or parents. Instead they are characterised by a firm attachment to some activity outside the school. This enables them to arbitrate on their experience from perspectives taken not only from family and school but from contacts made elsewhere in the community – so that, where aspirations suggested by one experience prove unattainable, alternative aspirations are available.

Among other enticing fragments of evidence that the achievement of the future is enhanced by acquisition of a number of perspectives on self and situation, is the evidence of Bazalgette's (1971) Young Adults Resources Project. On the basis of the experience of the project, Bazalgette argues that, in order to gain access to and use of their own authority as adults, young people need opportunities to interact with established adults – who will be able to use their understanding of adulthood-in-the-world in their dealings with the young people – and also opportunities to fulfil adult roles themselves alongside such contacts in the community.

The term that Bazalgette and his colleagues (Reed *et al.*, 1980) have gone on to use to refer to at least part of that loosely-connected web of help and influence is 'network'. They describe an experiment in which individual working people – with the sponsorship of their employers and the agreement of their trade unions – make themselves available as 'working coaches' to a workshop for a small group of unemployed school-leavers. With the help of a support team funded by the Manpower Services Commission, each coach has developed a programme of help for the youngsters, incorporating contacts with local employers, visits and discussion groups. The workshops meet once a week over a period of six months. The central feature of the experiment is the way in which it brings together working people and school leavers. They were formerly 'inhabitants of different worlds, whose values and attitudes to life appeared to be incomprehensible, in many respects, to each other'. The experiment provides an opportunity for them to 'see the world through each other's eyes'.

Reed *et al.* suggest two sorts of gains which the young people can make from such encounters. First, 'as young people and (the leader) become more willing to see the world through each other's eyes, they begin to see new possibilities in the situation they encounter'. In short, the young adults are released from some of the assumptions in which a limited environment, and a limited school curriculum, have entrapped them.

They acquire more concrete information about what the world of work means, they learn that there are other ways of interpreting and configuring that information, and their behaviour becomes more exploratory. Having more than the one way of looking at yourself in the world is the base for personal autonomy (Law, 1981). Second, as they learn to test and change their own assumptions by exposure to the assumptions of others, the young adults become more able to trust and act on the basis of their own feelings. They show less inclination to withdraw from conflict (like victims), more inclination to risk venturing out and to 'take authority for themselves'. They become 'fighters', not least in taking a more active role in searching for job opportunities, and continuing to persist in that search when earlier attempts draw a blank. Personal striving is the apex of personal autonomy (Law, 1981).

The evidence concerning how people receive help from community contacts leads directly to the sorts of conclusions suggested by Hopson and Scally (1978) concerning the need for community-based, paraprofessional help in counselling. Indeed, it leads beyond such conclusions, for it argues the usefulness not only of paraprofessionals but of a wider range of members of the community who would not pretend to any such designation. A community-interaction reading of career development theory suggests that designated guidance practitioners do not have – and should not seek – a corner on guidance. Clients can – and should – get help from people who have no guidance training, credentials or designation for guidance. The help that is available from professionalised and institutionalised practitioners is – and should be – interwoven in the experience of the client with a wide range of other sources of help and influence. For the professionalised and institutionalised practitioner to imagine that somehow he or she can – or should even try to – accept sole responsibility for the guidance of clients would be a bad case of delusions of professional grandeur. The professional, whether he or she plans for it or not, is – and should be – working with others.

### PLURALISTIC GUIDANCE IN AN UNPREDICTABLE SOCIETY

I argued at the beginning of this paper that thinking about career development is continuously reconfiguring evidence, seeking to resolve problems left by previous generations of theory, and gaining acceptance on the basis of a congruence with the cultural and social context in which it is set. Community-interaction theory does convincingly reconfigure available evidence, and – in particular – helps to resolve problems left by the juxtaposition of self-concept and opportunity-structure theory. It can also be argued that it is congruent with many of the preoccupations of our own social and cultural context.

At present, a combination of steeply rising unemployment figures, an accelerating rate of change in the opportunities offered by the labour economy, and an increasing rate of social change and technological development, are all conspiring to thrust on people at least puzzlement, and at worst threat, concerning the future. It is not only that we know that the lives of our youngsters will be different from the lives of their parents: we also know that we do not know in what *ways* those lives will be different. Change has become self-begetting. In changes brought about by wars, floods, recessions and failed harvests, there is the possibility of abatement and recovery time. But many of the changes now occurring in our society are cumulative and irreversible in their effects. This situation is very hard on people who seek simple, abiding and unambiguous solutions to life's problems. Unpredictability is threatening, and the sense of threat is currently diffuse and pervasive. It is reflected, for example, in a mistrust of inaccessible legislative, executive and commercial monoliths which seem to threaten the purity of our living spaces and to erode any residual capacity we may have to influence our individual destinies. It is linked to changes in the labour economy that undermine the basis upon which we have learned to understand our place in society, and that threaten to impose upon us swathes of time off work – time which we are not sure we are going to know what to do with. It is also linked to our sense of the accelerating capacity of science and technology to extend the power of an invisible elite, enabling them to take actions the possible – intended and unintended – consequences of which terrify our imaginings. We no longer believe in the inevitability of improvement, or even of survival.

One articulate reaction to the threat is – like that of Schumacher (1973) – to demand the re-structuring of society on a more human scale, and to gain a way of understanding what is happening which is more comprehensible than the macro-statistics of massive and impersonal national and international perspectives, paying more attention to what might be called the 'ecology' of human participation in society. Contemporary preoccupation with ecology nicely symbolises the nature of the reaction. For ecology is the study of habitats, and helps us to understand the ways in which changes within and beyond the boundary of the habitat can radically alter the use that individuals can make of their living space.

A pluralistic network conception of guidance based on a community-interaction theory of career development is highly congruent with such a reaction. It takes account of people's need for a human scale and texture to the nature of the problems they confront. Significantly, Reed *et al.* (1980) specifically draw a parallel between what they are attempting to develop and Schumacher's notion of 'intermediate technology'. Indeed, much of the evidence cited in support of a community-interaction theory of career development could, very readily, be re-stated using the language and concepts of ecology; for – like ecology – it focuses attention on a mid-range of phenomena, broader than the individualistic concepts of psychology-based theories, yet not so impersonally broad as the functionalist sociological theories. Unpublished attempts have already been made by my colleague Eddy Knasel to re-state some of the concepts of career development in terms derived from behavioural ecology.

In a rapidly changing and unpredictable environment it is – extending the ecological metaphor – the capacity of individuals rapidly to regulate, acclimatise and develop their behaviour which will prove to be critical. Accordingly, the call is increasingly for an education service which will help young people to develop the capacity to cope with ambiguity and unpredictability in their futures, to have more than one way of conceiving of possible selves in possible futures, to have the kind of flexibility of mind which is capable of abandoning a useless perspective in favour of a useful one, to find a sense of self in a world crowded with conflicting messages. Of the evidence we have examined, that relating to the outcomes of a conception of guidance based on a community-interaction theory of career development – in which a plurality of perspectives can lead to the use by the individual of a range of ways of thinking about possible selves in possible futures – seems to offer the best promise of an appropriate response.

## CONCLUSION: TOWARDS IMPLICATIONS FOR PRACTICE

Theories of career development stemming from differential, developmental and humanistic psychology suggest 'applied-psychological' roles for the guidance practitioner (Hughes, 1976). The preoccupations of guidance are focused upon the ways of helping the client internally to use the data of his or her experience. What is external to the client is a 'given', not a central preoccupation. The helper is interested most in how what is going on *inside* the client influences the achievement of his or her life chances, and how it may be changed.

On the other hand, theories of career development stemming from functionalist sociology suggest very little in the way of a role for the guidance practitioners. Indeed, such theories have proved the least fruitful in generating a parallel theory of guidance. K. Roberts counselled the counsellors to cultivate a 'due sense of modesty' concerning what they might be able to do to help their clients break the dies which have been cast for them. Attention is upon the levers in the 'big-picture' system, all of which are *outside* the range of significant manipulation by the client or his or her helper.

The strength of theories of career development stemming from a community-interaction approach is that they too focus the attention of the practitioner on the world beyond the introspective psychology of the individual, but that they focus on that part of the external world which is proximately in a process of exchange with the individual – in other words, with the sources of expectation, feedback, support, modelling and information which form part of the warp and weft of the client's day-to-day experience. The difference between such mid-range socio-logical focuses, and those of the 'big-picture' focuses of functionalist sociology, is that the former are more accessible to intervention and change. R.J. Roberts' contention that the constructions of the group are accommodated to those of the individual ('the socialiser is socialised') suggests that the network of help and influence may be changed by its experience. The community-interaction perspective provides guidance practitioners with an accessible theatre and a manageable scenario for 'social change' (Watts and Herr, 1976) and for 'intervention in the system' (Law, 1979) which is short of bloody revolution. It engages the interested attention of the practitioner in what happens beyond the consulting room and the classroom, and in how that world might – in small, organic ways be changed. Such a theory of guidance casts the practitioner in the role of 'applied sociologist' as well as 'applied psychologist'. Some aspects of such a role have been explored elsewhere (Law, 1980; Watts *et al.*, 1981). Further explorations of the role of guidance practitioner as applied sociologist will appear in a future paper.

## REFERENCES

Bazalgette, J.: *Freedom, Authority and the Young Adult*. London: Pitman, 1971.
Beck, C.: *Philosophical Foundations of Guidance*. New York: Prentice-Hall, 1963.
Bernstein, B.: 'Social Class and Linguistic Development: a Theory of Social Learning'. In Halsey, A.H., Floud, J., and Anderson, A.C. (eds.): *Education, Economy and Society*. London: Collier-Macmillan, 1965.
Bordin, E.S., Nachmann, B., and Segal, S.J.: 'An Articulated Framework for Vocational Development'. *Journal of Counseling Psychology*, Volume 10, 1963.
Carter, M.P.: *Home, School and Work*. Oxford: Pergamon, 1962.

Daws, P.P.: *A Good Start in Life*. Cambridge: CRAC, 1968.

Daws, P.P.: 'Are Careers Education Programmes in Secondary Schools a Waste of Time? – a Reply to Roberts'. *British Journal of Guidance and Counselling*, Volume 5 No. 1, 1977.

Daws, P.P.: 'The Socialisation-Opportunity Structure Theory of Occupational Location of School Leavers: a Critical Appraisal'. In Watts, A.G., Super, D.E., and Kidd, J.M. (eds.): *Career Development in Britain*. Cambridge: CRAC/Hobsons, 1981.

Dovey, K.A.: 'Politics and Guidance: an Overview of the South African School Guidance Service'. *British Journal of Guidance and Counselling*, Volume 8 No. 1, 1980.

Edmonds, T.: 'Applying Personal Construct Theory in Occupational Guidance'. *British Journal of Guidance and Counselling*, Volume 7 No. 2, 1979.

Fogelman, K.: 'Educational and Career Aspirations of Sixteen-Year-Olds'. *British Journal of Guidance and Counselling*, Volume 7 No. 1, 1979.

Ford, J.: 'Comprehensive Schools as Social Dividers'. *New Society*, 10 October 1968.

Goldman, L.: *Using Tests in Counseling* (2nd edition). New York: Appleton-Century-Crofts, 1961.

Gould, L.: *Matching the Unskilled by Job Preference*. London: Employment Services Agency, 1976.

Gupta, Y.P.: 'The Educational and Vocational Aspirations of Asian Immigrant and English School Leavers – a Comparative Study'. *British Journal of Sociology*, Volume 28 No. 2, June 1977.

Hargreaves, D.: *Social Relations in a Secondary School*. London: Routledge & Kegan Paul, 1967.

Hayes, J.: *Occupational Perceptions and Occupational Information*. Bromsgrove: Institute of Careers Officers, 1971.

Hill, J.M.M.: *Transition from School to Work*. London: Tavistock, 1969.

Hollingshead, A.B.: *Elmtown's Youth*. New York: Wiley, 1949.

Hopson, B., and Scally, M.: 'De-Mystifying and Deprofessionalising Counselling: the Work of the Counselling and Career Development Unit'. University of Leeds, 1978 (unpublished paper).

Hughes, P.: 'The Place of Psychology in Counsellor Education'. *Psychology Teaching*, Volume 4 No 1, 1976.

Jackson, B., and Marsden, D.: *Education and the Working Class*. Harmondsworth: Penguin, 1962.

Kahl, J.A.: 'Educational and Occupational Aspirations of "Common Man" Boys'. *Harvard Educational Review*, Volume 23, 1953.

Karabel, J., and Halsey, A.H.: 'Educational Research: a Review and an Interpretation'. In Karabel, J., and Halsey, A.H. (eds.): *Power and Ideology in Education*. New York: Oxford University Press, 1977.

Kirton, M.J.: *Career Information: a Job Knowledge Index*. London: Heinemann, 1979.

Kline, P.: *Psychology of Vocational Guidance*. London: Batsford, 1975.

Law, B.: 'The Careers Adviser: Tinker, Tailor, Psychologist, Sociologist'. *Careers Adviser*, Volume 3 No. 4, 1976.

Law, B.: 'Guidance Professions, Guidance Institutions and Guidance Communities'. *Collected Original Resources in Education*, Volume 4 No. 3, 1980.

Law, B.: 'Careers Theory: a Third Dimension'. In Watts, A.G., Super, D.E., and Kidd, J.M. (eds.): *Career Development in Britain*. Cambridge: CRAC/Hobsons, 1981.

Law, B., and Ward, R.: 'Is Career Development Motivated?' In Watts, A.G., Super, D.E., and Kidd, J.M. (eds.): *Career Development in Britain*. Cambridge: CRAC/Hobsons, 1981.

Lawton, D.: *Social Class, Language and Education*. London: Routledge & Kegan Paul, 1968.

Maizels, J.: *Adolescent Needs and the Transition from School to Work*. London: Athlone, 1970.

Miller, G.W.: *Educational Opportunity and the Home*. London: Longman, 1971.

Pirsig, R.M.: *Zen and the Art of Motor Cycle Maintenance*. London: Bodley Head, 1974.

Plowden Committee: *Children and their Primary Schools*. London: HMSO, 1967.

Reed, B., *et al.: The Working Coach in Action*. London: Grubb Institute, 1980.

Roberts, K.: 'The Entry into Employment: an Approach Towards a General Theory'. *Sociological Review*, Volume 16, 1968.

Roberts, K.: *From School to Work*. Newton Abbot: David & Charles, 1971.

Roberts, K.: 'The Social Conditions, Consequences and Limitations of Careers Guidance'. *British Journal of Guidance and Counselling*, Volume 5 No. 1, 1977.

Roberts, K.: 'The Sociology of Work Entry and Occupational Choice'. In Watts, A.G., Super, D.E., and Kidd, J.M. (eds.): *Career Development in Britain*. Cambridge: CRAC/Hobsons, 1981.

Roberts, R.J.: 'An Alternative Justification for Careers Education: a Radical Response to Roberts and Daws'. *British Journal of Guidance and Counselling*, Volume 8 No. 2, 1980.

Roe, A.: *The Psychology of Occupations*. New York: Wiley, 1956.

Rogers, C.: *Client-Centered Therapy*. Cambridge, Mass.: Riverside Press, 1951.

Rosenthal, R.: 'Interpersonal Expectations'. In Rosenthal, R., and Rosnow, R.L. (eds.): *Artifact in Behavioral Research*. New York: American Press, 1968.

Rutter, M., *et al.: Fifteen Thousand Hours*. London: Open Books, 1979.

Samler, J.: 'Psycho-Social Aspects of Work: a Critique of Occupational Information'. *Personnel and Guidance Journal*, Volume 34 No. 6, 1961.

Schumacher, E.F.: *Small is Beautiful*. London: Blond & Briggs, 1973.

Shertzer, B., and Stone, S.C.: *Fundamentals of Guidance*. Boston: Houghton Mifflin, 1971.

Speakman, M.A.: 'Sociological Perspective on Development Theories of Occupational Choice'. *Careers Adviser*, Volume 3 No. 3, 1976.

Strodtbeck, F.L.: 'Family Integration, Values and Achievement'. In Halsey, A.H., Floud, J., and Anderson, C.A. (eds.): *Education, Economy and Society*. London: Collier-Macmillan, 1965.

Super, D.E.: *The Psychology of Careers*. New York: Harper & Row, 1957.

Super, D.E.: 'A Life-Span, Life-Space Approach to Career Development'. *Journal of Vocational Behavior*, Volume 16 No. 3, June 1980.

Veness, T.: *School Leavers: their Aspirations and Expectations*. London: Methuen, 1962.

Watts, A.G., and Herr, E.L.: 'Career(s) Education in Britain and the USA: Contrasts and Common Problems'. *British Journal of Guidance and Counselling*, Volume 4 No. 2, 1976.

Watts, A.G., Law, B., and Fawcett, B.: 'Some Implications for Guidance Practice'. In Watts, A.G., Super, D.E., and Kidd, J.M. (eds.): *Career Development in Britain*. Cambridge: CRAC/Hobsons, 1981.

Weir, P.J.: *Significant Others' Influence on the Vocational Development of Australian Form Three Students*. PhD thesis, University of Wisconsin-Madison, 1977.

Willis, P.: *Learning to Labour*. Farnborough: Saxon House, 1977.

# COMMUNITY INTERACTION: A 'MID-RANGE' FOCUS FOR THEORIES OF CAREER DEVELOPMENT IN YOUNG ADULTS

## BILL LAW

### POSTSCRIPT

Re-reading the 1981 article now, I can see that it was yet another of my greedy attempts to get two birds with one stone! I can also now see that I was ignoring a third already in my hand.

### METATHEORY?

I was trying for what – if I had known the term then – I might have called *metatheory*. It uses a more general explanatory frame for a variety of theories about who-gets-to-do-what.

I have cleaned up this act a bit since then, and now use the diagram in figure 3. The diagram tells a story (columns 2–5), beginning with matching and leading to networking techniques. But it also (column 1) links techniques to theories and socio-political considerations. It is a more elegant portrayal of what I set out as *matching, humanistic*, and *functionalist* theories in the first few pages of the 1981 article; and it provides a single

*Figure 3:* **The growing up of careers education and guidance: coalitions of ideas and actions**

| 1 | 2 | 3 | 4 | 5 |
|---|---|---|---|---|
| TECHNIQUES | Matching | ------------------------------ > | | |
| | | Enabling | -------------------- > | |
| | | | Coaching | -------- > |
| | | | | Networking > |
| THEORIES | Differential | ------------------------------ > | | |
| | | Self-concept | -------------------- > | |
| | | | Structural ------------ > | |
| | | | | Interactive > |
| PERCEPTIONS OF SOCIETY | Expanding | ------------------------------ > | | |
| | | Problematic | -------------------- > | |
| | | | Restricted | -------- > |
| | | | | Unpredicted > |
| IDEOLOGIES | Scientific | ------------------------------ > | | |
| | | Humanistic | -------------------- > | |
| | | | Functional | -------- > |
| | | | | Pluralistic > |

column for *community interaction* theory. It would, I think, have helped to have put this diagram in the 1981 article – which still explains its structure.

This linking of careers theory, not only to practice but also to socio-political ideas, has been particularly useful in international settings. It helps to explain the more or less consistent way in which, in all societies, guidance work evolves from matching to networking techniques – and, no doubt, beyond.

An important feature of the diagram is that it portrays all the influences of earlier stages as still with us (for example, computer-assisted guidance, and Records of Achievement and Individual Action Planning, are – at least in part – implementations of differential theory). It suggests that the four sets of techniques do not supplant one another, but complement each other. The right side of the diagram, therefore, represents guidance work as a series of coalitions between accumulating ideas and actions.

This has implications for teambuilding, which suggested my bravest use of it in the UK. I used the four sets ideas (columns 2–5) as a rationale for the implementation by teachers of pre-vocational programmes (such as the Technical and Vocational Education Initiative) (Law, 1986). I cannot say that it has attracted much attention. I take a small comfort from the fact that Bernstein's (1967; 1971) analyses of integrated curriculum in open schools was a much more impressive rationale for TVEI. And, as you know, they speak of little else in the Department of Employment!

### NEW THEORY

The last dozen-or-so pages of the 1981 article was the product of exasperation with both Ken Roberts' opportunity-structure theory and Peter Daws' use of self-concept theory. I like and admire them both but I did not believe either of their theories. Rob Roberts' 'alternative justification' helped a lot: he was the trail blazer. But – unlike a good many Chicago-school sociologists – I wanted *evidence*. My article was substantially a secondary analysis of other people's evidence. Since then real researchers have found better evidence (notably Collin, 1983; R.J. Roberts, 1985; Smith, 1986; Young *et al.*, 1988).

In my own staff-development work, one of the most useful features of the 1981 article has been the *expectation-feedback-support-modelling-information* model. I have extended it: it now reads 'models encountered, feedback received, expectations sensed, support received, impressions formed, *and contacts made*. In this form it provides a particularly useful framework for understanding experience-based programmes (such as work experience). If work experience can be analysed as '(1) being here..., (2) doing this . . . , (3) . . . *with Nellie*', then community-interaction theory emphasises what – and how – students gain from 'Nellie'. It suggests that the *encounters* carry the experience-based freight. This has catalysed ideas about how a progressive curriculum can best support experience-based work (Law, 1986[1]; Law *et al.*, 1991). But its insistence on the importance of the *social* interactive process has been out of kilter with the dominant (libertarian and performance-focused) thinking of the 80s. Maybe that is why it has attracted so little attention.

You will have noticed the irony: my 'metatheory' predicted nothing (well, very little) of what happened during the first ten years after its publication!

### BETTER THAN I KNEW?

Nonetheless, I hold to the view that career development is usefully thought of in terms of biography – and biography is structured by *encounters*. I now like best the way in which this describes and explains change-of-mind. Being able to see it all another way is the catalyst for creative career development. Rob Roberts was on to this long before me: it was the basis of his 1980 article.

Rob Roberts and I agreed with Ken Roberts that career development is substantially a sociological phenomenon. Career roles are forged within, but also – most significantly – *between*, persons. But we disagreed that role is best thought of as functional compliance. Career roles are forged from both agreement and *disagreement*.

Disagreement thrives on the realisation that there are few (structural and functional) fixed, the-same-for-everybody concepts informing career development. What, to some, might appear objective and unproblematic structures of adult and working life – such as, 'self', 'work', 'wealth', 'male', 'technology' and 'enterprise' – are actually social constructions incapable of supporting any single definition. Different people see things differently. So your definition of any of these terms attaches you to some *social* constituencies more than to others. 'Work' (and all those other words) is, therefore, a social 'ligature': it affords you part of your social identity. But you have 'options' concerning where you attach it in the social web (Dahrendorf, 1979).

More dangerously, 'knowing'-things-differently alters the course of events. Changed thought changes action. Think differently about, say, 'women's work', and you will behave differently. The more varied the people you encounter, the more choice you will have about what to think. Change comes from encountering and exchanging with new people. You can change the attachments: indeed you *will*, as you think and exchange your thoughts (a forthcoming article (Law, 1992) indicates how such transactions of agreement and disagreement provide useful bases for workable concepts of autonomy).

All of this has a great deal to do with 'role' – sex-role, work-role, social-role. Sociological concepts of role lie close to the root of much of what we call careers education. It is a useful concept to careers work because it enables us to speak of 'self' and 'situation' in one breath. It relates who gets to do what, at whose behest, and for whose purposes. The notions of 'role' and 'narrative' are – of course – semiologically very close. Career *is* a role narrative – actually a biography.

Community interaction shows how other people's stories give us each a clue to our own. I now hold to it because it illuminates the clues which help us all – black and white, female and male, in inner-city and leafy suburb – to see how *different* our story *might* be . . . if that's what we want.

### NOTES

[1] Law (1986) was, incidentally, the 'future paper' I promised in 1981. I could not get it into a *BJGC* article!

### REFERENCES

Bernstein, B.: 'Open Schools, Open Society'. *New Society*, 14 September 1967.
Bernstein, B.: 'On the Classification and Framing of Educational Knowledge'. In Young M.F.D. (ed.): *Knowledge and Control*. London: Collier-Macmillan, 1971.
Collin, A.: 'A Mid-Career Perspective on the Opportunity Structure-Occupational Choice Debate'. *British Journal of Guidance and Counselling*, Volume 11 No. 1, 1983.
Dahrendorf, R.: *Life Chances*. London: Weidenfeld & Nicolson, 1979.
Law, B.: *The Pre-Vocational Franchise*. London: Harper & Row, 1986.
Law, B., Hughes, B., and Knasel, E.: *Careers Work*. Manchester: Open College, 1991.
Law, B.: 'Autonomy and Learning About Work'. In Collin, A., and Young, R. (eds.): *Interpreting Career*. New York: Praeger, 1992.
Smith, D.V.L.: *The Community Interaction Approach to Occupational Choice – a Study of Fifth Form Leavers*. Unpublished PhD thesis, University of London, 1986.
Young, R., Friesen, J., and Pearson, H.: 'Parents, Adolescents and Career Development'. In Campos, B. (ed.): *Human Development and Counselling Psychology*. Porto: University of Porto, 1988.

# CAREER(S) EDUCATION IN BRITAIN AND THE USA: CONTRASTS AND COMMON PROBLEMS

## A.G. WATTS AND EDWIN L. HERR

*An analysis of the meanings attached to 'careers education' in Britain and to 'career education' in the USA reveals a number of important differences, each of which identifies questionable assumptions in the careers education model emerging in Britain. Attention is also addressed to three major problems which have received inadequate attention in both countries: the socio-political aims of career(s) education, the extent to which it should be concerned with paid employment, and the relationship between the content of careers education curricula and the institutional structures within which these curricula are based.*

The last few years have seen the parallel emergence in Britain and the USA of two educational movements which sound very much the same: the careers education movement in Britain, and the career education movement in the USA. Despite their similar titles, the two movements differ in several major respects, and an analysis of these differences may help to address attention to important assumptions in the British model which have received too little discussion to date. At the same time, the movements share several common problems and dilemmas, and here too some sharing of perspectives and experience may be of value.

### CAREERS EDUCATION IN BRITAIN

At root, the main focus of careers education in Britain has been on the concept of career decision-making. The DES survey defined three objectives (DES, 1973, para. 14):

**1.** To help boys and girls to achieve an understanding of themselves and to be realistic about their strengths and weaknesses.
**2.** To extend the range of their thinking about opportunities in work and in life generally.
**3.** To prepare them to make considered choices.

It saw this 'zone of critical decision' as occurring 'between the ages of 13 and 17 and in some cases well beyond these years' (para. 2), and suggested that a policy for careers education should be implemented in two stages: first a divergent process of exploration, and second a convergent process leading to a decision (para. 15).

First published in the *British Journal of Guidance and Counselling*, Volume 4 No.2, July 1976.

The same three components – self-awareness, opportunity awareness, and decision-making – also underlie the definitions of careers education used by Hayes and Hopson (1971), the Schools Council (1972), Watts (1973) and the Schools Council Careers Education and Guidance Project (1973). In addition, Daws (1969) and Watts (1973) include the concept of preparation for transition – preparing students for the transition to the post-school environment and for the personal adjustment that will be required. A possible conceptualisation of the relationship between these four components is indicated in figure 1. The binding element is the concept of career decision-making: the first three components are concerned with the *formulation* of career decisions; the fourth with the *implementation* of those decisions at the school-leaving stage. The main objective, then, has been to help the student to acquire concepts, skills and information which will help him to formulate and implement the career decisions that immediately face him, though some attention has been paid to the fact that they will also help him when facing subsequent career decisions – indeed it is this notion of equipping students with enduring resources for career development which is one of the main justifications for an educational approach to careers guidance as opposed to the talent-matching approach that was dominant until the late 1960s (see e.g. Watts, 1973, pp. 4–5).

*Figure 1:* **The basic components of careers education**

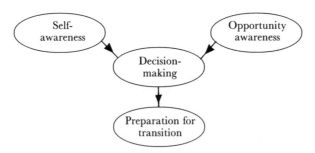

If these are the basic objectives of careers education, however, it is also true that other, broader objectives have been accreted to it. The Schools Council (1972), for example, adds 'an awareness of social involvements and responsibility', and the Schools Council Careers Education and Guidance Project (1973) sees one of its objectives as being that of 'helping children to understand their responsibility to the community' – 'teaching the social skills necessary for development of sound personal relationships and the toleration of other people's opinions'. This objective is only loosely related to the concept of career decision-making, and is perhaps more immediately recognisable as 'social education'. Although for practical purposes of curriculum development careers education can healthily and economically be integrated with social education and indeed with such other areas as moral education and health education (see Daws, 1971), it is conceptually confusing to annex parts of those other territories and still to retain the label 'careers education'.

Similarly, the DES report – having for most of the time conducted its enquiries in the more limited terms quoted earlier – ends by defining careers education as being concerned with the whole area of 'preparation for adult life and with the acquisition of knowledge and development of skills which have relevance for the future':

> 'Implicit in the continuous process are: self knowledge; the exploration of the material world and the people who live in it; the training of the intellect; the development of the creative and aesthetic senses; the challenge of moral principle and the response to it; the awareness and understanding of ethical values. Careers education is not a new concept; it identifies and accentuates certain specific features in the profile of general education familiar to every secondary school teacher' (DES, 1973, para. 163).

It is difficult not to feel that 'careers education' is here being defined so broadly that it no longer has any distinctive identity: it is becoming synonymous with 'education', and indeed 'any secondary school teacher' will probably feel that he can regard what he and his school are already trying to do as being 'careers education' in these terms. If the earlier parts of the report had been based on so broad a definition, they would hardly have been so preoccupied with careers libraries, careers conventions, work experience schemes, and the like.

Perhaps the basic confusion here is between careers education as a specific curriculum centred around the concept of career decision-making, and careers education as a broader philosophical standpoint which seeks to influence the whole curriculum – and indeed the whole structure – of the school. The latter is often used to support the former, but in the end its ramifications go much deeper and wider. Even if it is defined more precisely than in the DES report, however, it can take at least two very different forms. The first is a plea that the curriculum and the structure of the school should be much more 'relevant' to adult life and particularly to the world of work. The important questions of who is to define what is 'relevant', and whether they are to define it in terms of short-term or long-term needs, are left unresolved by this kind of statement, but frequently the implication is that what the school does should be much more relevant to the immediate needs defined by employers. 'Careers education' can also however be used as a plea for greater attention to the autonomy of the individual within the educational system, both in terms of equipping him to make autonomous choices about what kind of person he wants to become and what adult roles he wishes to play, and also in terms of structuring the educational system itself in a way which allows him to take more control over what he learns and why.

The conflicts between these two philosophical approaches are present also in the American concept of 'career education', and since the American movement has been more 'philosophical' in character than the parallel British movement, they will be discussed in greater detail later. In Britain, the dominant use of the term 'careers education' has been not philosophical but to describe a specific curriculum centred around the concept of career decision-making: the gulf between the philosophical and more concrete uses of the term which was evident in the DES report has also been evident in the way in which careers education has been implemented. At the time of the DES survey, 70% of schools had set up a careers education programme in this more limited sense of the term, though in perhaps a third of these cases it was provided only for *some* of the school's students (DES, 1973, pp. 7 and 9).

## CAREER EDUCATION IN THE USA

Since 1971 the US Office of Education has undertaken to implement a major reform and redirection of the American educational structure. The term which has been used to describe this movement is 'career education'. It has been interpreted in many different ways, but in general these interpretations have differed from the British use of the term 'careers education' in four fundamental respects.

The first difference relates to *length*. In the USA career education at school level has been seen as a process starting not at the age of 13 but on entrance to kindergarten, and then proceeding systematically through elementary, junior high and senior high schools, and on into higher education. The most influential model has been that promulgated by the US Department of Health, Education and Welfare (1972, p. 5), which sees grades K–6 (ages 5–11) being concerned with career awareness, grades 7–9 (ages 12–14) with career exploration, and grades 10–12 (ages 15–17) with career preparation: this model has been followed in many of the curricular schemes which have subsequently been developed in individual states. This contrasts dramatically with Britain, where formal careers education is concerned exclusively with what Super and Jordaan (1973) term the 'exploration' stage of career development, and the 'growth' stage is left to the tender mercies of natural forces. Of course, much work done in British primary and middle schools is concerned with development of self-awareness, awareness of the structure of the local community, and so forth. But it is not at present focused in a way which allows the relevance of such work to career development to be made explicit and integrated into an ongoing developmental structure. The basic questions being posed here are: (**a**) whether the growth phase requires, and is responsive to, intervention, and (**b**) if so, how structured that intervention needs to be.

A second difference relates to *depth*. The main approach in the USA has been not to establish careers education as a new subject in the curriculum, but to infuse it into other subjects right across the curriculum. In part this has been a tactical decision: American schools do not have careers teachers even in the primitive form that British schools have them, and therefore had no obvious basis on which to build a 'stand-alone' approach; moreover, the pressures on, and vested interests in, the existing structure of the curriculum, would have made such an approach difficult to implement effectively. This latter argument has also been used to advocate an infusion approach in Britain (Avent, 1972). In part, however, the American decision was also a strategic one, based upon a recognition of the implications for the curriculum as a whole of any genuinely thorough attempt to implement the objectives of career education. In this sense, career education becomes an attempt to orient the whole curriculum around the aim of helping students to identify and develop their individual abilities and interests and to relate these abilities and interests to possibilities within the world of work. Such an approach requires the accretion to each subject of certain curriculum content that may not have been there before, and it also in many cases requires a questioning of the focus of the existing curriculum content. It poses the question of whether the general British approach – that of setting up a separate 'course' – does not allow the objectives of career education to become *contained* in a way which severely restricts the chances of achieving those objectives.

A third difference between the American and British approaches relates to *breadth*. The matrix developed by the federally-funded project at Ohio State University, which has been influential on many state systems, saw eight 'elements' running across the thirteen grades (Center for Vocational and Technical Education, 1972). The first five of these – 'self-awareness', 'educational awareness', 'career awareness', 'economic awareness', and 'decision-making' – are broadly compatible with the first three elements in the British model outlined earlier in figure 1. But the final three – 'beginning competency', 'employability skills', and 'attitudes and appreciations' – enlarge the fourth British element ('preparation for transition') in two major ways: first they are concerned explicitly with the development of work habits and attudes which are necessary for entering and keeping a job, and second they are concerned with the development of specific vocational skills. Indeed, one of the basic objectives for career education laid down by Marland (1971) – who as US Commissioner of Education was largely responsible for launching the career education movement – was that 'every student leaving school will possess the skills necessary to give him a start in making a livelihood for himself and his family, even if he leaves before completing high school'. This concern with specific skill training is open to at least two major objections: first, that training does not create jobs, and that therefore there can be no guarantee that it will lead to employment; and second, that with the ever-increasing pace of technological change, specific skills quickly become obsolescent, so that schools may better serve their students by concentrating on basic skills like literacy and numeracy and on broadening their students' interests and attitudes in a way which will make them flexible and adaptable. The answer to these objections has been to try to relate the skills not to specific occupations but to clusters of occupations – of which the US Department of Health, Education and Welfare (1969) has defined 15 (cf. Training Services Agency, 1975a) – and thus to break the separation of so-called academic and vocational education (Herr, 1972, p. 38). In Britain, on the other hand, the careers education movement in schools has kept itself separate from the concern with vocational training, and has respected the traditional British view that such training should properly be left to employers and to other post-school institutions like colleges of further education.[1] This raises the question of how far effective vocational exploration can be separated from vocational training, both in terms of content – training can provide a very useful form of exploration – and in terms of students' motivation. The latter is particularly important in the American model: to focus students' attention on careers for 13 years without ever equipping them with any specific employment skills would be likely to cause great frustration. It may also however merit more discussion than it has received hitherto in Britain.

This leads to a fourth contrast between the British and American approaches, which is that despite (or perhaps because of) the broader and more utilitarian nature of the American approach to career education, it is also more aware of the constraints which the school environment imposes. In addition to the widely-developed school-based model of career education, with which we have been concerned so far, three other models are being created: an employer-based model which is for adolescent students and, in a few cities, uses employment settings for educational purposes;[2] a less well-developed home-based model which is for adults and adolescents who are neither employed nor in education, and seeks to co-ordinate the use of mass media and career education resources; and a rural/residential-based model which in one isolated location is exploring the possibility that entire disadvantaged rural families can experience lasting improvement in their economic and social conditions through an intensive programme at a residential centre (Career Education Development Task Force, 1973). None of these is currently as well-developed or as widely-implemented as the school-based model. It is however interesting that in Britain the Training Services Agency (1975b) has recently pointed out the difficulty of doing effective careers teaching in schools in which most teachers lack knowledge of industry and commerce, and has suggested the establishment of post-school 'gateway' courses which could cover many of the areas that careers education schemes aim to cover. The three other American models raise the issue of whether the school is the best base for careers education even as defined in Britain (although they have not yet succeeded in seriously challenging it in practice). They also raise the issue of whether careers education ceases when the student leaves school, or whether it needs to be seen as an ongoing process related to the long-term pattern of career development.

### COMMON PROBLEMS

It will thus be seen that the American concept of career education differs from the British concept in a number of basic ways, each of which identifies important questions for those involved in careers education in Britain. In addition, both the American and the British movements face a number of common problems and dilemmas, and it is to these that we shall now turn.

**Socio-political aims**. Perhaps the most important of these problems – and the least discussed – is the implicit socio-political aim of careers education. As Evetts (1973) points out, all educational theories are, in the end, political theories. But careers education is *directly* concerned with the relationship between education and the allocation of life-chances, and is therefore political in a particularly direct sense, especially in a society which is characterised by considerable variations of remuneration and status between different occupations. Four possible approaches can be identified.

First, careers education could be primarily an agent of social control, adapting individuals to the career opportunities which realistically are open to them. In a meritocratic society, this would involve both adapting less-able students to less-skilled occupations, and raising the aspirations of able students from deprived backgrounds. Implicit here are the *right* to take decisions about who is 'able' and who is not, and the *capacity* to do so in terms which are educationally defensible and related not only to present but also to future societal needs. In careers education terms, it requires restricting in a subtle way the nature of the occupations presented to each student, and placing some emphasis on the dignity of all work. Many would see the latter as a 'con', particularly if it coexists with the concept of 'choice': Sessions (1975, pp. 315–316), for instance, says that to tell young working-class people 'that there is satisfaction and dignity in that which is their probable economic destiny is not making it possible for them to have "freedom to choose" – it is rather telling them that they should be satisfied with their lot in life'. According to this argument, careers education is concerned with propagating myths which will help to maintain the existing employment system (see e.g. Grubb and Lazerson, 1975).

Such arguments might lead to a second approach to careers education, which is to see it primarily as an agent of social change. The more individually-oriented approaches examined below may implicitly include social change as a by-product or subsidiary aim, but an approach which focuses *primarily* on social change might for instance see its function as being to make students aware of how exploitative the employment system is. This basically Marxist approach is prescriptive and value-laden, and the concept of 'false consciousness' (i.e. that those who perceive the employment system as non-exploitative have not understood its true nature) is self-sustaining in much the same way as the Catholic concept of an 'informed conscience': it assumes a single 'reality' which will be accessible to those whose eyes have been opened to the truth. It also ultimately sacrifices the immediate health of the individual to the long-term health of the society: if the individual believes that work has dignity, this may give him much greater self-esteem and fulfilment, but this is seen not as a positive outcome but as an impediment to social change. If utopias turn out to be chimerical, such arguments are ultimately nihilistic.

Some of the same objections can also be made to the third approach, which is to see careers education primarily as an agent of individual change. It is for example argued that careers education should be concerned with raising the aspirations of able students from deprived groups like girls, immigrants, and working-class students. This objective, as we have seen, was also present to some extent in the social-control approach, but here the concern is less with increasing the economic prosperity of the society – which in social-control terms may have to be balanced against other considerations – than with improving the life-chances of the individual. The aim is not to help such students make decisions consonant with their own value-system – influenced as it must be by the values of the subcultures from which they come – but with alerting them to, and pushing them towards, decisions consonant with the dominant value system of the society, so increasing their life-chances. Such arguments have some of the prescriptiveness of the two earlier approaches, in that they assume that the interests of the individual will best be served by subordinating their existing values and accepting the instrumental superiority of societal values (Hamblin, 1974, p. 247). Little weight is attached to the problems of adjustment which, for instance, upwardly-mobile working-class students commonly experience (see e.g. Jackson and Marsden, 1966); nor to the possibility that in conforming to the goals of career advancement fostered by a materialistic and status-conscious society, girls for example will sacrifice roles which might provide them with much greater personal fulfilment (cf. also LoCascio, 1974). There is also the problem of raising expectations which society may not be able to meet. This has happened recently with graduates both in the USA and in Britain: expectations of vocational advancement have led more students to apply for higher education; this has led to an expansion of higher education at a pace which has exceeded the change in the skill-mix of the economy; the result has been a frustration of the very vocational aspirations which set the process in motion (Watts, 1974). This is likely to cause considerable individual discontent: as Runciman (1966) has pointed out, the *objective* degree of inequality in society needs to be distinguished from the *felt* inequality, which is experienced only in relation to the reference groups with which those in the lower levels of the occupational hierarchy habitually compare themselves; but the effect of raising aspirations is to extend these reference groups, thus – if the aspirations are frustrated – increasing the sense of relative deprivation. It is interesting that the mismatch between the output of graduates and the number of graduate-level jobs has been one of the most frequently-cited justifications for more attention being paid to career education in the USA (see e.g. Marland, 1971). But if educational institutions are to be concerned with raising the aspirations not of all students from deprived backgrounds but only of those above certain levels of ability, then they face the same problems of selection that, as we have seen, they face with the social-control approach.

The fourth approach to careers education – the non-directive approach – avoids some of these pitfalls by seeing its primary aim as being simply to make students aware of the full range of opportunities, and helping them to be more autonomous in choosing the alternative suited to their needs and preferences. This approach is much more pluralistic than the other three models: it recognises that different students will have different values, and the validity of these differences; it also recognises plurality within society. As with the individual-change model, however, it does not pay any attention to the question of whether society will be able to meet the individual expectations raised by this careers education process, or to the dysfunctional consequences both for the individual and society if it does not. Moreover, the extension of the field of choice could well lead to a situation of what Toffler calls 'overchoice' – 'a time when choice, rather than freeing the individual, becomes so complex, difficult and costly, that it turns into its opposite' (Toffler, 1971, p. 257).

A closer examination of these four approaches indicates that they can be distinguished along two dimensions: one concerned with whether the primary focus is on society or on individuals; the other with whether the approach basically accepts the *status quo* or is concerned with changing it in prescribed directions. Although in figure 2 each is represented as being divided into two discrete categories, for practical purposes they are perhaps better regarded as continua. The designers of a careers education scheme will inevitably find a place somewhere within the two-dimen-sional space represented by the continua. Our concern is that at present they too frequently do so without being aware of the assumptions and implications which have been outlined in this discussion.

**The work ethic**. A related dilemma is the extent to which careers

*Figure 2:* **Four approaches to careers education**

| | Focusing on society | Focusing on individuals |
|---|---|---|
| Change | Social-change approach | Individual-change approach |
| *Status quo* | Social-control approach | Non-directive approach |

education should be concerned with paid employment. There is no doubt that one of the strong forces behind the American career education movement has come from those who have seen it as a moral counter-force to a possible collapse of the Protestant work ethic. A British observer, for example, has reported the movement being described as 'a staggering reassertion of the importance of the work ethic by an administration which has been concerned with the deleterious effects of that sort of individual autonomy which, lacking a central core of shared belief, seemed likely in the late 1960s to threaten the very fabric of American society' (Brennan, 1974, p. 37).

The functional value of such an aim even in relation to a social-control approach to careers education is highly questionable at a time when the capacity of the economy to absorb the population in paid employment appears to be diminishing. People are leaving education later, working shorter hours, retiring earlier, and living longer (see e.g. Central Statistical Office, 1974), and all these trends seem likely to continue (see e.g. Kahn and Wiener, 1967). Moreover, it seems likely that many workers will have to be prepared to face periodic bouts of unemployment even while they are 'economically active'. The futility of a narrowly-based concept of careers education in this situation was expressed graphically by an unemployed County Durham school-leaver:

'You know all that careers work we did at school. It's just a big waste of time. They never told us how to be unemployed' (quoted in Institute of Careers Officers, 1972).

There are profound social and political issues at stake here. The work ethic may be socially functional in a society which 'needs' as much of its manpower as possible to be engaged in economic production. But in a society where this is not the case, it becomes highly dysfunctional: it raises expectations which the society is not able to fulfil, and the result is likely to be considerable individual distress and social unrest.

Such dangers are particularly great where – as in Britain and the USA at the moment – the ideology of social equality has led to pressure from groups which in the past have been content to accept low-status or dependent roles. The realisation that in a work-oriented society status is associated with work roles has for example led to pressure from women to enter the labour force, and to have the same opportunities and pay as men. Again, it has been argued that a significant cause of student unrest over the last ten years has been the student's lack of an accepted social role (e.g. Hatch, 1972; see also Silver, 1965), and the same kind of explanation has been advanced for the distress and anomie experienced by many old people once they retire (e.g. Burgess, 1960, p. 20). Either our society has to find ways of providing paid employment for a much larger proportion of the adult population; or it has to find ways of enabling people to achieve social status and self-esteem without being dependent on paid employment; or it has to face the consequences of doing neither. Only if it takes the first course – and there is no sign of this either in Britain or in the USA – will it be socially functional for careers education to be concerned with reinforcing the work ethic. If it does not do this, then arguably the task of careers education should be precisely the reverse: to weaken the work ethic and emphasise the satisfaction which can be achieved *outside* work.

The arguments against a narrowly work-centred approach to careers education are equally strong if attention is focused not on the welfare of the society but on the welfare of the individual. Not only do all the arguments advanced above apply here too, but in addition attention has to be paid to the fact that many even of those who do work for major portions of their lives draw their main satisfactions outside their occupations, viewing their jobs in purely instrumental terms as providing the means to implement their non-work aspirations (see e.g. Dubin, 1956; Goldthorpe *et al.*, 1968). The implication of this is that if careers education is concerned with helping individuals to find identity and self-fulfilment in terms of their own values, an exclusive focus on work roles will be of limited value to those for whom work is not likely to be a 'central life interest' (Dubin, 1956): not only will it totally neglect those roles which are likely to bring them most satisfaction, but it will fail to realise that for them it is only in relation to these other roles that work roles are likely to have meaning.

It would seem then that there are strong arguments for careers education to be concerned not just with work roles but also with family roles, community roles, and leisure roles. Hoyt (1975, p. 304), for example, has tried to do this by redefining work to cover 'conscious effort, other than activities whose primary purpose is related to either coping or relaxation, aimed at producing socially acceptable benefits for oneself or for oneself and others'. He points out (*ibid*) that such a definition includes work done as part of leisure time, together with the work of the volunteer, of the full-time homemaker, and of the student; and elsewhere states quite explicitly that 'we are not primarily concerned with making people feel a societal obligation to work, but instead with helping each individual discover ways in which work can become a meaningful and rewarding part of his or her life' (Hoyt, 1974, p. 3). Nonetheless, he also goes on to argue in relation to Maslow's needs structure (Maslow, 1954) that 'we have spent too much time attempting to meet student self-actualisation needs and too little time meeting their prior needs for survival and for security' (Hoyt, 1975, p. 307) – implying a clear preoccupation with adaptation to paid employment. The same preoccupation is also evident in the balance of most careers education materials developed both in the USA and in Britain. Such attention as has been paid to the questions raised in this section has tended so far to result in rhetoric rather than any real attempt to tackle their implications for careers education.

**Content and structure**. A final dilemma to which more attention needs to be paid is the relationship between the *content* of careers education – as exemplified in the curricula developed to date – and the *structure* within which these curricula are based. We return here to the distinction made earlier between careers education as a specific curriculum centred around the concept of career decision-making, and careers education as a broader philosophical standpoint which seeks to influence the whole curriculum and the whole structure of the school. Questions about the relationship between them can be posed in relation to each of the elements of careers education outlined earlier in figure 1. For example, is it possible for students to engage in honest, deep and comprehensive exploration of *self* in institutions which they perceive to be largely concerned with controlling them and assessing them in relation to a rather limited set of intellectual skills? Is it possible for students to develop *decision-making* skills in institutions which give them very little control over their day-to-day lives: for instance, is it possible for students to prepare adequately for complex and crucial career decisions in institutions in which they are not even permitted to choose what to wear? Again, is it possible for students to explore adult *opportunities* and to prepare adequately for the *transition* to adulthood in institutions which are largely closed off from the community around them?

It is indeed arguable that the structure of many schools, far from facilitating the development of skills, concepts and information in each of these areas, actually inhibits the development which – in a world without schools – would have occurred naturally. In this sense the attempt to establish careers education curricula in schools can be seen as a doubly ironic instance of the omnipotent claims of the 'schoolmen' (Lister, 1974): not only are formal efforts needed to compensate for the 'deskilling' which the structure of schools has produced, but these efforts are to form part of – and therefore to bolster – the curricular infrastructure of the very institutions responsible for the deskilling. In this way the schoolmen's myth that learning only takes place within educational institutions starts to become reality – a self-fulfilling prophecy.

As we have seen, the American career education movement seems to have been more aware than the parallel British movement of the constraints imposed by the school environment. Neither movement however has yet really addressed itself to the basic questions about the structure of schools which are posed by a rigorous and systematic attempt to achieve the aims of careers education. In the end, such an attempt must pose many of the same questions which have been posed by the deschoolers (see e.g. Illich, 1971). These include the extent to which learning can satisfactorily be separated from action, and the extent to which community and work environments can be harnessed as learning resources (Bremer and von Moschzisker, 1971; Coleman, 1972; Panel on Youth, 1974). Perhaps for example the best way to develop vocational maturity is not to do endless preparatory work in classrooms, but rather to allow students to make and implement vocational decisions earlier, while at the same time recognising and supporting the exploratory nature of these decisions.

## CONCLUSION

We have attempted in the latter part of this paper to identify some of the basic issues to which those involved in careers education need to address themselves if they are to stand any chance of being effective. The movements both in the USA and in Britain have so far been over-pragmatic. They have been concerned with process rather than outcomes, with doing something now rather than pausing to think about its aims and whether it is the best way to achieve those aims. Careers education is beginning to establish a foothold within education on both sides of the Atlantic. If it is now to develop some roots, and to avoid becoming a ritualised tool through which the educational system can protect itself against some of the attacks to which it is vulnerable, then these issues merit much more attention than they have received to date.

### NOTES

[1] This not to say that this view is always carried into practice: cf., e.g., typing courses in schools, and the growth of linked courses with colleges of further education.

[2] This has recently been renamed the 'experience-based' model, and its terms of reference have been extended to include other kinds of community settings.

### REFERENCES

Avent, Catherine: 'The Integration of Careers Education with Other Subjects'. *The Careers Teacher*, Spring 1972.

Bremer, John, and von Moschzisker, Michael: *The School Without Walls*. New York: Holt, Rinehart & Winston, 1971.

Brennan, E.J.T.: 'The "Vo-Tech" in the Context of the 1970s'. *Trends in Education*, No. 33, May 1974.

Burgess, Ernest, W.: *Ageing in Western Societies*. Chicago: University of Chicago Press, 1960.

Career Education Development Task Force: *Forward Plan for Career Education Research and Development*. Washington, DC: National Institute of Education, 1973 (mimeo).

Center for Vocational and Technical Education: *Developmental Program Goals for the Comprehensive Career Education Model*. Columbus, Ohio: Ohio State University, 1972 (mimeo).

Central Statistical Office: *Social Trends No. 5, 1974*. London: HMSO, 1974.

Coleman, James S.: 'How Do The Young Become Adults?' *Phi Delta Kappan*, December 1972.

Daws, Peter P.: 'The Role of the Careers Teacher'. *Careers Bulletin*, Autumn 1969.

Daws, Peter P.: 'Careers Education in the Secondary School Curriculum'. *Careers Quarterly*, Volume XXIII No. 4, 1971.

Department of Education and Science: *Careers Education in Secondary Schools*. Education Survey 18. London: HMSO, 1973.

Dubin, Robert: 'Industrial Workers' Worlds: a Study of the "Central Life Interests" of Industrial Workers'. *Social Problems*, Volume 3, January 1956.

Evetts, Julia: *The Sociology of Educational Ideas*. London: Routledge & Kegan Paul, 1973.

Goldthorpe, John H., *et al.*: *The Affluent Worker: Industrial Attitudes and Behaviour*. Cambridge: Cambridge University Press, 1968.

Grubb, W. Norton, and Lazerson, Mervin: 'Rally Round the Workplace: Continuities and Fallacies in Career Education'. *Harvard Educational Review*, Volume 45 No. 4, November 1975.

Hamblin, Douglas H.: *The Teacher and Counselling*. Oxford: Blackwell, 1974.

Hatch, Stephen: 'Change and Dissent in the Universities: an Examination of the Sources of Protest'. In H.J. Butcher and Ernest Rudd (eds.): *Contemporary Problems in Higher Education*. London: McGraw-Hill, 1972.

Hayes, John, and Hopson, Barrie: *Careers Guidance: the Role of the School in Vocational Development*. London: Heinemann, 1971.

Herr, Edwin L.: *Review and Synthesis of Foundations for Career Education*. Columbus, Ohio: Ohio State Center for Vocational and Technical Education, 1972 (mimeo).

Hoyt, Kenneth B.: 'Answering the Critics of Career Education'. *SRA Guidance Newsletter*. March-April 1974.

Hoyt, Kenneth B.: 'Career Education: Challenges for Counselors'. *Vocational Guidance Quarterly*, Volume 23 No. 4, June 1975.

Illich, Ivan D.: *Deschooling Society*. London: Calder & Boyars, 1971.

Institute of Careers Officers: *About Unemployed Young People*. Bromsgrove: ICO, 1972.

Jackson, Brian, and Marsden, Dennis: *Education and the Working Class*. Harmondsworth: Penguin, 1966.

Kahn, H., and Wiener, A.J.: *The Year 2000*. Toronto: Collier-Macmillan, 1967.

Lister, Ian: 'The Challenge of Deschooling'. In Ian Lister (ed.): *Deschooling: a Reader*. London: Cambridge University Press, 1974.

LoCascio, Ralph: 'The Vocational Maturity of Diverse Groups: Theory and Measurement'. In Donald E. Super (ed.): *Measuring Vocational Maturity for Counseling and Evaluation*. Washington, DC: National Vocational Guidance Association, 1974.

Marland, Sidney P.: 'Marland on Career Education'. *American Education*, November 1971.

Maslow, A.H.: *Motivation and Personality*. New York: Harper, 1954.

Panel on Youth: *Youth: Transition to Adulthood*. President's Science Advisory Committee. Chicago: University of Chicago Press, 1974.

Runciman, W.G.: *Relative Deprivation and Social Justice*. London: Routledge & Kegan Paul, 1966.

Schools Council: *Careers Education in the 1970s*. Working Paper 40. London: Evans/Methuen Educational, 1972.

Schools Council Careers Education and Guidance Project: *Frame*. London: Schools Council, 1973.

Sessions, John A.: 'Misdirecting Career Education: a Union View'. *Vocational Guidance Quarterly*, Volume 23 No. 4, June 1975.

Silver, Harold: 'Salaries for Students'. *Universities Quarterly*, Volume 19 No. 4, September 1965.

Super, Donald E., and Jordaan, Jean Pierre: 'Career Development Theory'. *British Journal of Guidance and Counselling*, Volume 1 No. 1, January 1973.

Toffler, Alvin: *Future Shock*. London: Pan, 1971.

Training Services Agency: *Grouping of Skills*. London: TSA, 1975(a).

Training Services Agency: *Vocational Preparation for Young People*. London: Manpower Services Commission, 1975(b).

US Department of Health, Education and Welfare: *Vocational Education and Occupations*. Washington, DC: US Government Printing Office, 1969.

US Department of Health, Education and Welfare: *Career Education*. Washington, DC: US Department of Health, Education and Welfare, 1972 (revised edition).

Watts, A.G.: 'A Structure for Careers Education'. In Ray Jackson (ed.): *Careers Guidance: Practice and Problems*. London: Arnold, 1973.

Watts, A.G.: 'Higher Education and Employment'. *Universities Quarterly*, Volume 29 No. 1, Winter 1974.

# CAREER(S) EDUCATION IN BRITAIN AND THE USA: CONTRASTS AND COMMON PROBLEMS

## A.G. WATTS AND EDWIN L. HERR

## POSTSCRIPT

Re-reading our paper a decade and a half later, some parts read as historical statements of situations long past; other parts still seem relevant and pertinent. At least one aspect of the paper is embarrassing: the unashamed use of sexist language, for which we repent.

Judging from citations in the work of others, the paper appears to have been found useful in two main respects. The first was its comparative analysis of careers education in the UK and career education in the USA. The second was its analysis of the range of possible socio-political aims underpinning career(s) education programmes. What more can be said on these matters in 1992?

### THE COMPARATIVE ANALYSIS

In the USA, the term 'career education' has declined in its influence and visibility. Certainly there are major school districts and other institutions that continue to use the term (Katzman, 1989). Many however now prefer to describe similar programmes using such terms as 'career development' or 'pre-employment skills'. This has been due in part to the withdrawal of federal support for career education initiatives across the nation: the Career Education Incentive Act of 1977 was repealed in 1981. It also suggests though that the breadth of the concerns embodied in the US use of the term were ultimately too broad to be contained within a term capable of much narrower definition. Certainly the debate about the role of the school in preparing students for work – a debate which career education helped to re-initiate (Herr, 1987) – has continued to be a matter of widespread concern. In particular, it has been a prominent feature of a series of reports from private foundations, government panels, etc., with titles such as *Nation at Risk* (National Commission on Excellence, 1983). These reports have analysed and prescribed remedies for the deficiencies of the nation's schools in nurturing the country's intellectual capital on which its future economic competitiveness depends. Most of the reports, however, have ignored career education *per se* either as part of the problem or as part of the solution.

Meanwhile, careers education in the UK for a while also declined in significance. Its high point was when in the 'Great Debate' initiated by the then Labour Government in 1976, it was regarded as one of the five 'fixed points in the curriculum' in, particularly, the fourth and fifth years of secondary school (DES, 1977). As time went by, however, it became increasingly subsumed within three other curriculum trends: social and personal education (for the 'pastoral curriculum'); school-industry links; and broader curricular initiatives designed to introduce a stronger concern with vocational application across the curriculum as a whole – notably the Technical and Vocational Education Initiative (Watts, 1986). When the new Conservative Government issued its consultative document for the National Curriculum, careers education was not even mentioned (DES, 1987).

Since then, careers education has staged something of a revival, drawing – interestingly – on some features of the American concept as described in our 1976 paper. In terms of *depth*, careers education and guidance is now officially defined by the National Curriculum Council (1990) as one of a number of 'cross-curricular themes'. The notion of some separate provision, either as a separately timetabled subject or as part of separately timetabled personal and social education, is not ruled out, but considerable emphasis is given to the desirability of infusing careers education as much as possible into other subjects across the curriculum. Moreover, in terms of *length*, careers education is no longer viewed as being confined to the later years of secondary school but is seen as being relevant from the age of 5 (see also HMI, 1988). There are however continuing concerns about whether there are strong enough supports for the cross-curricular themes, or whether they will be squeezed out by the pressures imposed by the statutory parts of the curriculum, particularly once TVEI – which includes mandatory contractual provision for careers education and guidance – comes to an end.

### THE SOCIO-POLITICAL ANALYSIS

Our analysis of the socio-political aims underlying careers education and guidance has subsequently been applied in more detail to the issue of unemployment (Watts, 1978; 1983) and to work with girls (Watts, 1985). In the latter case, for instance, traditional careers education programmes saw their role as being to inform girls about the areas of employment that conventionally welcomed women – teaching, nursing, etc. – and about how these could be combined with child-bearing and child-rearing: such programmes can be viewed as performing the 'social control' function of conditioning girls to accept women's traditional roles. In the last few years, there has been stronger emphasis on presenting role-models of women who have managed to succeed in traditionally 'male' areas, thereby in some respects becoming the exceptions that have proved the rule: this represents an 'individual change' strategy. In some programmes it has been extended into a more thoroughgoing attempt to explore the sexism which restricts opportunities for so many women, and the social changes required if such limitations are to be removed: this represents a 'social change' strategy. Other programmes are concerned that such emphases, if taken too far, may restrict the choice of girls who want to adopt 'traditional' roles, and accordingly attempt in a 'non-directive' way to permit space for girls to make – and feel good about – *either* 'non-traditional' *or* 'traditional' choices if they so wish.

It is important to note, however, that 'non-directive' here does not imply 'passive': within a society in which opportunities for women are very circumscribed, such an approach would revert to the 'social control' function of reinforcing the *status quo*. Instead, strong elements of consciousness-raising are needed so that these girls who enter traditional roles do so from choice rather than from conditioning. This illustration poses the more general question of whether a 'non-directive' approach requires some element of the 'social-change' approach if it is genuinely to foster individual autonomy. But how does one get the balance right? How does one extend horizons and make available new values, whilst still respecting and supporting the individual's existing values and their right to choose?

This continues to be a critical question in careers education and indeed in all guidance work. We believe that our model has helped illuminate it, but that more attention than in our original account needs to be given to the interaction between the four approaches. In this respect we consider that on reflection it might be helpful to re-frame figure 2

*Figure 3:* **Four approaches to careers education** (revised version)

|  | Social *status quo* | Social change |
|---|---|---|
| Focusing on societal interests | Social-control approach | Social-change approach |
| Focusing on individual interests | Individual-change approach | Non-directive approach |

in the different form shown in figure 3. Doing so addresses attention to the linkages between the two boxes on each of the vertical dimensions: individual change in conformity with existing dominant societal norms can reinforce the social *status quo*, just as a truly 'non-directive' approach requires some attention to ideas which potentially subvert it.

### REFERENCES

Department of Education and Science: *Educating Our Children*. London: HMSO, 1977.

Department of Education and Science: *The National Curriculum: a Consultation Document*. London: DES, 1987.

Her Majesty's Inspectorate: *Careers Education and Guidance from 5 to 16*. Curriculum Matters 10. London: HMSO, 1988.

Herr, E.L.: 'Education as Preparation for Work: Contributions of Career Education and Vocational Education'. *Journal of Career Development*, Volume 13 No. 3, 1987.

Katzman, S.: 'A Response to the Challenge of the Year 2000'. In Hanson, R. (ed.): *Career Development: Preparing for the 21st Century*, chapter 2. Knoxville, Tennessee: Department of Technological and Adult Education, University of Tennessee, 1989.

National Commission on Excellence: *A Nation at Risk: the Imperative for Educational Reform*. Washington, DC: Government Printing Office, 1983.

National Curriculum Council: *Careers Education and Guidance*. Curriculum Guidance 6. York: NCC, 1990.

Watts, A.G.: 'The Implications of School-Leaver Unemployment for Careers Education in Schools'. *Journal of Curriculum Studies*, Volume 10 No. 3, 1978.

Watts, A.G.: *Education, Unemployment and the Future of Work*. Milton Keynes: Open University Press, 1983.

Watts, A.G.: 'Vocational Guidance in the Curriculum'. *Educational and Vocational Guidance Bulletin*, No. 44, 1985.

Watts, A.G.: 'The Careers Service and Schools: a Changing Relationship'. *British Journal of Guidance and Counselling*, Volume 14 No. 2, May 1986.

# OPEN LEARNING AND GUIDANCE

## DIANE BAILEY

*The expanding and diverse area of open learning is described and difficulties of definition addressed. Rationales for its relationship with guidance based on the learning opportunities structure, the confluence of teaching and guidance, and the concurrence of goals between open learning and guidance, are identified. Models of guidance in relation to open learning are indicated, together with some of the issues these raise. A framework for the analysis of open learning and guidance is suggested, based on the policy objectives of providers (enablement, enfranchisement, cost-effectiveness) and on the components of learning (content, media, styles). The survey indicates a need for better evaluation strategies and a closer scrutiny of what is 'opened' for whom.*

### PROLOGUE: RITA, JUDE AND THE OPENING OF LEARNING

'There's something external to us which says "You shan't!". First it said, "You shan't learn!". Then it said, "You shan't labour!". Now it says, "You shan't love!".'
Thomas Hardy, *Jude the Obscure*, VI.2.

Willy Russell's naturalistic comedy, *Educating Rita* (1981), about the liberation of a working-class woman through the agency of the Open University, has had considerable recent success. Part of its appeal lies in a skilful modernisation of industrialisation's most durable narratives: self-help and the parish boy's progress. Rita travels not from log cabin to the White House, but from a state of educational dispossession to one of owning an understanding of Shakespeare and Ibsen. Her self-actualisation also involves a transformation of style and a shedding of her redundant marriage. In spite of its misleading impression that the OU offers one-to-one weekly tutorials, it is a narrative with which many open learners can identify.

Almost a century before, *Jude the Obscure* (1895) mounted a comprehensive interrogation of the potent myths of upward mobility and individualistic advancement, as popularised in Samuel Smiles' *Self Help* (1859) and its sequels. Hardy's self-taught hero, maturing from bird-scarer to stonemason, is progressively disenfranchised from every adult role, as parent, lover, citizen, worker and learner, by systems constructed to regulate and to delimit access. Learning, labour and love, as the

---

First published in the *British Journal of Guidance and Counselling*, Volume 15 No.3, Sept. 1987.

epigraph above asserts, are correlated as interpenetrating sites of social and economic reproduction. Jude functions as the exposing image of the contradictory nature of these systems and of their sustaining narratives. His aspirations are towards the classics and theology, the curriculum of privilege and power. The more avidly he pursues these by home study, the more vehemently is he rejected by the colleges which refuse to legitimate his learning – in letters that constitute a kind of anti-guidance. By a deeper irony, the more he learns about his own situation, the less he is fitted to participate in any institution, educational, occupational or social. Extra-mural in a very literal sense, he chalks on the college gates the words of Job: 'I have understanding as well as you; I am not inferior to you ...'.

*Jude*, with its post-Darwinian and post-Benthamite hero, is a terminal novel in several senses: *fin-de-siècle*, Hardy's farewell to fiction, and a terminus of the *bildungsroman* or novel of education. It remains a classic exposition of the closure of learning and of the active tensions this produces in individual lives. *Educating Rita*, superficially the more appropriate tract for our times, encompasses a less radical view of the opening of learning. The initially obscure Rita is empowered with a new role, a new voice and wider life choices. But the text can declare this only by a fairly drastic reductionism. Access, for example, is construed chiefly as a matter of legislation. *Rita* largely reproduces, without ambiguity, the consoling narratives of self-help and the hairdresser's progress. Educating Jude was and is a more problematic enterprise.

## OPEN LEARNING: THE CURRENT SCENE

Open learning is now a growth area. It represents a collection of strategies rather than a discrete mode, one band within the learning opportunities spectrum. It has flourished in the same climate as modularised courses, individualised curricula and work-related experiential learning which also characterise the Youth Training Scheme, the Certificate of Pre-Vocational Education and the Technical and Vocational Education Initiative (Phillips, 1986). Indeed, 'graduates' of these schemes will be future candidates for the proliferating open-learning schemes for adults. Increasingly, colleges are establishing open-learning units to convert existing courses to packages or to provide drop-in facilities.

The current open-learning map is difficult to draw. One subset of open learning is the distance and correspondence schemes, in which learner and tutor are geographically separated. Wolsey Hall and the

National Extension College continue to offer external degrees, GCEs and many vocational and professional qualifications by home study. Collaborations between NEC and colleges or the voluntary sector have resulted in schemes like Flexistudy and its clones, combining elements of face-to-face and distance study.

More recent features are the Open Colleges Federations. These are regional consortia of providers from adult, further, higher and community education, and from careers and educational guidance services. The object of federation is to improve access by proactive and interventionist policies: alternative entry requirements, credit transfer, combined curricula, team teaching, outreach work, child-care facilities, and energetic guidance and advocacy. The Federations target educationally disadvantaged groups: 'women, ethnic minorities, the disabled, those with few, if any, formal qualifications, the unemployed, the elderly and people with special needs' (North London Open College Network brochure). These activities are relatively small-scale in terms of the total operations of the participating bodies: it is a federation of parts rather than of wholes.

The largest landmarks in the open-learning landscape are the Open University, which from 1971 has offered degree courses on an open-access basis, and the Manpower Services Commission's Open Tech Programme, which between 1983 and 1987 initiated over a hundred schemes developing work-related learning. To characterise these two as oriented respectively towards education and training would be misleading. The Open University's undergraduate programme includes about 160 courses, many of them potentially vocational. The Continuing Education programme includes community and health education, in-service teacher training, scientific and technological updating and the Open Business School. A 1980 study reported that two out of three undergraduates tried for better pay, promotion or a job change as a result of their studies (Open University, 1986). Conversely, the Open Tech has generated models of work-related open learning wider than the training for 'technician and supervisory levels' originally envisaged (MSC, 1982). First, there are schemes producing multi-media learning packages, aimed at occupational groups (laboratory technicians, nurses), at particular industries (tourism), or at clusters of transferable skills (robotics). Second, there are large-company schemes, based at ICI, Austin Rover and Lucas, which are converting or augmenting existing training by the use of computer-based learning, company-specific packages and on-site resource centres. Third, there are open-learning delivery systems based on local education authorities or on regional consortia (e.g. Taytec) which offer employers or individuals a menu of learning packages, well-equipped open-access centres or mobiles, with tutoring and guidance arranged and paid for as required.

This rapid survey of open-learning country shows it as increasingly and variously populated. Developers have an understandable sense of ownership in their preferred versions. But the very elasticity of the term can be convenient, bridging the often unhelpful distinction between education and training. 'Open' has an ambivalent syntactic status, as mainly adjective but partly verb, making 'open learning' potentially an imperative as well as a substantive. 'Open' suggests both the creation of new opportunities and the removal of old barriers. 'Learning' shifts the emphasis from institutions to individuals – especially helpful in relation to adult needs in a 'post-education society' (Evans, 1985).

## OPEN LEARNING AND GUIDANCE: RATIONALES

What are or should be the relationships of guidance, considered as a family of practices and theories, to these proliferating schemes? Most policy makers and practitioners acknowledge that, in whichever of its incarnations it appears, open learning necessitates some kind of accompanying guidance. Different rationales for the relationship are advanced. One concerns the *learning opportunities structure*. Open learning multiplies options, both in terms of the total number of routes to a particular learning end and of the subsidiary choices attendant on any one route. There are more schemes available, offering more permutations of modules. The argument is that educational guidance has a key role in the matching of clients' clarified needs to the available learning opportunities. Open-learning structures make this guidance role at once more necessary, because of the bewildering multiplication of schemes, and more possible, through a closer matching of personal preferences. One broad inference from this argument is that the multiplication of options necessitates a plural approach to guidance in terms of what it does, who provides it, and what technologies are used.

A second argument stresses the *changed role of the teacher/tutor/trainer in open learning*. Open learning marks the vanishing point of the 'disappearing dais' much discussed since the sixties *à propos* student-centred learning (Whitehead, 1966). In those open-learning models in which the main teaching artery is the package of linked texts, tapes, kits or programs, the tutor is displaced from main subject authority towards the guidance roles of counselling, encouragement, coaching in learning skills, or advocacy. A study of tutors in open learning has shown how wide is the interpretation of that role (Clarke *et al.*, 1986). The Open University's title 'tutor-counsellor' reflects the integration of roles, as do titles of industrial counsellor, mentor and facilitator used in various Open Tech schemes where often learners can choose a tutored or an untutored study route. The fundamental continuity of teaching and guidance has been argued by, for example, the Unit for the Development of Adult and Continuing Education (1985, para. 2.13.1):

'Guidance has always been part of the role of the good teacher and for most learners the teacher will be the only source of guidance once a course of study has begun.'

From the other side, the curriculum for counselling has been defined (Martin, 1985) as self-instruction or 'teaching in its best sense': that is, the 'giving away' to clients of the functional skills of exploration, understanding and action. This rationale rests on the melting of role boundaries in open learning. The more elective the learning mode, the more desirable becomes the elision of guidance and teaching.

A third argument stresses the *concurrence of goal* between open learning and guidance. Polemicists of open learning often define the end goal as increased independence in the learner, who is encouraged to identify her or his own learning objectives and to take increasing control over their realisation. Enhanced autonomy is frequently, if vaguely, invoked as contributing to or resulting from open learning. A large body of counselling theory across several specialisms postulates the counselling goal as increased self-management or self-actualisation by the client. This third rationale based on the high degree of congruence between open learning and guidance points to a shared vocabulary of client- or learner-centredness, a shared dynamic model of the person-as-learner and a shared investment in the technologies of learning.

These three rationales for the relating of guidance to open learning emphasise three different and correlative aspects of guidance: information-giving and the matching of needs to opportunities; in-course support for learning; and the long-term goal of progressive self-realisation. These three processes are respectively appropriate, perhaps, to the person as enquirer, the person as (enrolled) learner and the person as a whole. All three processes have been recognised in recent discussions. The Unit for the Development of Adult Continuing Education (1986) has made recommendations for a national strategy to develop more stable, equitable and accessible guidance services and to improve on the unco-ordinated and volatile provision of the last decade (Watts, 1980).

The UDACE model of guidance, augmenting earlier models (ACACE, 1979; 1982; Butler, 1983; Hopson, 1985), comprises a range of distinct, but inter-related, processes. The Open Tech project on guidance and open learning defined guidance similarly as a range of helping activities (Bailey, 1987):

*Informing:* providing clear, accurate, unbiased and relevant information to the individual, in the forms and at the pace most useful to her or him.

*Advising:* making suggestions based on the helper's own knowledge or expertise for the individual to consider.

*Counselling:* working in a non-directive way with individuals to help them explore and assess their needs and the options available to them.

*Coaching:* creating or structuring a learning experience so that the individual can practise and gain new knowledge, skills or perceptions.

*Assessment:* gathering and giving information about the individual or about specific aspects of the individual (abilities, aptitudes, performance, values, interests, etc.).

*Advocacy:* taking action on behalf of and with the agreement of the individual or group.

*Feedback to systems:* providing information to organisations on the experiences or problems of individuals which require changes in the system.

Guidance and open learning are both aimed at removing blocks to learning, with different combinations of help appropriate at four stages of development: pre-entry, enrolment, in-course and exit (see figure 1). All stages can be protracted and intermittent, with numerous variables affecting guidance provision. Help may be sought out by the learner or laid on by the scheme or the employer. Guidance may be embodied in people or be mediated by low or high tech. It may be available from professionals (careers, educational or personal counsellors), from para-professionals, from those with other main roles (managers, supervisors, administrators), from peers, colleagues or family. Potentially, the routes to and through open learning are legion and the learner constituency enormous. A matching, symbiotic guidance provision would be equally flexible and available. However, the empirical conjunction of open learning and guidance practice is raising several issues.

*Figure 1:* **The learning sequence: a guidance matrix**

| | Informing | Advising | Counselling | Coaching | Advocacy | Feedback to systems | Assessment |
|---|---|---|---|---|---|---|---|
| **PRE-ENTRY** | – range of options<br>– finance<br>– OL scheme details<br>– company intentions | – levels of difficulty<br>– need for preparation<br>– pros and cons of OL<br>– job prospects | – reviewing needs<br>– awareness raising<br>– appraising current work role<br>– coping with blocks | – decision making | – employer contacts OL scheme for employee<br>– guidance helper contacts scheme for client<br>– scheme contacts LEA on fees | – by OL scheme to companies on training needs<br>– to funding agencies on grants | – formal aptitude tests<br>– self-diagnosis of capabilities |
| **ENROLMENT** | – specific details on packages, practicals, tutorials, methods of payment | – study skills<br>– order of modules | – choosing a programme<br>– understanding OL<br>– boosting confidence | – learning management skills | – scheme approaches employer about time off, fees, support<br>– helpers contact careers service etc. on job prospects | – to validating bodies on credit exemptions | – informal (vocational) assessment |
| **OL LEARNING** | – use of libraries<br>– update of modules available<br>– whereabouts of other learners | – where to study<br>– who can help | – using assessment constructively<br>– learning styles<br>– coping with blocks | – running self-help groups<br>– planning time<br>– using telephone support<br>– handling self-assessment questions | – referral to counsellor or guidance specialist<br>– liaison with employer/trainer | – from employer on work performance<br>– to MSC on gaps in provision<br>– to colleges/employers on OL | – range of assessment from tutor, trainer, peer, self |
| **EXIT** | – new range of learning options<br>– data on jobs | – where to get specialist help next | – appraisal of current position<br>– exploration of new needs | – writing up reports<br>– applying learning to workplace practice<br>– self-preservation | – referral for further training<br>– liaison with Jobcentre or careers service | – to/from guidance agencies on OL as a form of training<br>– to employers' bodies | – reprofiling<br>– final assessment |

## ISSUES

*Pre-entry guidance*, a broad church of interests rather than a single agency or culture, is deeply and problematically implicated in the major issue of adults' access to learning. One sizeable element in this issue is the operational separation of educational and vocational guidance, manifest not only in the constitution of the main agencies, but in workplaces and institutions. Because much recent open learning is work-related, the lack of coherence here may be exacerbated. In any event, the workplace will become an increasingly important context for guidance – not least because of the possible emergence of the paradoxically 'involuntary' open learner. Providers of open learning, either subsidised or self-financing, cannot offer comprehensive and independent guidance to all enquirers. Accurate referral requires time, energy and good-quality information – resources not likely to be available in many schemes. In the absence of a rationalised and clearly signposted national system, guidance from learning providers is likely to exist in a necessary but uneasy relationship with their marketing operations.

*Post-entry guidance* is a matter of the support systems which attach to particular open-learning schemes. As they emerge, these pose interesting questions: Is the innovation that characterises much of the curriculum design and educational technology also evident in the design of support systems? How dominant is the Open University model of counselling and what kind of progeny has it produced? What models, styles and levels of guidance are embedded in support systems: remedial/universalist, pro-active/reactive, problem-centred/growth-oriented, purist/eclectic? Does the professed opening of learning lead to a consequent opening of guidance in terms of – say – role changes and role accretions, the expansion of lay counselling, shifts in workplace relations and authority structures? What level and style of training for guidance roles is desirable and possible? The politics of guidance is an underdeveloped area. Open learning may prise some of its fissures slightly further apart. Ready collusion with the seductive terminology of openness can block a systematic evaluation of just who is learning what. A sense of proportion points to the persisting closure of most learning systems for many people for much of the time.

### A FRAMEWORK FOR ANALYSIS

One framework for the analysis of open-learning schemes is that suggested by the policy objectives, or the institutional motives that bring them into being. There are three main groups here: the adoption of open learning as *enablement* – making learning more convenient and facilitating participation; as *enfranchisement* – making learning opportunities more equal and extending participation to new groups; and as *cost-effectiveness* – providing learning more cheaply than by equivalent schemes. These three are not mutually exclusive, separable or explicit in fully operational schemes. They correspond roughly to what have been seen as three definitive requirements for an effective national education system: the augmentation of individual choice, of social justice, and of economic effectiveness (Halsey, 1983).

This framework concerns the 'why?' of open learning. A complementary one concerns the 'how?'. This distinguishes three main components of schemes: the *content* – what is learned and how a curriculum is constructed; the *learning styles* – the range of ways by which learners pursue their learning objectives; and the *learning media* – the selection of technologies through which learning and guidance are delivered. Clearly these three are interdependent. The choice of medium, for instance, can reinforce a particular learning style. But their correlation can be complex and contradictory rather than simple or causal, as can the wider correlation between the why and the how of open learning. The following sections look at various schemes and the relevant guidance issues in terms of these two linked frameworks of policy objectives and of scheme components.

## ENABLEMENT

There is no doubt that open-learning schemes have enabled people to learn more conveniently. Marketing messages often concentrate on their 'own pace own place' dimension, sometimes with the dubious corollary that this promotes autonomy. Early on, the Open University was known as 'the university of the air', with an emphasis on its ubiquity rather than on its open-access policies. The blocks of circumstance are easier to point to than those of psychology and ideology.

A hierarchy of the major blocks to participation might extend from purely environmental factors to profoundly personal factors:

*External*      Geography
                         Fixed timetables
                         Lack of ladders and bridges to learning
                         Inappropriate curricula and pedagogies
                         Pre-requisite entry qualifications
                         No child-care facilities
                         Cost
                         Employers unconvinced of the value of training
                         Specific work experience needed

Stereotyping by age, race, sex, class and physical fitness
Role conflicts
Pressures of time
Isolation and lack of support
Legacy of poor learning experiences
Poor self-image (as not-a-learner)
*Internal*     Unclear motivation

This is a crude schematisation that ignores the social, material and ideological construction of experience. It also ignores the dynamic interplay of factors in the experience of most people: give women child-care facilities and they gain confidence; shift the physical contours of education and people are jolted out of what George Eliot called 'their habitual selves'. But a reductive list does show where open learning is operating most effectively, towards the external pole. Guidance, however, operates primarily with individuals towards the internal pole, with its feedback role exerting pressure for change on more external factors.

Open Tech schemes that offer role-based, skills-based or industry-wide curricula have been particularly effective in designing learning opportunities that realise the 'own pace own place' ambition. The scheme for site managers developed from an existing college syllabus by the Construction Industry Training Board (launched 1984), and that for pub managers developed by the British Institute of Innkeepers (launched 1985), both combine elements of distance, work-based and experiential learning so as to circumvent problems of place and time. Learning is taken to the building site and the pub. Their different guidance strategies both try to harness the existing management skills and energies of their target occupational groups.

The pub business scheme suggests that learners get off-job seminars through the brewery companies and that they also locate their own mentors as allies in learning. A dual workbook helps the learner choose a mentor and helps the mentor undertake the role. The mentor may offer subject expertise, help with study management, or simply listening time. S/he may even police the process – more minder than mentor. The relationship is essentially contractual, the two parties deciding its scope, nature and duration, with no cost to the scheme. This revival of what one writer calls 'an age old practice in a knowledge-based society' (Gerstein, 1985) is now well advanced in America (Krupp, 1985) and more slowly advancing in British open-learning schemes, though without as yet much evaluation of its benefits.

The scheme for site managers has developed a more formal, plural and costly approach to guidance. The lynch-pin is the tutor whose roles encompass the initial marketing of the scheme, pre-entry counselling, subject teaching of all modules, negotiating assignments, assessment, advocacy to employers and systematised feedback. All tutors are trained and supported from a central unit. In addition, the learners get guidance sheets (on using libraries, etc.), occasional teleconferences, and a system of profiling. Profiling, begun before enrolment, involves completing a self-appraisal exercise, first alone, then in consultation with a tutor, to identify learning needs and to plan a programme (or opt out). The profile acts as a basis for regular progress reviews. An early evaluation of the scheme (Hawkes, 1984) reported considerable user satisfaction, and by 1986 over 150 people were enrolled on tutored routes, with over 8,000 packages sold, one large company using these successfully for in-company training (PA Management Consultants, 1985).

These two schemes are reasonably representative of the growing number of work-related open-learning systems, many fostered by the Open Tech. Their guidance strategies, exemplifying respectively support initiated by the learner and support provided by the scheme, show that innovation *is* active in the more invisible area of support, as well as in tangible package production. Participation in such schemes is still, however, minimal. There are an estimated 100,000–200,000 site managers, for example. The occupational grapevine and the multiplier effect spread information slowly and open learning still lacks a clear public definition. Schemes' pre-entry guidance and publicity have to be confined to likely entrants. Convenient learning has costs and limits.

## ENFRANCHISEMENT

It is often non-physical forms of institutionalisation which prove most recalcitrant: the ideological construction of knowledge and its containment within discrete disciplines; the mechanisms for recognising and certificating what is known; the privileging of one kind of knowledge over another, of the abstract over the concrete, of the written over the oral, of the cognitive over the affective, of the instrumental over the inspirational, of the male over the female. Changes here will hardly be effected by schemes concerned mainly with contingent factors. Enfranchisement implies a radical transfer of power. When Gentile, under Mussolini, proposed apparently liberal reforms in education, Gramsci (1971 ed.) objected:

'But as with most idealistic conceptions of education, "freedom" reflected only that which was compatible with the existing social and economic order. So that where the philosophers strove towards the higher ideals of education, the structure of the education system itself denied those very ideals.'

Open-learning initiatives range from those with a high degree of compatibility with the 'existing order' to those that are marginal or oppositional. In the first group come schemes focused on skills shortages (robotics, information technology), on favoured learning populations (small-business people), on employer-sponsored provision (practical training facilities) or on grant-attracting areas (Open University INSET courses). At the other end of the scale come schemes for disadvantaged groups or those exercising positive discrimination (Open Colleges Federations, women into technology schemes, law for ethnic minorities courses).

Open Colleges aim primarily to enfranchise new participants, though institutional survival is also a motive. There is evidence that pooling and reallocating resources and working intensively at local levels does effect changes in who learns. The Open College of South London currently has 3,000 enrolled students, with 1,000 involved in a flexible drop-in learning programme. Some external barriers remain: you will find a crèche when you attend, but you still have to get there at set times. The adaptation, rather than deconstruction, of the curriculum is achieved by access courses, some accreditation of experience, credit transfer and a broad restructuring of the existing provision into four levels:

(**a**) Basic literacy and numeracy (with links to schools and to the 16–19 provision).
(**b**) The application and development of basic skills (with links to voluntary and paid work).
(**c**) The application and development of conceptual skills (with further links to voluntary and paid work).
(**d**) The application and development of critical and evaluative skills (with links to higher education).

Whilst arguably retaining a hierarchical structure to learning, this does rationalise the bewildering array of courses into an approachable form. Participants are encouraged 'to develop a habit of identifying themselves with a curriculum rather than with an institution'. Guidance is integral to this process and to the accompanying 'continuous process of staff development'. Central to the approach is unhurried counselling and assessment at pre-entry, advertised and available on an outreach basis.

Also integral are peer support and co-counselling, accurate advocacy and regular feedback to providers. The aim is to compensate for the missing institutional base with co-ordinated support. The model is highly interventionist, but essentially marginal and small-scale.

On a larger scale, the Open University has enfranchised new groups, but how far and how radically is arguable. Open access was seen as contributing to social equality by the Labour administration founding the university in 1969 (Perry, 1978). In 1980 it was reported that less than 20% of each entry were manual workers, that only three out of ten of these graduated, and that they took longer to complete the degree than others (Evans, 1985). However, *Into the 1990s*, responding in 1986 to the green paper on higher education, reported that one in two new undergraduates had blue-collar fathers, compared with one in five of mature entrants to other universities (OU, 1986). Obviously these figures may reflect the difference between the socio-economic groups of students and of students' parents rather than a change over time. The evidence that the university has served older cohorts of the population (median age of entry 32–33) and those with disabilities is less equivocal. It also serves the unemployed to some extent, though 70% to 80% of its undergraduates are in paid employment and applications from the South-East predominate. The Open University currently appears Janus-faced, retaining its enfranchising aspect alongside an emphasis on its 'market potential' and consistency with 'government policy preferences' (McNay, 1986).

The role of guidance in these processes is notoriously difficult to evaluate. Who enters the system is determined by many factors beyond the quality of the enquiry service, though who stays in it is closely affected by the quality of its counselling system. To assess the correlation between counselling and completion rates requires control groups that are rarely available. Studies of entrants considered at risk and given extra counselling suggest positive correlations (Thorpe, 1979). Models of collaborative schemes with other education, community and industrial agencies suggest a resulting wider entry (Turner, 1986). For this to happen, perhaps the guidance needs to be local, free-range and collaborative, rather than owned or managed by one provider, however benevolent.

### COST-EFFECTIVENESS

The MSC's consultative paper on the future of open learning stressed cost-effectiveness in conjunction with flexibility as one important benefit to providers (MSC, 1985). Most respondents to the paper proved to be in favour of MSC's incorporating Open Tech developments into their wider training programmes (Hilgendorf and Welchman, 1985). The arguments for cost-effectiveness rest on the capacity of open learning to cope with small and irregular groups of learners, to respond to training needs quickly and without disruption to production schedules and, ultimately, to lower resistance to change by introducing transferable cross-sector training and by involving people co-operatively. The implication is that open learning, through its flexible, adaptive nature, can improve the fit between organisational needs and training programmes, between labour-market demands and the available pool of skills, and even perhaps between market forces and individual aspirations. In so doing, wastage is reduced.

The relationship between guidance aims and cost-effectiveness is complex. Providing guidance, even if low- and high-tech resources are ingeniously deployed so as to release staff for the work they do best, can be costly (Bailey, 1986a). Schemes that give customers a choice of supported or unsupported routes make it necessary to put price tags on elements of education that have been hitherto unquantified or submerged in general budgets. Inexperienced learners, however, do not necessarily know at the outset which route they want, or what they will get for their money. They need pre-entry guidance to help them determine their post-entry guidance. Good learning materials have high development costs which may or may not be offset by low delivery costs. Increasingly, elements of support are being built in, as guidance on study skills or time management, self-assessment, advice on learning resources and peer-groups, and needs analysis through workbooks or computer programs. But these often presuppose confident, experienced users, whereas many need (often costly) coaching in basic learning skills to function as independent learners.

Many schemes cannot offer independent guidance at pre-entry, since the cost of this must be recouped through enrolment fees. Marketing and guidance objectives are only partly consistent with each other and partly discrepant. Marketing is aimed at the employer or at the individual as consumer; guidance is aimed at the individual as learner or as a whole.

'Captive' learners in company schemes may have at worst a shotgun alliance with open learning and at best a jointly negotiated training programme. ICI's Open Tech scheme aims for the latter. Groups being trained initially are office staff, craftsmen, engineering design staff and process operators, with extensions planned to supervisors and managers. Ten centres in the UK provide on-site computer terminals with appropriate software and self-study units. Trainees book in for learning that is mainly self-paced and self-assessed. Support is dependent on workplace role changes, in a company climate shifting generally to more open styles. A hierarchy of potential objectives for the open learning scheme has been proposed by Foggo (1986):

Extrinsic motivation; management-led

- ❖ to get basic essential training to do the job;
- ❖ to improve effective job performance;
- ❖ to produce a more rounded capability (gain a wider grasp of the context of the job);
- ❖ to prepare for a new job or career, in or outside the company;

Intrinsic motivation; self-initiated

- ❖ to pursue personal interest.

The assumption here is that more guidance will be needed at the extrinsic pole. Initial recruitment has been management-driven, but training programmes have been developed through joint consultation. Trainers whose past roles were as 'arrangers and record keepers' are now contributing to writing courseware, to advising and tutoring, and to acting as advocates. So far, participants' responses have been very positive and a computerised scheme evaluation, based on elements of a repertory grid, is now running. Cost-effectiveness is demonstrable from the ratios of development capital to potential employees trained, by comparison with alternative training methods. Most learning is done in company time and guidance costs are absorbed. In addition, ICI hopes to sell computer-based training packages to other companies here and abroad.

This model of open learning, however, is not readily transferable to other training situations. Size is important, as is the company culture and the availability of development capital. A report by PA Management Consultants (1985) claims that many companies see training as essentially task-related and are, therefore, likely to develop and assess open learning in rather narrow ways:

'This desire to "control" Open Learning might be thought to conflict with the principles of "own time, place and pace", but we suggest that it is inevitable in the context of the training policy of most large organisations' (para. 3.3).

Where the company draws up a narrowly instrumental training agenda, the gap between organisational and individual goals may widen. Where – adding insult to injury – open learning is perceived as a way of transferring training costs to individuals who learn in their discretionary time with no compensation, many of the psychological benefits of open learning evaporate. Guidance then can become merely remedial and ameliorative. Reluctant trainers coaxing reluctant learners through self-study packages may smack of schooldays for some, and the question arises: 'Cost-effective for whom?'

### THE CONTENT OF LEARNING

Open learning is extending the possibilities of individualised curricula and customised training programmes. Modularisation is a key feature in this. The *à la carte* menu approach to programme construction and the importation from America of concepts such as contract and negotiated learning increase the consumer's control over what is learned and in which order, and allow the provider to meet differing levels of need simultaneously. Open learning now encompasses a very wide range of subjects, from zoo-keeping to counselling skills, from highways maintenance to Wittgenstein (Lewis, 1984). Greater choice necessitates more help and information for enquirers. Multi-module schemes often now provide course planners, maps or simple pre-entry diagnostic tests. General open-learning information, however, is still fragmented. The *Open Tech Directory* collates Open Tech information only. The Materials and Resources Information Service (MARIS-NET) provides access via Prestel to the largest available database of open-learning packages and resources, with a guidance software package that sifts and routes users on entry.

Clearly, an increased control over content is likely to result in more relevant and committed learning. There remain, though, questions about how extensive the learner's ownership of the curriculum can be. Open learning can loosen the cement around the blocks of knowledge or produce smaller bricks but the main edifices still stand. The extension of practices such as continuous assessment and individual or group projects is shifting curriculum design slightly towards the learner, but syllabuses are largely controlled by institutions and examining bodies, which have sometimes proved resistant to open-learning approaches. Modularisation does not in itself create new configurations of knowledge.

The impressive array of of the Open University's menu raises questions about the practice of guidance in relation to an open-learning curriculum. The longer the menu, the greater the need for continuity of counselling. In the Open University, the tutor-counsellor of the foundation year retains the counselling role as the learner progresses through various courses and changes of tutor. First-in-line counsellors and tutors are part-time, regionally based and highly divergent in their role interpretations (Carr, 1983). They operate in ambivalent territory between the centre and the learner, between the given nature of the course materials and the subjectivity of their clients, mediating syllabuses and assignments which they have had no part in constructing. One critique of the Open University argues that its purportedly liberal policies mediate and instrumental view of knowledge (Harris and Holmes, 1976). The centralised production of materials and the dominance of assessment both serve to formulate behavioural objectives to which successful learners accommodate themselves, rather than developing a personal praxis. The packaging of knowledge leads to its commodification.

This account, however, ignores the whole tier of part-time support where the position appears more contradictory. Tutors and counsellors are not merely conduits of the curriculum, serving purely adaptive functions in relation to a centralised control. Packaged learning merely makes visible many assumptions that are unexamined within traditional courses. All curricula reproduce socially organised knowledge. Course producers, learners and tutors do not simply represent 'them', 'us' and 'the intermediaries', respectively, but are in complex ways participants in the wider production of knowledge. The mediators have their own meanings and agendas, including the counsellor's and advocate's responsibility to help learners to use the curriculum rather than being used by it and to question and appraise it within their own construct systems.

### LEARNING STYLES

A learning style is any preferred method or constellation of techniques which an individual uses to progress towards a learning objective. One influential model of learning styles is Kolb's circular and cyclical one which articulates the concrete-abstract dimension with the active-reflective one (Kolb, 1976; 1984). To what extent learning styles are a consequence of teaching styles is of importance to open-learning providers. Some schemes such as open-access centres aim to create multi-learning environments. The use, for example, of practical kits and work-based exercises matched with more expositionary texts tries to stimulate both learning by doing and learning from discussion (or from exegesis as it sometimes turns out), spanning Kolb's active-reflective dimension.

A plurality of learning components is not, however, the same as a plurality of pedagogies, and there is no necessary equation between pedagogies and learning styles. A mismatch in the latter can be a cause of dysfunctional studying. There is evidence that some Open University students adopt a predominantly instrumental approach, eliminating all elements – broadcasts, experiments or text – not directly relevant to assessed assignments (Harris and Holmes, 1976). Self-help groups which centralise collaborative learning models are, typically, marginal and of minority interest (Bailey, 1983). Most significantly, open-learning tutors and learners still experience the pull of authoritarian pedagogies and the transmission model of education. One study of open-learning tutorials noted that tutors talked for up to 70% of the time and that exchanges were characteristically of the closed question-and-answer type (Murgatroyd, 1980). Tutor and students apparently colluded in reinstating the former as the key distributor of knowledge, despite the acknowledged presence of other sources – texts, broadcasts and learners.

There is evidence that people who have several distinct and considered motives for learning, both intrinsic and extrinsic, succeed better than those with few and unexamined motives (Gibbs *et al.*, 1982; Laurillard, 1979). Similarly, the recognition that learning styles are not 'givens' but are variables over which the learner can come to exercise some control may be a mark of maturity and of competence in open learning. One in-course guidance role is to raise learners' awareness and to help them manage their learning styles.

Many open-access centres are trying to develop multiple learning environments. Individual work stations face outwards, with optional areas for group work. Administrators and receptionists are accessible and trainees at adjacent carrels can develop co-operative styles. Because learners work individually, tutors can circulate and the pressure to revert to classroom styles is diminished. Outreach and the specific involvement of trainers can extend the learning environment to the learner's workplace. Where there is little workplace support for sponsored trainees, there is a likely reduction in motivations, styles and sources of guidance.

### LEARNING MEDIA
Many open-learning schemes depend entirely on a particular selection of

technologies for the realisation of their objectives. Specific technologies may be applied to materials production, to course design, to the delivery of learning or to the management of the system. A recent study provided an impressive survey of media currently used in distance education: text, word-processors, computers, radio and television, satellite and cable, video-cassettes and video-discs, audio-cassettes, home kits, telephone, CYCLOPS, teletext and viewdata systems (Bates, 1984). It has been argued that the penetration of new technology can transform adult education (Gerver, 1984), as did the spread of literacy and cheap print in the last century. The applications of such technologies to guidance are also interesting, if less well advanced. The best developed areas are probably vocational guidance (Watts, 1986), distance/telephone coun- selling for personal and educational circumstances, and the large national databases of MARIS for open-learning information and ECCTIS (Educational Counselling and Credit Transfer Information System) for course information.

In open-learning schemes, such applications are piecemeal and relatively undeveloped (Bailey, 1986b). Many schemes with com- puterised record systems are slowly extending these to give, for example, feedback to support staff on learners' progress, with cues to take action, as happens in the Open University. Systems with optical mark readers for analysing multiple choice answers can extend their use to guidance functions such as profiling. The NEC's MAIL (Micro-Aided Learning) service can provide fast computerised feedback to learners on assign- ments or on diagnostic tests. Such feedback can include some breakdown of performance, with suggestions for action. Schemes such as at Austin Rover and ICI, which deliver computerised training in the workplace, include self-diagnostic testing and assessment.

Several schemes use audio- or video-cassettes to induct entrants into open learning, though these are necessarily general in approach and often serve promotional as well as guidance ends. Learners and tutors communicate extensively by audio-tape, which has benefits and costs different from either the correspondence or telephone alternatives. The telephone remains the preferred medium for counselling activities. One OU region is currently experimenting with prerecorded Advicelines on such topics as exam anxiety or course exploration. Some Open Tech students were reported as wanting quicker routes to their helpers by, for example, answerphones. There is evidence, however, that where the initiative rests entirely with the learner, the take-up of telephone guidance is low and is focused on course content. The Library and

Information Sciences distance learning scheme has experimented with a highly proactive model in which counsellors phoned their students regularly. The scheme is costly, but drop-out after two years is low.

Despite these examples, innovation in technology-assisted guidance in open learning is limited. There is little in – say – coaching in study skills or learning styles, in vocational exploration or the clarification of learning priorities. Reasons for this lack in innovation are numerous: development is expensive and many outcomes of guidance are unquantifiable. Providers often have no scope to take longer views of their learners' needs. Moreover, there is little substantial research into the experiential aspects of technology beyond reports of general user satisfaction. One isolated study into painful emotions in open learning discusses the 'soothing sub-routines' built into certain computer programs (Snell, 1985). But there is little systematic investigation of how various media position the user – as learner, enquirer, or consumer – or of the medium-as-message. There is also little traffic between current research on educational technology and that on reading relations, semiotics, discourse theory and the media as constitutive of the subject. If, in post-structuralist terms, there is no access to uncoded experience, then the encoding of knowledge and of guidance practices is of more than incidental importance.

## CONCLUSION

The variety and pluralism of open learning is encouraging. But there is a need for more discriminating evaluation of both the objectives of particular schemes and the specific kinds of opportunity they create. It is this kind of knowledge – of the particular outcomes of learning, of the costs, benefits and conflicts of interest involved, and of the cognitive and affective experiences of participants – that informs good guidance. Open learning in all its manifestations has designs on the learner who in turn has her or his own designs. Those involved in guidance, as planners or practitioners, need clarity as to where their responsibilities lie. From this can follow the innovation and development in guidance that will help open learning.

The (doomed) learning project of Jude the Obscure eventually became not to get into college, but to define the conditions of his own obscurity, to heal personal and historical dislocations and to join the past to the future.

## REFERENCES

Advisory Council for Adult and Continuing Education: *Links to Learning*. Leicester: ACACE, 1979.

Advisory Council for Adult and Continuing Education: *Adults – their Educational Experience and Needs*. Leicester: ACACE, 1982.

Bailey, D.: 'Samuel Smiles Revisited: Helping Yourself in the Open University'. *Teaching at a Distance*, No. 23, Summer 1983.

Bailey, D.: 'The Cost of Guidance in Open Learning'. Hertford: National Institute for Careers Education and Counselling, 1986(a) (mimeo).

Bailey, D.: 'Technology-Assisted Guidance and Open Learning Systems'. Hertford: National Institute for Careers Education and Counselling, 1986(b) (mimeo).

Bailey, D.: *Open Learning and Guidance: a Manual of Practice*. Hertford: National Institute for Careers Education and Counselling/Manpower Services Commission, 1987.

Bates, A.W. (ed.): *The Role of Technology in Distance Education*. London: Croom Helm, 1984.

Butler, L.: *Educational Guidance: a New Service for Adult Learners*. Milton Keynes: Open University, 1983.

Carr, R.: 'Post-Foundation Counselling Revisited'. *Teaching at a Distance*. No. 24, Autumn 1983.

Clarke, A., Costello, M., and Wright, T.: *The Role and Tasks of Tutors in Open Learning Systems*. Cambridge: Industrial Training Research Unit/MSC, 1986.

Evans, N.: *Post-Education Society: Recognising Adults as Learners*. London: Croom Helm, 1985.

Foggo, T.: 'Open Learning in ICI'. *Open Learning*, Volume 1 No. 1, February 1986.

Gerstein, M.: 'Mentoring: an Age Old Practice in a Knowledge-Based Society'. *Journal of Counseling and Development*, Volume 64, October 1985.

Gerver, E.: *Computers and Adult Learning*. Milton Keynes: Open University Press, 1984.

Gibbs, G., Morgan, A., and Taylor, E.: 'Why Students Don't Learn'. *Institutional Research Review* (Open University), No. 1, Spring 1982.

Gramsci, A.: *Selections from the Prison Notebooks* (translated by Hoare, Q., and Noel Smith, G.). London: Lawrence and Wishart, 1971.

Halsey, A.H.: 'Schools for Democracy'. In Ahier, J. and Flude, M. (eds.): *Contemporary Education Policy*. London: Croom Helm, 1983.

Harris, D., and Holmes, J.: 'Openness and Control in Higher Education: Towards a Critique of the Open University'. In Dale, R., *et al*. (eds.): *Schooling and Capitalism*. London: Routledge & Kegan Paul/Open University Press, 1976.

Hawkes, R.: 'Site Management Open Tech Project: Internal Evaluation Report'. Academic Service Unit, University College, London, November 1984 (mimeo).

Hilgendorf, L., and Welchman, R.: 'Consulting About the Future of the Open Tech Programme'. Tavistock Institute of Human Relations, December 1985 (mimeo).

Hopson, B.: 'Adult Life and Career Counselling'. *British Journal of Guidance and Counselling*. Volume 13 No. 1, January 1985.

Kolb, D.A.: *Learning Style Inventory: Technical Manual*. Boston: McBer, 1976.

Kolb, D.A.: *Experiential Learning*. Englewood Cliffs, NJ: Prentice-Hall, 1984.

Krupp, J-A.: 'Mentoring: a Means of Sparking School Personnel'. *Journal of Counseling and Development*, Volume 64, October 1985.

Laurillard, D.: 'The Process of Student Learning'. *Higher Education*, Volume 8, 1979.

Lewis, R. (ed.): *Open Learning in Action: Case Studies*. London: Council for Educational Technology, 1984.

McNay, I.: 'Open Market for the Open University?' *Open Learning*, Volume 1 No. 1. February 1986.

Manpower Services Commission: *Open Tech Task Group Report*. Sheffield: MSC, 1982.

Manpower Services Commission: *The Future Development of Open Learning: Consultative Paper*. Sheffield: MSC, 1985.

Martin, J.: 'Self Instruction: a Curriculum for Counseling'. *Journal of Counseling and Development*, Volume 64, October 1985.

Murgatroyd, S.: 'What Actually Happens in Tutorials'. *Teaching at a Distance*, No. 18, Winter 1980.

Open University: *Into the 1990s: The Role of the Open University in the National Provision of Part-Time Higher Education*. Milton Keynes: Open University, 1986.

PA Management Consultants: *Open Learning in Large Companies: Report of a Pilot Project*. Sheffield: Manpower Services Commission, 1985.

Perry, W.: *Open University*. Milton Keynes: Open University Press, 1976.

Phillips, P.: 'Modular Learning – Theory and Practice'. *Newscheck*, Volume 3 No. 5, March 1986.

Snell, R.: 'Painful or Unpleasant Emotions: A Challenge for Open and Distance Learning'. Lancaster: Centre for the Study of Management Learning. University of Lancaster, 1985 (mimeo).

Thorpe, M.: 'The Special Student Support Scheme'. *Teaching at a Distance*, No. 15, Summer 1979.

Turner, J.: 'Wensum Lodge Open Learning Project'. *Open Learning*, Volume 1 No. 1, February 1986.

Unit for the Development of Adult Continuing Education: *Helping Adults to Learn*. Leicester: UDACE, 1985.

Unit for the Development of Adult Continuing Education: *The Challenge of Change: Developing Educational Guidance for Adults*. Leicester: UDACE, 1986.

Watts, A.G.: 'Educational and Careers Guidance Services for Adults: I. A Rationale and Conceptual Framework'. *British Journal of Guidance and Counselling*, Volume 8 No. 1, January 1980.

Watts, A.G.: 'The Role of the Computer in Careers Guidance'. *International Journal for the Advancement of Counselling*, Volume 9, 1986.

Whitehead, F.: *The Disappearing Dais*. London: Chatto and Windus, 1966.

# OPEN LEARNING AND GUIDANCE

## DIANE BAILEY

## POSTSCRIPT

### THE CONTEXT OF WRITING

The lexicon of education and training in the UK is full of terms with unstable and contested definitions. Two of the most problematic must be 'open learning' and 'educational guidance'. The article above was an attempt to map the complex relationship between the two in the mid-1980s. After the steady development of correspondence colleges and the Open University through the seventies, the eighties saw an acceleration in open learning. The Open Tech Programme (1983–87) stimulated development across diverse, even discrepant, cultures: large and small firms; Local Education Authorities and further education; professional associations, training boards and unions. At this point, open-learning schemes differed markedly in their dimensions of openness, their vocabularies of learning, and the support networks available to their potential learners.

Given the pace of change, the volatility of the terminology and the lack of evaluative research, mapping the open-learning/guidance relationship seemed an ambitious task. As a cartographer I was limited but had some first-hand knowledge of the terrain. I had worked part-time for the Open University since its inception, as well as in more orthodox university and polytechnic contexts. I had also worked for three years in an Educational Guidance Service for Adults, followed by work on an action-research project developing guidance policy and practice in the Open Tech. Questions about adult learning posed within these various sites had common themes, if different emerging solutions. How far can the guidance world's taken-for-granted assumptions of independence, non-directiveness and client-centredness be transferred to provider-led programmes? Whose needs and objectives are paramount in any open-learning scheme? What is the relationship of guidance to marketing, and of counselling to tutoring? Given the interlinked triad of educational, vocational and personal development, how can pre-entry and post-entry guidance be designed (and afforded) to meet adults' needs?

The article attempted a framework to bring together the discourses of open learning and guidance, plotting rationales for their relationship. It was part of a dialogue taking place within institutions and interest groups, but very little across them. This may be why reactions were mainly at the level of information, not argument: in particular, surprise at the range of open learning and approaches to support current in the UK.

## FIVE YEARS ON

As an analysis of competing versions of open learning, the article still seems relevant. In retrospect, its limitations seem not so much in its suggested taxonomy and models of guidance but in its middle-range concentration on the structural features of particular schemes. This misses at one end the macropolitics of national directions, and at the other the micropolitics of personal practice – the orientations, skills and values of those in guidance roles. Perhaps this simply means that my own view has become more politicised.

## OPEN LEARNING REVISITED

New features in the open-learning landscape include the government-initiated Open College, now focused mainly on corporate clients (Tait, 1991), and the Open Polytechnic (now called the Open Learning Foundation), with over twenty participating institutions commissioning courses jointly but delivering them locally (Hardy, 1991). From 1989 the Open College of the Arts has provided mixed-mode learning in graphic arts, and the Open College Networks (not to be confused with the Open College) have expanded across many regions to improve access for under-represented groups. In addition, open learning is now a strategic element in training, from banking to nursing.

Alongside this expansion, the debate has continued on how far open learning is enfranchising or whether its rhetoric of individual choice masks an instrumentalism directed at meeting labour-market needs cheaply (Rumble, 1989). The specific issue of student support has been far less debated and researched. If 'progressive' open learning has been hijacked for purposes of social control in the post-Fordist economy to the extent that some commentators claim (Edwards, 1991), then those in support roles must experience tensions, given the person-centred basis of most guidance theory. However, it still seems more likely that, as the article argued, open learning is neither inherently democratic nor instrumental, but a heterogeneous family of approaches within which guidance can individualise and humanise the learning process.

## GUIDANCE: FROM THE MARGINS TO THE CENTRE?

Since the article was written, educational guidance has become more visible, with the improved networking of local agencies and better staff development, stimulated by the National Educational Guidance Initiative. Significantly, more guidance training is available by open learning (e.g. Bailey *et al.*, 1990). The 'traditional' end of the post-compulsory spectrum is also developing strategies for co-ordinated pre-entry and post-entry guidance, as in the current UDACE/CNAA project on Guidance in Higher Education (Herrington, 1991). This move towards integration contrasts with student counselling and careers guidance as discrete opt-in services, the pattern in most higher education institutions (Hooper and Stone, 1989). Such integration is the norm in open-learning schemes, though the level of guidance is often limited by resources, and there may be no equivalent to the specialist therapeutic and careers counselling found on campuses. If the academic curriculum is contained in learning packages, then support staff, together with technological resources, can concentrate on other needs: assessing prior learning, counselling, providing feedback and study skills help, negotiating action plans, and advocacy. The more guidance moves from the margins to the centre in learning design, the more comprehensive can be the approach to learner support.

### CONCLUSION

Attempting a mapping exercise today, I would indicate more clearly contradictions in national policies, apparent in the ambivalent progress of the Open College, the expansion of the OU in the UK and Europe, and the White Paper on further and higher education (DES, 1991) which separates vocational and leisure provision and pays slight attention to adults and to guidance. Meanwhile, the Careers Service is having to re-argue that 'impartial guidance can only be provided by someone without a vested interest in provision' apropos its relationship to Training and Enterprise Councils (Chubb, 1991). It is this macro context which determines the longer-term opening of learning.

The remapping should also attend more closely to the micro level of practice, as well as defining guidance activities at pre-entry, enrolment, in-course and exit stages. Recent work is providing a more finely-grained account of the processes and skills needed to help learners progress (Oakeshott, 1991). More problematically, debates on equal opportunities have progressed to analyses of unequal outcomes. This includes work on gender in both counselling (Chaplin, 1988) and distance education (Faith, 1988), and on ethnicity and the monoculturalism of most education. More radically, individualism itself, the binding concept of open learning and Rogerian-derived guidance, is being appraised as a construct of liberal humanism which is neither value-free nor, in any analysis of social oppression, adequate. The guidance practitioner (or manager) now needs to be not just multi-skilled but reflexively aware of how practice itself replicates and constitutes closure for some adults.

While the article seems to offer valid models and relevant discussion, therefore, recharting the territory in the 1990s would mean not only recognising the advances in open learning and guidance but also engaging with the wider politics of access.

### REFERENCES

Bailey, D., Docherty, A., Hawthorn, R., Opie, L., Hodgen, L., and Mares, P.: *Counselling in Educational Guidance.* Cambridge: National Extension College, 1990.

Chaplin, J.: *Feminist Counselling in Action.* London: Sage, 1988.

Chubb, P.: Letter to *The Guardian*, 22 October 1991.

Department of Education and Science/Department of Employment: *Education and Training for the 21st Century* (2 vols.). Cmnd. 1536. London: HMSO, 1991.

Edwards, R.: 'The Inevitable Future? Post-Fordism and Open Learning'. *Open Learning*, Volume 6 No. 2, June 1991, pp. 36–42.

Faith, K. (ed.): *Towards New Horizons for Women in Distance Education.* London: Routledge, 1988.

Hardy, D.: 'The Open Polytechnic'. *Open Learning*, Volume 6 No. 2, June 1991, pp. 55–59.

Herrington, M.: 'Guidance in Higher Education'. Newsletter of the UDACE/CNAA Project, No. 2. Leicester: Unit for the Development of Adult Continuing Education, May 1991.

Hooper, R., and Stone, L.: 'A Survey of University Counselling in the United Kingdom and Some Observations on Evaluation'. *British Journal of Guidance and Counselling*, Volume 17 No. 1, January 1989, pp. 49–58.

Oakeshott, M.: *Educational Guidance for Adults: Identifying Competences.* London: Further Education Unit and Unit for the Development of Adult Continuing Education, 1991.

Rumble, G.: '"Open Learning", "Distance Learning", and the Misuse of Language'. *Open Learning*, Volume 4 No. 2, June 1989, pp. 28–36.

Tait, A.: 'Distance Education in the United Kingdom Today: Current Trends'. *American Journal of Distance Education*, Volume 5 No. 2, 1991, pp. 42–47.

# INDEX